Existence and
the World of Freedom

PRENTICE-HALL INTERNATIONAL, INC., *London*
PRENTICE-HALL OF AUSTRALIA, PTY., LTD., *Sydney*
PRENTICE-HALL OF CANADA, LTD., *Toronto*
PRENTICE-HALL FRANCE, S.A.R.L., *Paris*
PRENTICE-HALL OF JAPAN, INC., *Tokyo*
PRENTICE-HALL DE MEXICO, S.A., *Mexico City*

Existence and
the World of Freedom

JOHN WILD
Northwestern University

Prentice-Hall, Inc. *Englewood Cliffs, N.J.*

To Cynthia and Mary

Preface

This book results from lectures, conferences, studies, and personal reflections during the past five or six years in which I have been concerned with the further development of a radically empirical philosophy. This philosophy has much in common with present-day phenomenology and existential philosophy, but, in our own American tradition, it goes back to the insights of William James. This new empiricism is now engaged in an intensive and disciplined exploration of the human life-world, and it has already shown that this world can no longer be discussed as a chaos of disordered and subjective impressions. Rather, it is now emerging as a vast and far-ranging horizon with distinctive orders and structures of its own.

In the first part of this book, I have tried to give a coherent statement of the major results so far attained. In the latter portions, I have tried to shed some light on areas that are still obscure and to indicate further regions that need to be explored. I hope that this book will suggest to American readers the importance of the exploratory work that is now proceeding and will perhaps help some of them to carry it on further. If so, it will have fulfilled my purpose.

Certain chapters of the book are based upon previously published articles and public lectures, and I wish to make the following acknowledgments. Chapter 4 is a revised version of my presidential address before the Fifty-Seventh Meeting of the Eastern Division of the American Philosophical Association at Yale University, December 28, 1960, and I wish to thank Mr. Lewis Hahn, Secretary of the National Association, for his permission to include this material in my book. Approximately one half of Chapter 2 is taken from an article entitled "Existentialism: A New View of Man," published in the *University of Toronto Quarterly*, XXVII, 1 (October 1957), 79–95. The substance of Chapter 3 was published under the same title in *The Philosophical Review*, LXVII, 4 (October 1958), and that of Chapter 11 in *The Journal of Bible and Religion*, XXX, 4 (October 1962). I am grateful to the editors of these journals for their permission to reprint these articles. Chapter 6 appeared in *Experience, Existence and the Good: Essays in Honor of Paul Weiss*, ed. Irwin C. Lieb, copyright by Southern Illinois University Press, 1961, and reprinted with the permission of Southern Illinois University Press. The substance of Chapter 9 has been accepted for the volume of *Essays in Honor of Charles Hartshorne*, and I am grateful to Mr. Eugene Freeman of the Open Court Publishing Company for allowing me to use it here.

Finally, I wish to express my appreciation to Mrs. Barbara Whitney for her most effective secretarial assistance in preparing my manuscript for publication, and also to thank Mr. H. L. Dreyfus and the other graduate students at Harvard and Northwestern Universities who, during the last five years—by their pointed questions and exacting criticism—have helped me to avoid many blind alleys and to keep my thinking on the move.

J. W.

Contents

Part I

The Present Situation in Philosophy

Chapter 1

Concepts of Man

The purpose of this book is to acquaint the reader with a new way of thinking that is growing in the Western world of our time, and with certain fundamental insights already achieved. We shall begin, in Chapter 2, with a general account of existential philosophy and its radically empirical method, now known as phenomenology. In the next chapters—3, 4, and 5—we shall turn to the exploration of the human world which it has inaugurated, and to some of the well-confirmed results of this exploration. After this, in Chapters 6 and 7, we shall consider the more radical conception of human freedom which is developing out of these investigations.

We shall then illustrate these methods by exploring with the reader certain specific facts of the life-world; responsibility, in Chapter 8, and devotion and fanaticism in Chapter 9. Following this, we shall show how this new way of thinking offers us new approaches to two traditional questions of general interest: What is the relation of the individual to the group (Chapter 10)? and what is the evidence, if any, for the existence of divine transcendence (Chapter 11)? We shall conclude, finally, in Chapter 12, with a consideration of the new light that has been shed by these explorations on the nature of the humanistic disciplines and their relation to the sciences.

Before embarking upon this exploration, let us now turn to certain concepts of man that are now alive and active in the West. Since, as we shall try to show, man cannot be separated from the world in which he exists, this will also introduce us to corresponding ways of understanding the world, and will give us an initial orientation with respect to the present situation of philosophy. We shall restrict ourselves to Western culture, and, within this culture, to five living ways of thought and life which are widely known, and which have all received disciplined philosophical attention: (1) the rationalist view of the Greeks and medieval "Christian" thought; (2) the naturalism which relies on modern science; (3) positivism, the latest expression of modern scientism; (4) the nonreligious existentialism of thinkers like Jean-Paul Sartre; and finally (5), the religious existential thought of philosophers like Jaspers and Marcel, and of theologians like Niebuhr and Bultmann. This is not an exhaustive list. But the claim perhaps may be reasonably made that it represents those views which are most influential in the West.

We are dealing here not merely with abstract views of man and the world but with ways of existing in the world. In order to gain a vital understanding of what they share in common, as well as how they differ, it may be well for us to have an image in mind. This may not only serve to stimulate our imagination (always necessary for understanding the acts of man) but also to work out a concrete way of speaking which can save us much time.

Imagine a military plane in time of stress, with an English-speaking crew of five men, forced to make a crash landing on a glacial field high up in the Himalayas. The plane is severely damaged, its instruments beyond repair, all extra equipment lost, including rope. The men emerge alive with burns on the body and arms, but with their legs intact. They are able to build a flimsy shelter, and to save from the wreckage barely two days' supply of food and a small portable radio receiving set in bad condition. They land in the early morning and are surrounded by light snow and mist. But they remember from the air that the field is surrounded by a wall of peaks on every side. Near their shelter by the plane one of them notices what seem to be human tracks leading south. Following the tracks for a quarter of a mile, they come to a depression which turns out to be a glacial crevasse at least nine feet wide at the top. They cannot see whether the tracks continue on the other side. With further exploration they discover that they are surrounded, within an area of about one square mile, by crevasses at some points much wider, but gradually being covered by snow.

The next day the snow gives way to light mist, which breaks unevenly at intervals; at the first break they see a white object in the crags to the north, which one member suggests is a tent. During another such interval they see and hear a plane overhead, and feel that they may have been observed. Soon after, they receive a broken message over the radio in English. Something seems to be said about an exploring party that may be attempting to rescue them but which is at least two days away. There is doubt as to whether this is the meaning of the message. They are clearly in a desperate position. No one of them can last in the cold more than three or four days. What are they going to do?

There is general agreement, at least in the West, that man has either fallen or has been thrown by powers beyond his control into a seriously threatened condition. The fact that he has various kinds of insight and powers of action in accordance with this knowledge has never been seriously doubted. It is also agreed that we are surrounded by natural objects which do not act at random but according to more or less orderly patterns which must be considered in forming our plans for the saving of man. Finally, it is clear to all that in our history obscure signs have been offered of friendly assistance from sources beyond our ken. Some such image as we have just suggested is appropriate to express these common factors. Let us then accept it to stand for the general situation of man-in-the-world to which all parties agree. But this situation is shot through with ambiguity. It can be interpreted in very different ways to support very different modes of action.

Let us now see if we can use this image, crude and oversimple as it may be, to suggest the five divergent ways of life with which we are here primarily concerned, beginning with the traditional rationalism of the West, as exemplified in Aristotelian and Thomistic thought. Let us first consider this world of rationalism in terms of our image, which may give us the basic feeling, and then proceed to interpret it in more abstract, conceptual language which may give us a more exact understanding.

The Man of Faith in Reason and Order, Who Waits

This man has emerged from the wreckage with only minor bruises and burns. His eyes are in good condition, and he is full of confidence and hope. He clearly remembers the view he obtained as the plane came in, and the valley that lay ahead to the south. To him the facts are basically clear, and he argues that they must simply be accepted. The confused tracks are pointing to the south and the break in the mountain barrier from which the exploring party departed, and to which they will return. The plane, of course, observed them, for the message came soon (one half hour) after. Help is on the way. Friends are coming from over beyond. Let us not trust subjective fancy nor take unnecessary risks. The picture is essentially clear. We must act in accordance with what we know: strengthen our shelter, and devise a bridge from the wreckage. Snow is gradually covering the crevasse. When it is safe, we can cross it and move to the south to meet our rescuers. But since help is surely coming, the thing to do now is to wait.

This may serve to portray the attitudes and the world of the man of reason, as he has loved to call himself throughout our history, since the time of the ancient Greeks. The world of this man is an independent, cosmic order, already fixed and established completely apart from him. He has great respect for the visions of those in the past who saw the cosmos from a higher and clearer point of view. He is himself a part of this great order, by no means and in no sense its center. Such a view he dismisses as an irresponsible subjectivism, to be avoided at all costs. Nevertheless, he holds that man occupies a lofty place in the order of nature which, on the whole, supports his aims and desires—which is very reasonable of it.

Recognizing his lost and fallen condition, he is ready to listen to friendly messages coming from beyond, and to accept them as genuine, particularly if they fit with what his reason tells him. His mind is objective and outwardly directed, and he is not bothered by any acute self-consciousness. He tries to regard himself as one complex object among many others in a great world order that is an unconscious projection of his subjective needs. He supports this conception by all manner of self-evident propositions and deductive arguments, which he calls *objective* and *unbiased* thinking. If he empties his mind of bias, and simply looks at a thing, its truth will come floating in without hindrance.

According to this man of objective thought, freedom is simply to act in accordance with the rational order of things—which hardly ever means anything very new, since this order is already fixed and pre-established. To do something that has never been done before is to flout the cosmic order, and has myriad reasons against it. Hence he embraces a backward-looking ethic of self-realization, which aims at perfecting and completing a self whose nature and capacities are already given with birth. He makes no sharp distinction between individual existence and that of the group, which is simply larger and includes the former as a whole includes its part. But the proper law of the group is the very same as the law that guides his personal action. Hence, when in a minority, he can be quite stubborn in defending what he feels to be the reason of things. Error is due to what he calls *willful confusion, bias,* and *subjective caprice.*

This traditional man of reason admires the objective attitude of science which, like his own rationalism, is always impartial and detached. But each of the sciences has a provincial territory of its own, and all of them must be fitted into a broader philosophical and theological frame. It is only these *basic* disciplines which have a right to make judgments of intrinsic value. Science is either neutral to value or, at best, in the practical sciences, concerned with means rather than ends. The aim of science is to find law and order; the aim of human action, to establish it in both the individual and the group. This order is much more important than freedom, which, indeed, can be properly defined only in terms of orderly action. Wherever it is found, the eccentric, the exceptional, the unique is to be distrusted, in science as well as in society. In the active sphere especially, it is better to do nothing than to break the group solidarity or to take an unwarranted risk.

Ever since the time of Plato, this rational man has mistrusted and discounted the moving, ambiguous world of lived experience. He has preferred to retire in immobility to a region of abstract systems where he can reside in quiet and security. This is a world of peace and order—the faith of a man who waits.

The Man Who Trusts Science and Nature— the World of Tragedy

This second man emerges from the wreck with only minor bruises. But he is far more sober and skeptical. He doubts the "clear view" of Number One as they came in, and remembers great waves of mist. He did not see, and doubts whether anyone saw, a valley to the south. After carefully examining the confused tracks, he points out that some point south and some point north, but that the latter are superimposed upon the former, which shows that the wandering party left toward the north, he thinks from the measured lengths, at a much slower pace. This party of not more than two men is probably also lost and perhaps in a worse condition. No help can be expected from them.

As to the plane, it probably did not observe them at all, for they had nothing conspicuous to show. As to the message one half hour later, God knows where that came from, to whom it may have been directed, and where the rescuers, if any, are. He refers to the many lacunae in the message, and doubts the whole optimistic interpretation of his friend, which is merely wishful thinking. There are probably no rescuers on their way to *them*. They must rather examine the nature of their situation, be guided by what they find, and act accordingly.

He encourages his friend, Number Three, in his attempt to make something like snowshoes, canes, and bridging gear to cross the crevasse. The next clear day he closely studies the crevasses, testing their width and depth. In the afternoon, he notices what he takes to be a break in the mountains to the west through the scattering clouds, and carefully measures the snow and ice now covering the crevasse. His conclusion is quite clear, and he argues for it at length.

The hope of receiving aid from friends in the beyond is a snare and a delusion. This is mere wishful thinking. They must follow the indications of nature and act for themselves without trusting in imaginary friends. They should spend their time constructing the necessary apparatus. Then with snowshoes and bridging tackle, they should cross the crevasse at a narrow point, make for the west, and, husbanding their food, try to descend the mountain on their own. In this way, they might manage to last eight days and thus reach safety at last.

This scheme has much against it because of their weakened state and their ignorance of the country. There is perhaps one chance in a hundred. Nevertheless this chance must be taken, since it is the only one offered by the situation and the laws of nature. We ourselves are natural beings under this law. If it is to crush us, we must accept this fate, for there is no higher power. If, however, we devote ourselves to understanding it, and act accordingly, we may succeed in saving ourselves. This is how it looks to modern man, Number Two, who trusts in nature and science.

This picture may serve as a concrete illustration of the attitude of naturalism which had illustrious representatives in ancient Greece, in Hellenistic and Roman times, among the Stoic philosophers, and now in the Anglo-Saxon countries. The naturalist has much in common with the man of reason. His world also is a natural order established completely apart from him, but not so rigidly fixed, and subject to change and evolution. Nevertheless it works by regular laws which can be understood and used for the satisfaction of those peculiar, human desires that also belong to nature. Like his older ally, the man of reason, the naturalist prides himself on his objectivity, and believes that he is himself only a natural object among many others in the vast ongoing flux of nature. But he cannot accept any divine theology.

Any idea of a superhuman friend behind phenomena is wishful thinking and anathema to him. Nature is just what it is, and man is a tiny ephemeral part. Nevertheless, this insignificant creature somehow does not belong. Within himself, he carries an order of his own which he stubbornly chooses to pursue on his own. He is like a turtle caught in the midst of a floor of swinging dancers. He senses, indeed, that there is an order here, but it is not his. It is rather an array of swaying, ruthless forces that will crush him in the end. Man belongs to nature, and yet does not belong. Nature is the only source of meaning. There is nothing beyond. And yet this source is meaningless. Man is an insignificant part of a vast, inhuman order and yet he must oppose and master it.

This paradox, lying at the very heart of naturalism, sets the stage for tragedy, and appears in every major manifestation of this age-old creed.

Thus, nature itself is determined and predictable. Man, on the other hand, is free and unpredictable in his basic choices. But instead of opting for consistency and eliminating one or the other of these alternatives, the naturalist has always asserted both together, in accordance with his sense of tragedy. Thus, as Sydney Hook has recently maintained, man is both free and determined at the same time. He is caught in a web of inexorable natural laws, enslaved by them. And yet, he is free to understand and master them, though in the end they must sweep him on to death. This is the essence of tragedy.

To be really free is to pursue one's desires and to act in accordance with the nature of things. This leads the naturalist also to an ethic of self-realization. Like the rationalist, he looks not so much forward as backward to the desires and interests he already has. What is right is to satisfy as many of these as possible—the greatest good of the greatest number. As in rationalism, the group takes precedence over the individual, the common over the personal good. But the individual naturalist can be quite stubborn in defending his ideals against a consensus which he takes to be out of line with nature.

Like the rationalist, he believes that vice is due to ignorance. But this is an ignorance of empirical fact, which can be corrected only by scientific observation and logic. The naturalistic mind has little sense of mystery, and distrusts any faith that goes beyond the evidence as subjective fantasy. He prides himself on being hard-boiled, unsentimental, and having his feet on the ground.

Of all living philosophers, the naturalist has the highest respect for objective science, both natural and social. He believes that value is a kind of fact, and that moral questions can be solved by factual investigation. He makes no sharp distinction between the *ought* and the *is*, and enjoys committing the so-called naturalistic fallacy. He dreams of a time when the human sciences will catch up with the physical sciences, and man will at last control his destiny. Then the good will be subject to exact calculation, and the maximum realization achieved. At the same time he recognizes, but also tries to forget, the thought that it will all come to nothing in the end.

This is the world of Number Two, the hard-boiled man with his feet on the ground, who trusts hard facts of nature and science. In the concrete situation, he is ready to embark the whole group on a desperate venture into the unknown, with one chance out of a hundred for success. In the back of his own mind, as he speaks with his disillusioned courage, and in the minds of those around him who listen, there looms a tragic sense.

The Man of Science Who Senses Its Limits

Number Three is a small man who emerges from the wreck with painful burns on the legs and body bruises. Nevertheless, he can work with his hands; and being encouraged by Number Two, he spends the first day carefully examining the nearby crevasses and then using his technical skill in piecing together a bridgelike structure from the wreckage of the wings. This, he thinks, might be strong enough to support them as they wriggle over the abyss, if it is not too wide. But he is not at all enthusiastic about this plan. He agrees with his friend, Number Two, about the tracks pointing in opposite directions. These tracks, he shows, have been recently made. Hence, the party is probably nearby wandering on the glacier, perhaps in as hapless a state as they themselves.

He gives further convincing reasons for doubting that the radio message is directed to them, or, indeed, that any definite interpretation is possible. Only five words and a Chinese accent are clear, and these are consistent with any number of possible meanings. They may be able to devise climbing tools and to cross the crevasse. But then where are they?—12,000 feet up in the crags of an unknown peak, and three days' food at the best. They may as well follow the plan of Number One and wait where they are, though this also is not auspicious. The facts are quite clear, such as they are, and tools may be devised. But these facts and instruments dictate no single course of action.

Of course, he wishes to survive. This is a fact of nature. But he brings equally cogent arguments against every idea that is suggested. When asked what he himself advises, he has nothing constructive to offer. The situation is ambiguous. No one solution is better than any other. He will abide by the decision of the majority, which seems to be now that they should wait, at least two days, for equipment to be prepared. But the final choice must be arbitrary. They may as well toss a coin.

This world has much in common with that of the naturalist, though the positivist has an even more exaggerated respect for the objective methods of science. These methods alone can establish hard facts, which are the bedrock of any knowledge worthy of the name. Like the naturalist, he believes that these observable, empirical facts can be fitted into a framework of laws, some of which are already known. On the basis of these laws, reliable predictions can be made and technical instruments devised for the control of nature. His mind has been thoroughly trained in this logic of science and technology, and for him this is all the logic there is. For any idea that there may be other disciplined ways of approaching the concrete, he has only bitter scorn. This is confused and sloppy thinking, masquerading as some kind of science. Broad speculative theories that cannot be confirmed by sensory fact are not only false, they are meaningless. If the author of a theory cannot specify a way in which the theory might be disconfirmed, he is sinning against the spirit of reason, and merely wasting time.

By holding rigorously to this notion of verification, the positivist has been able to exercise a purifying critique of objective thought, revealing many confusions and unfounded, pretentious claims. In all these ways, he has been a forceful, though sometimes difficult, ally of scientific rationalism and naturalism. But here we must notice a sharp and basic difference.

His critical acumen has enabled him to grasp the limits of science and so-called reason. More particularly, he has seen that to look at a value-laden project from the outside is not the same as to live it through from the inside. Hence the famous formula, science is neutral to value. No amount of factual information can dictate, or even indicate, a final value. Technology provides us with means only, not with ends. This reminds us of traditional rationalism, but the common formula only points to a radical gulf. The rationalist holds that there are higher objective sciences, metaphysics and theology, which can determine the final end by factual analysis. For the positivist, on the other hand, this is a sheer delusion. There are no "higher sciences" determining what we ought to do. This is a wishful projection from our human insecurity. No *ought* can be derived from an *is* of any kind: no value from any kind of fact.

This holds of the "value" of freedom also, which cannot be objectively observed by science. Freedom, therefore, is absurd. Hence positivistic analysis has rejected the naturalistic notion that one can be free and determined at the same time as a jumble of confusions. The empirical facts of "nature" do not require an ethics of self-realization nor any other kind. Virtue is not knowledge, and the dream of a scientific Utopia is just another wish projection. In science, personal bias must be sacrificed to impersonal impartiality; what I alone can see to what anyone can see. But the attempt to turn this into an ethical principle of personal subordination to the common good is to indulge in a baseless metaphor. Hence, positivistic thought has given us a cogent defense of the open society where individuals are free to act on their own.[1] Ethics, like poetry and music, is not science. It occupies another realm, and has a rationale of its own.

But when we ask where this realm is and what is its rationale, the positivist gives us no unambiguous answer. It is simply a matter of personal choice, and we are confronted with an undiluted relativism. Should we do this or should we do that? Should we choose freedom or tyranny? What do we mean by *person*, by *choice*, and by *free-*

[1] Cf. K. Popper, *The Open Society and Its Enemies* (Princeton, N.J.: Princeton University Press, 1950).

dom? If they are beyond the competence of science, how then do we understand them?—and how are we to clarify this understanding? To these questions we receive no coherent answer from positive man. He stands on the borderline of science, and points beyond in silence. But this is a meaningful silence, and out of this silence something strikingly different and novel may emerge.

Existential Man Who Is Ready to Leap

Numbers Four and Five emerge from the wreckage shaken and bruised. But they are able to walk and see. Number Five, in fact, has managed to salvage the binoculars he carries with him, though they are badly cracked. They help to gather what can be saved from the debris, and to measure the depths and sides of the chasm that lies directly before them. But these members of the party are more concerned with getting a bird's-eye view of their surroundings than to discover more exactly where they are.

On the first day, it is they who take the longest part of the journey along the crevasses by which they are encircled. On this journey, they discover a ridge from which a better view may be obtained. The first day is too misty. But the second morning they climb the ridge and spend several hours in the bitter cold waiting for a view. When the clouds finally break and the plane appears, one takes off his red jacket and waves. The other focuses his glass on the valley to the north, and finds the small white tent in the crags with a moving human figure at the side. Examining the terrain, he sees that beyond the crevasse the ice seems smooth in this direction.

Returning to the party after the message has been received, Number Five points out a basic defect in the accepted plan. Their only real hope is to contact the rescue party which is coming either for them or for the mysterious wanderers in the tent. But they have been too preoccupied with the immediate technical problem of crossing the crevasse. It will take two days to finish the bridging gear while they are consuming their last crumbs of food. Suppose they cross: What then? At this time, the rescue party will be reaching the glacier at a valley either to the north or to the west. If this party comes upon the people in the tent, they may return at once. If not, they may start looking for the plane. But we will then be wandering on a glacial surface of 400 square miles in the mist and snow. With no stable base to aim at, under these conditions the two parties will never meet. They will both perish in the snow and ice.

In either case, *time is of the essence.*

The main group must stay by the plane, which may have been sighted, and where there is some shelter. Meanwhile, I, Number Five, will leap across the crevasse to the east, where it is only nine feet wide and covered in part with ice. Then I will make for the tent to the north, where I may gain information. If not, I will descend below the cloud line to observe the country. If I see a searching party, I will join them. If not, I can get a sense of the passes, and after I return to you, only a half day after you are ready with the bridge gear, we can cross the crevasses, and even then we may be able to get down. But I will need a first-aid kit, and some extra food for the tent people, if they are out of food or injured. Such is the project of Number Five.

His companion, Number Four, agrees that something must be done now or they will perish in the snow. But he does not share the optimism of his friend. It is more than doubtful that a rescue party is on the way. It is likely that the people in the tent are injured or starving, and therefore a mere liability. In any case, they have no food to spare. Finally, and most important of all, he does not really believe that either he or his friend can make the leap over the crevasse, at least nine feet wide and with no smooth approach. Nevertheless, if his friend fails, he is ready to make the attempt, which is the only chance they have. Since I must die anyway, I may as well die with a sense of self-respect.

Such are the projects of the men of existence, Numbers Four and Five. They are ready to share their ideas, but the others disagree. Nevertheless, they will not be dissuaded. They have made up their minds in the light of a clear view of *their total situation* and of evidence known to all. Hence, they are not moved by the many counter-arguments offered. It may have been an unfriendly plane; there may be no rescue party; the tent people may know nothing; and the crevasse may be too wide. But they have now decided and are ready to take the risk. They leave and prepare for the leap.

Numbers Four and Five present us with a point of view which differs radically from the others. While our image is oversimple and imperfect, it may suggest to us something of the new existential mode of thought that is now revolutionizing philosophy and theology in the West. Let us first try to interpret the new attitude shared by Numbers Four and Five in common, and then briefly turn to what distinguishes them from each other.

The rationalist and the naturalist are aware of a region of lived experience which they dismiss as something "subjective," and try to suppress until they find out the "objective" truth. Hence their gaze is primarily directed toward an external system which they passively receive by "observation." They try to fit themselves and their "interests" into this objective system and then, from its various laws and structures, try to deduce what they should do. The positivist sees that this cannot be done because of the incommensurable character of this "subjective" element. But for him it is neither a world nor even a region. Because of his objective orientation, it is merely an irrational, surd element to which he points in silence.

For the first time in our history, the existential thinker has at last seen that this surd element is an overarching historical world of action with structures of its own. Agreeing with the positivist that this world can never be fitted into the objective frame of scientific fact, he sees that a movement, precisely the opposite, must be performed. It is the various regions of scientific fact that must be ultimately fitted into this broader horizon, and interpreted in the light of what is now referred to as the *Lebenswelt*. It includes not only subjective factors, but objective factors as well, both joined together in overarching structures of its own.

Hence, as we have noted in our image, the efforts of Numbers Four and Five to get a wider grasp of their actual situation, which is not constituted by scientific facts alone. It is constituted rather by what we can call *historic facts* or *world facts*, which include their own feelings and projects as well. They are, in fact, the center of a world whose final meaning rests on their own resolution and choice. Hence they are not only more widely oriented than the rest, but more self-conscious as well. Without any apologies, they use the first personal pronoun in their speech. Truth is not merely the passive assimilation of objective facts; new questions may be asked to get new answers. And, finally, this growing truth must be not only observed from the outside by a detached point of view, but lived through from the inside. Whether it helps us, and how, will depend on what we do.

The existential thinker is now aware of a deeper dimension of human freedom, quite strange to the Western tradition of philosophy up to the time of Kant. This must lead him to be highly critical of

16

traditional theories. The rationalistic view of "freedom of the will," as action in accordance with a pre-established order, is far too narrow and leads to determinism in the end. The same is true of naturalistic attempts to identify freedom with special forms of determinism (action from internal causes, for rational ends, etc.). All such theories attempt to fit freedom into an alien objective frame, and therefore destroy it.

The positivist rightly sees that it cannot be fitted into any such frame. But he does not see far enough. As Kant perceived, freedom belongs to a world of its own, the world in which we live and exist. It is not restricted to certain special events within this world, like acts of will; for, as history shows, man is free to choose different styles of life and different global meanings. Hence, while freedom cannot be clearly focused as a scientific fact, it underlies science, and pervades the *Lebenswelt* as a whole in all its forms and manifestations. This radical, constitutive freedom, as we may call it, is new to the history of Western thought. It is possessed, to a very limited degree, by human groups and institutions which always tend toward a backward-looking policy of self-realization directed to a pre-established end. Such a policy is, indeed, necessary for the existence of individual persons. But once in existence, the human person, whose world horizon is wider, is able to question all such ends, and to exercise a far more radical and open freedom. This person will question a group concensus and accept being in a minority; even a minority of one.

As against rationalism and positivism, existential thought will agree with naturalism that a close cooperation between philosophy and the sciences of man, especially history (if this is to be called a science), is possible. But if it is to be fruitful, such cooperation will depend on the further development and application on both sides of what is now called the *phenomenological method*. This method does not restrict itself to the examination of measurable objects, but also takes into account the "subjective" attitudes and intentions that are always correlated with such objects—trying to reveal these total relational structures as they are lived from the inside. It is capable of broadening our human understanding, making us more keenly aware not only of the objective signs of other persons (tents) but of the unique persons themselves, living in unique worlds of their own. It has already led to widely confirmed and striking results, not only in philosophy but in psychiatry, anthropology, and the disciplined study of religions.

Phenomenology has now probably shed sufficient light on the human *Lebenswelt* to rule out traditional interpretations of our immediate experience, like rationalism, naturalism, and positivism, as unduly reductive and inadequate to the evidence. But it would be highly erroneous to suppose that it has ended, or ever will end, in a final metaphysics. This would be inconsistent with the radical human freedom, of which we have spoken, that lies at the root of its revelations. The world in which we exist is open to a vast variety of divergent interpretations. Some evidence is accessible, but not enough to rule out other alternatives. Society, through its individual members, and these individual persons, themselves, must choose in some way; and as William James, the first American existential philosopher, cogently points out, these choices are never certain, but always attended by risk. Other possibilities are open.

Let us now conclude by briefly characterizing two of these, now actively defended by disciplined thinkers, and already symbolized in our image by Numbers Four and Five.

This way of life is symbolized by Number Four (Camus and Sartre). He has made a radical choice, and lives in a meaningful world of his own. This world is ordered to his survival and that of the group with which he is identified. Like the naturalistic way, it is closed to transcendence and mystery. Beyond man, there are no saving powers at work; only meaningless, alien forces. Other humans live in worlds of their own and must solve their problems for themselves. So while Number Four is aware of the strangers in the tent, he is not prepared to sacrifice himself for them. He has taken account of all that he knows clearly, and has decided shrewdly and courageously for himself and his friends.

What lies beyond, what he does not know clearly, must be like the alien stuff that he knows around him, only on a larger scale. These forces reduce him to the performance of repetitive functions, and to a meaningless death in the end. With mystery reduced in this way, life becomes absurd—a sharper and starker version of a Greek tragedy that man makes for himself. Nevertheless, for the sake of a certain authentic dignity that man feels as a real possibility, this heroic choice is worth making. Why?

To give any reasons in answer to this question would be a dissolution and degradation of what is genuinely human in man.

The way of life, symbolized by Number Five (Heidegger, Bultmann, Marcel), is more open and flexible. He recognizes the ambiguity with which freedom is pervaded and surrounded. Instead of reducing mystery to the alien forces he knows, he knows that he does not know. Hence, his world is open to the possibility of saving forces from beyond. He feels that freedom, if left to itself, will waste away. How, indeed, can freedom be actualized without offering itself to something beyond, to which obedience is owed? But this obedience must be freely rendered, this sacrifice freely offered.

Hence, for Number Five, freedom itself points to the possibility of saving forces beyond. Nevertheless, he knows that he cannot remain inactive. They will not save him automatically and by rule. They are a call to decision, requiring action and risk on his part. This, I believe, is the existential pattern of the living "religious" thought of our time. In being open to transcendence, it is also open to the transcendence of other men. Number Five, of course, wants to save himself and his friends. But he is not finally caught in an ethic of self-realization. In the face of transcendence, other possibilities open up before him. He is not only aware of the others in the tent, he is willing to risk the whole project by giving up food to them.

There may be no saving mystery, in which case all is absurd. But then again there may. So why not take the risk? The other ways lead ultimately to tragedy, and tragedy is fine and great.

But is tragedy enough?

Chapter 2

Human Existence
and Phenomenology

World of
existence

Having worked out an image through which we may gain some
feeling for the different living philosophies of the West in our time,
let us now turn to the last of these, which we have called the philosophy of existence. It is with this mode of philosophizing that we shall
be henceforth concerned. There is one thing about it which we did
not consider in connection with the image. This is its relative novelty. Ever since the time of Plato, who thought of it as an under-
ground cave in which only fleeting shadows could be seen, the world
in which we actually exist has been disparaged and ignored by
disciplined philosophy. For Plato, the whole point of life was to climb
out of this cave into which we have fallen, and to ascend toward
higher regions. Following him, our existence in this shadow world
has been discounted as confused, unstable, and subjective.

Plato

We might summarize this neglect of subjective existence as follows. Classical philosophy held that it could be dealt with as an
object of some kind, a complex essence with derived properties and
accidents. This turned out to be inadequate. Modern philosophy
realized that something was missing and speculated about a transcendental subject beyond the finite person. No one ever thought of
studying seriously the finite existence of the human person as lived
from within.

Classical

Modern

Then suddenly, more than a hundred years ago, during the reign
of Hegelian philosophy in Europe, a young Danish thinker, Sören
Kierkegaard, reflecting on Hegel's claim to have assimilated the

whole of Christian life into his system, became aware of this objectivist trend in modern thought, and attacked it with great penetration and originality. There is a great difference between Christian faith as observed from the outside, and as lived from within. The former attitude is detached and uncommitted. Its object is a timeless, abstract essence. The latter is passionately concerned and committed. It is not a theory about some abstraction, but a concrete personal faith. This personal faith cannot be included within any conceptual system. To think about Christianity is not the same as to exist as a Christian.

But one who is trying to exist in this way has a peculiar inner access to his own existence. He may describe it and contrast it with other modes of existence which are radically opposed. Kierkegaard devoted his keen powers of observation and his great literary talents to this task, embarking on a new exploration of the hitherto neglected region of the so-called "subjective." This exploration has since borne amazing fruit. Kierkegaard saw that modern thought, by neglecting the "subjective," had really neglected existence, for existence cannot be clearly envisaged from the outside. It can be adequately understood only from within. Feelings like boredom, melancholy, anxiety, and despair cannot be seen and measured. They must first be lived to be grasped as they really are. Our thought tends to lose itself in its object and to forget itself. But if we are really to understand this peculiarly human manifestation of man, we must understand it in relation to the thinker of the thought, as the guiding light of his existence. According to Kierkegaard, by grasping our existence we can understand thought, but by thought alone we shall never understand existence.

In inaugurating this new study, Kierkegaard was also inaugurating a new approach to philosophy, which is now called *existentialism* and has been manifested in manifold and divergent forms. Both Heidegger and Marcel have repudiated this term, because of their wish to dissociate themselves from certain doctrines of Sartre with which it has become associated in France; but as we need a general term to refer to the common features of this new philosophy, we shall continue to employ it—though in a sense much broader than that of Sartre. By existentialism we shall mean a new mode of thought, initiated by Kierkegaard, which attempts to approach the problem of being by a careful study of personal existence as concretely lived. It differs from classical realism in denying that such existence can be adequately understood by the use of objective categories such as thing, time, and space in their traditional senses. It differs from modern idealism in holding that the transcendental self is the human person in the concrete, and that he and his human world are open to disciplined empirical study. This new philosophy is still far from being in a finished state. It is too early to expect any complete and rounded doctrine. We shall restrict ourselves primarily to certain insights of Kierkegaard concerning central structures of personal life and its limits, which have been further developed by Heidegger and have been widely accepted.

Human Existence and Its Limits

According to the naturalist, the human body is a physical object with definite boundaries, which is surrounded by other physical objects in geometric space. Private experience occurs within these boundaries, giving us a confused and distorted picture of ourselves and of the real world of science. The existentialists have shown that these views are not supported by the actual evidence. Let us now consider this evidence from an existential point of view.

A physical object simply lies before us with its various properties as something there, *on hand,* to be gazed at from a detached point of view. It lies within a geometric space, any point of which is like any other, at various measurable distances from things. But if we look carefully at the objects round about us, we shall find that they are not like this at all. The chairs and tables and windows of this room, for example, are implements *at hand,* inviting me to action. They are not just there, but *there for something.* The book is ready to be opened. The window invites me to gaze outside. This environing space does not consist of positions, each one of which is like any other. It is rather made up of *different places,* above me on the ceiling, below me on the floor, before me on the table. The things are either in their places or just lying around. The room is a region oriented with respect to other regions, and this region is not merely the sum of the things that lie within. It has a structure of its own. Thus when I enter the room I do not first have to count up the separate objects to know where I am. I must first grasp the region as a whole before I can grasp the places of the different implements. Each region is for something, and points beyond itself to further regions. Taken together, they point to an ultimate object of care, for the sake of which they all are. This is that ultimate horizon which I call *the world*, and within which I myself and all the beings I know are now located. Wherever I go, my world goes with me. Without a world-field surrounding him, there can be no human person.

A similar correction needs to be made with respect to the naturalistic view of time as a succession of "nows." On this view, the past has no reality of its own. When the past really was, it was a *now*. But now it is no longer. The future is a not-yet-*now*. What first occurs is the past, then the present, and last the future.

According to Heidegger, this conception of time involves many misconceptions, not the least of which is the confusion of time with the things that happen in time. These things occur one after the other. But the different phases, or ecstasies, of time (past, present, and future) do not succeed each other in this way. They occur all together as parts of an integral structure of human existence, or not at all. Just as man is stretched out spatially into surrounding regions of care, so human existence, or *Dasein*, as Heidegger calls it, is stretched out temporally into the ecstasies (outstretchings) of time.

What I call the past is not all gone, because it never was all there. In its own time it had its own past and, even more important, its own future, which may overlap with my future and may be now sustained and repeated. As we shall see, it is such sustaining of human purpose and choice that alone gives unity and integrity to our existence. This existence cannot be enclosed within the limits of a physical organism, or squeezed within the confines of a specious present. As long as man exists, he is unfinished, always stretched out into the past and projected into the future. He can, of course, order his world in different ways. But some world he must have.

This field conception is already beginning to have a profound effect on depth psychology and psychiatry. It used to be held that mentally disturbed patients projected their internal feelings into the surrounding world, and that their accounts of what appeared to be going on around them were, therefore, of little importance. It is now being recognized that our feelings reveal the world to us, and that we are necessarily projected into a world-field. Hence a disturbed patient will necessarily involve a disturbed world. Thus the psychiatrist needs to listen to what the patient tells him of his world. He may be reporting facts quite as genuine as the internal phases of his disorder, and the former may provide important clues to the latter.

It is also being discovered that the human body and its organs are much more than what the surgeon or physician observes from the outside. This body is not merely a physical object to be seen and measured from a detached point of view. It is also a phase of personal existence. As Marcel says, I *am* my body. I do not merely have it as an instrument.

My body is not a thing from which I am separated. It is not even an instrument, for it is the necessary condition for the existence of any instruments. It is a part of me, a level of my being. Nevertheless there are other levels, like thoughts and choices which are quite distinct, and yet I am one person. If I say *I am mind,* I leave out the body. If I say *I am body,* I leave out the mind. If I follow Descartes in saying *I am both,* I cut myself in two. Is it not clear that we are fumbling for a more basic concept, neither mind nor matter, but broad enough to include both levels? *Being* is precisely such a concept, long reduced in our modern languages to a semidormant state. If we are to understand the unity of the human person, we must revive this "obvious" concept and put it to new uses. Thus in his penetrating discussion of the mind-body problem in the *Mystery of Being,* Marcel refers to the active being of the human person who *incarnates himself in his body,* and *who lives it.*

Of central importance for the understanding of personal existence is anxiety. The peculiar quality of anxious feeling was recognized in the classic literature of Christianity. In modern times, however, it has been neglected and ignored. Descartes, for example, does not even mention it in his treatise on the *Passions of the Soul.* Most of us are now aware that it has some importance for abnormal psychology, but we regard it as a morbid symptom of some kind which certainly plays no major role in normal life. Kierkegaard was the first modern thinker who recognized this strange phenomenon and challenged the prevailing invidious interpretation. He is followed in this by the existentialists of our time who agree on the importance of the role it plays in human existence. There are, of course, many different interpretations, but that given by Heidegger in *Sein und Zeit* is now the most carefully thought out and widely accepted.

Like Kierkegaard, he works out his conception of anxiety by contrasting it with fear, from which it differs in two basic respects. In the case of fear, I am afraid *of* some definite object approaching me *because of* its threat to some project or active phase of my being. The *of which* is always different from the *because of which.* Thus I am afraid *of* such and such an eye disease *because of* my research. In the case of anxiety, no such difference is observed. If we question a really anxious person as to precisely what it is he is anxious about, he will say: "I don't know, really nothing." If we ask him why—because of what is he anxious?—we elicit the same reply. What does it mean? What is this nothing?

In our everyday life, we are for the most part lost in the things we do, the functions we perform. Thus we say he is a lawyer or a doctor; she is a teacher or a nurse. These functions are interchangeable and can be performed by others. In personal existence, however, there is something unique and irreplaceable, which goes deeper than this. My own existence can be totally grasped only in the final perspective of my death. It is the whole of my being-in-the-world that I am anxious about, for the sake of this being itself as it might be, if its last possibilities were fully maintained up to the very end. This existence of mine is not just the functions I perform. It is not any of *the things* I do. It is precisely no-thing. The answer is correct.

The definite things that I fear may be strong and dangerous. But precautions may be taken; measures may be adopted to ward them off. Such dangers are usually shared by others. Even if not, they may give us advice and active assistance. The object of anxiety is nothing at all of this sort. It is now my very being that is at stake; not the various functions that might be done by others, but what I alone can do on my own responsibility; not this or that phase of my being, not the next ten days or the next ten years, but the whole of my being-to-the-end. Is my factual being-in-the-world as I am now the real being that I *have* to be? Such anxious questions as this cannot be answered by any resort to technological instruments. No calculating machine can answer them. No other can answer them for me. They may, however, be evaded.

I may run away from my anxiety when it begins to encircle me. I may discard it as a morbid delusion, deciding to be sensible and to go about my business. Here, too, I must face risks. But these are no longer a misty nothingness, but definite dangers against which definite precautions may be taken. This depersonalization of existence is, in fact, the easier way. Hence we may be able to glimpse what Heidegger means by his statement that the impersonal *one* of everyday life (*das Man*) is constantly evading his anxiety and attempting to replace it by derived forms of fear.

This strange feeling singles out the person by himself. Like death, it is something that I must face alone. It also brings me before those last possibilities of my total existence which elicit final choice. Hence Kierkegaard said that anxiety was the gateway to human freedom. As soon as we pass through this gateway we are confronted with the mysterious phenomenon of conscience, of which Heidegger has also presented a very penetrating analysis.

We now tend to picture conscience by the image of a courtroom scene in which, after a guilty action, I am called before a stern judge who passes a severe sentence by reference to fixed rules. According to Heidegger, this is a distorted picture which fails to do justice to the actual phenomenon in several important respects. It does not explain why we speak of conscience as "a distant voice" or "call," nor why we refer to "the goads and pricks" of conscience. These expressions would seem to suggest a summons to future action rather than an *ex post facto* judgment on acts already performed. The threat of conscience is not restricted to certain specific acts. It penetrates to the depths of our being, and threatens our rules and norms as well. How then is it to be interpreted? Heidegger's existential analysis of man enables him to answer this question in a way that is both original and revealing.

Most of us have abandoned ourselves to objective ways of thought and to the impersonal modes of everyday life. Kierkegaard has this in mind when he speaks of an acquaintance who was so detached and objective about his own affairs that in talking to him one felt he was listening not to the man himself but to a distant relative, perhaps an uncle. Usually, I do not say what I really think, nor act as I really choose. I say the sort of thing that one would say, and do the sort of thing that one does. This is my guilt, the futile, distracted being that I have been and feel myself now to be.

But man is always more than what he already is. He is also projected ahead of himself into the future, even into his last and final future. All men know that they face death. They are at least dimly aware of their final possibilities, of what they might be if they strained their capacities to the very limit. Since Kirkegaard called attention to it, this phenomenon, what we call personal wholeness or integrity, has been carefully analyzed by Heidegger and other existential thinkers.

The parts of a physical process can never exist all together at once. It achieves itself in successive stages. At a given moment it is not the past and not the future, but just what it is. The cognitive being of man gives rise to a very different structure. I not only grow out of the past like a plant: I am now the past that I have been. The future is not merely something external that may happen to me: by self-reflection and choice I can project my future. And insofar as I do this, I am now the future I project. Thus it is possible for man to achieve a new and distinctively human type of wholeness, the concentration of an integral past and integral future in a present act.

The most distinctively human acts have this sort of integrity. When confronted by them in history or in our own experience, we are impressed by the sense that in them the full force of a whole human life—future, present, and past—is being expressed. This is human existence in its most concentrated form. It may seem to occur in a single moment of critical decision. But as a matter of fact, such a moment requires a prolonged preparation and arduous discipline. Human action is always historical and rooted in the past. If integral action is to be achieved, the first step must be to accept a total responsibility for the past that I have been, with all the weakness, ugliness, and guilt that attaches to it. Then there may be a choice which will commit me only to a certain degree, with a certain part of my being, for several days or months or years, after which it is replaced by other choices. Such a life disappears into a past that is not maintained. It is lived successively like a process that runs off in time. The *whole* of the man is never engaged with the *whole* of his personality at a present moment, but only certain parts of himself that appear for an interval and then disappear. A genuine choice commits me with the whole of my being up to the very end. Such a choice must be renewed, and, to use a term from Kierkegaard, "repeated" from day to day. Otherwise the historic structure of life disintegrates, and its powers waste away.

The whole existentialist literature is saturated with a poignant sense of the fragility and contingency of man. From the time of Kierkegaard's bitter rejection of the Hegelian doctrine of an immanent, absolute spirit, it has been primarily a philosophy of finitude. This finitude is to be understood not so much in terms of absent properties as of pervasive obstacles which check the power of our free existence, and whose obstructive influence is present in every act that we perform. Certain obstacles are open to objective analysis. Once understood, we may take measures against them and sometimes, by the application of scientific intelligence, overcome them one by one. Other obstacles, however, are beyond them. They tower over our action like great walls we cannot climb, and through which we can never pass. Against these, technological instruments, in the end, are useless. They are the final and inexorable limits of our being. Jaspers has called them boundary-situations, and has described several with penetrating clarity.

One of them is the *situationality* of our existence. I may analyze clearly the difficulties of my present position, make shrewd calculations, and throw myself into the task of overcoming them. But if I succeed, it is only to find myself in another situation with further obstacles to overcome. Wherever I am, whatever I do, I am always in a situation. This is an unsurpassable limit of our existence.

Another such limit is what we call *chance*, which can never be clearly predicted and may always intrude at the last moment to upset the best-laid plans.

Conflict is a further limit of this sort. Though we may disguise it and try to conceal it from ourselves, it conditions our existence constantly and fundamentally. Every moment that I live deprives someone else of existence. My life is possible only through military conquests made by those who came before me. Its continuance, together with that of millions of others, now depends upon weapons of vast destructive power. No doubt the forms of conflict and competition may be changed. But to think of eliminating them entirely is to indulge in a futile dream.

As we have already noted, what we call *guilt* is another such ultimate limit. Here again we may try to run away from it and ignore it. But these attempts are futile. In the end, whatever I choose, whatever I do, I am always guilty.

Then there is the final limit of *death,* a dominant theme in the literature of existentialism, beginning with Kierkegaard. In it, all the marks of an existential limit emerge with peculiar clarity. That it is, all men are sure. I know that I am going to die. But I cannot see clearly beyond. I cannot pass through as I am. It may be postponed and pushed back by medical science, but *in the end* such measures are futile. It looms over me as an inexorable and inscrutable wall about which I can do nothing.

It is true that technical measures and manipulations are helpless against such limits. In this sense, nothing can be done. But there is another sense in which much can be done. To reflect upon these boundaries seriously is to raise the ultimate questions of our existence. The way we face them reveals the kind of being we are, for the way a finite being holds itself with respect to its ultimate limits is the very core of that being. Even an unconscious thing becomes diluted and confused when its limits are confused. But to be aware belongs to the being of man. Hence, to become evasive or confused about these limits is to confuse our existence at its very core. As Jaspers says: "authentic existence is possible only in the light of these ultimate boundaries."

Is there anything radically new about this philosophy? If we take account of the best existentialist writings, such as Kierkegaard's *Concluding Unscientific Postscript*, Marcel's *Metaphysical Journal*, Jaspers' *Philosophie*, and Heidegger's *Sein und Zeit*, an affirmative answer must be given.

Existential Thinking and William James

Existential thinking has developed a highly original and cogent criticism of the traditional conception of a philosophical system which is fixed and finished for all time. Human existence is always proceeding and never finished. Hence it cannot be systematized in this way. This traditional conception has now been replaced by a new way of understanding philosophy as a description and interpretation of our existence as it is lived in the concrete, and, therefore, in closer touch with the actual philosophic process that is ever proceeding in living men. Existential philosophy has shown that traditional philosophy, by neglecting what it called the confused, unstable, and subjective, has neglected existence, and has fallen into an abstract essentialism which is out of touch with being as it is. In exploring these regions of "the subjective" it has shed much-needed light on hitherto neglected phenomena, like mood and feeling, and new light on others, like time, death, conscience, and choice; though, as we shall see, many of these important insights have been achieved with the aid of phenomenology.

In its investigations of choice, it has helped to show that man not only possesses a freedom of action, but also a freedom of understanding himself in different ways, no one of which can be logically or rationally demonstrated. This has enabled it to work out a view of human freedom that is deeper and wider in range than traditional conceptions. In concerning itself with the long-forgotten horizon of being and its diverse modes of manifestation, it has been able to bring together many seemingly unrelated phenomena, and to overcome traditional dualisms like that of mind vs. body and subject vs. object. Kierkegaard was deeply concerned with the question of truth. Guided by his suggestions, existential philosophers of our own time have been able to show that, in addition to the truth of correspondence with which the tradition has been almost exclusively concerned, there is another kind of truth, called subjective truth by Kierkegaard, which is not restricted to objects, but which is able directly to reveal our lived existence as it proceeds, in its subjective as well as in its objective phases.

With the aid of phenomenology, these existential explorations have been carried on during the twentieth century by thinkers coming from very divergent backgrounds in different nations of the West. Among these, Dostoevski and Berdyaev must be mentioned in Russia; Ortega y Gasset in Spain; Bergson, Blondel, and Merleau-Ponty in France; and Husserl, Scheler, and Heidegger in Germany. It is widely believed that American and English philosophy never actively participated in this movement away from abstract system-building toward a more vital and concrete philosophy. But this is an error. The American thinker William James must certainly be mentioned in this connection, for in his own way he contributed to every one of the major phases of existentialist thought that we have indicated.

Like many of his distinguished colleagues in other lands, he was repelled by the academic abstractness of traditional philosophy, and, like Kierkegaard, attacked the pretentious claims of the great Hegelian system.[1] In seeking to work out a way of thinking less remote from our lived existence, he soon recognized that vast regions of experience lay neglected and hidden under the invidious epithet "subjective," and devoted himself to the exploration of these regions. In this exploration, which he pursued throughout much of his great text on *Psychology* and his later *Essays*, he shed new light on habit, not as it can be objectively observed in a laboratory, but as it is lived by existing persons,[2] on attention,[3] on the feeling or *Sentiment of Rationality*,[4] and on religious experiences, not as they are placed in an alien frame and externally interpreted, but as they are revealed

[1] Cf. "Hegel and His Method," Lecture III, in *A Pluralistic Universe* (New York: Longmans, Green, 1909).
[2] Cf. *The Principles of Psychology* (New York: Holt, 1893), I, pp. 120–127.
[3] *Op. cit.*, I, Ch. XI.
[4] *The Will to Believe and Other Essays* (New York: Longmans, Green, 1897).

by individuals living through them (*The Varieties of Religious Experience*).

Constantly on his guard against subjectivism, he was able to describe these phenomena and to catch their tone and existential style. Like other existential thinkers before and after him, he realized that freedom lay deeper in our human being than any mere indifference of a single faculty, the will; he devoted a lifelong attention to it, and in his *Psychology* identified it basically with the direction of mental attention to a single object of concern.[5] Always skeptical of the traditional dualism of mind vs. body, he struggled constantly to grasp human behavior integrally in a way that would do justice to both its "mental" as well as its "physical" aspects, and often used the word "existence" to grasp them in their being together.

Perceiving rightly that we cannot get outside our lived existence to make up propositions which may agree or disagree with it, he worked out many penetrating criticisms of the correspondence theory of truth. While he never arrived at a satisfactory formulation of his own pragmatic theory, he was right in groping for a more primordial kind of truth, which directly reveals our existence in the world as we live it, and which is confirmed by its historical fruitfulness. Like Kierkegaard, Jaspers, and other existential philosophers, he recognized the fragility and essential finitude of our human existence, and the element of risk that is always involved in the acceptance of any guiding faith. Though in his own country, James's ideas have been buried by different trends of thought associated with the word "pragmatism," they have been deeply studied and cultivated in Europe where, as we shall see, they have contributed to the movement now known as phenomenology, which it is now important for us to consider.

The Phenomenological Movement

What is now called the phenomenological movement began at the turn of the century with two thinkers, Franz Brentano and Edmund Husserl, who shared James's acute dissatisfaction with traditional philosophy as too abstract and remote from the given evidence. In their attempt to work out a way of thinking closer to our lived experience, they made a close study of British empiricism, which at that time was the best known "empirical" philosophy. As a result of

[5] *The Principles of Psychology, op. cit.*, p. 561.

this study, their attitude became very negative, and they criticized this account of experience as being highly inaccurate and distorted. In working out what he called a *radical empiricism,* James also criticized this supposedly empirical philosophy, with which he was very familiar, along similar lines. He especially stressed its reduction of experience to isolated, atomic units, called ideas or impressions, and its failure to do justice to the relational structures that belong to our lived experience.[6] Brentano first, and later Husserl, also recognized this defect in British empiricism, and focused their attention especially on the relational, or what they called the *intentional,* structure of human awareness that is always related to, or stretched out toward, its object. It was this conception which later led Husserl and Heidegger to their discovery of the human life-world, or *Lebenswelt,* as Husserl called it.

This meant the end of the ancient view that the human individual is a *subject,* or substance enclosed within itself, and that human consciousness is to be understood as the presence of atomic units of experience within this substantial container. It is true that consciousness begins with mental acts. But these acts are essentially related to their objects. Every desire is the desire *of* something, and every act of understanding is the understanding *of* something. In order to comprehend one pole of this relational structure, it is necessary to comprehend the other pole as well. For example, we cannot fully understand a fearful object unless we also understand the intentional act of fear that fears it. This discovery of the intentional nature of awareness opened up many new fields for exploration, and early phenomenological studies which tried to describe both the empirical object in its original evidence as it is given, as well as the intentional attitude to which it is given, shed a new light on many phenomena in the fields of ethics, religion, aesthetics, and even mathematics. But Husserl was a highly original thinker, never willing to remain on a single level of thought, but always raising deeper questions leading him to ever deeper levels.

He soon saw that the traditional conception of an external world beyond our immediate awareness was incompatible with the intentional structure of our lived experience. Since all our conscious acts and attitudes are stretched out into a field which is ready for any objects that may be given, we exist in a world that is in a certain

[6] Cf. "The World of Pure Experience," in *Essays in Radical Empiricism* (New York: Longmans, Green, 1943).

sense "subjective," and relative to man and his meanings, though this world horizon, which we carry with us wherever we go, is the broadest and widest horizon to which we have access. Everything that we sense or feel or understand has its place within this far-reaching horizon of the *Lebenswelt*. Husserl felt that the structures of this life-world were quite different from those of the scientific universe, as we shall call it, which abstracts from subjective feelings and attitudes, so far as this is possible. But how is this life-world to be grasped as a whole? Husserl's answer to this question took a special form, which it is important for us to notice.

According to him, in the natural attitude of everyday life our interest is outwardly directed, or centrifugal. We pay little or no attention to our own intentions as we live them through, but lose ourselves in the objects to which these intentions are directed and on whose existence and value we depend, once our intentions are established. As Husserl saw it, the whole phenomenological method required an abandonment of this naïve, outwardly directed attitude which dominates our daily lives. We must become conscious of the original attitudes and meanings on which we ourselves and the constitution of the world in which we exist are even more dependent.

Now according to Husserl, we have no clear awareness of our intentional acts as we live them through, for all consciousness is intentional, or directed to an object. Hence for him, the only way to understand the basic intentions which constitute our world is to gain a position outside it, from which we can view it as a whole, together with the basic intentions which make it possible. Husserl called the phenomenological observer in such an extra-worldly position *the transcendental ego;* and the gaining of such a position from which our whole subjective-objective existence in the world could be objectively viewed, *the transcendental reduction.* To attain this point of view, I must become indifferent to my own basic concerns, and even to existence, my own and that of other things and persons; for, unless I can get beyond them, I can never bring them before me as intentional objects to be understood. There is no doubt that this ideal has stimulated many useful and important investigations. But it is subject to the following two criticisms.

First, there are difficulties in even imagining a transcendental ego that is able to detach itself from all concrete existence to observe the world as a whole. One wonders if this is not a mere figment of idealistic fantasy, and if all the transcendental intentions which are supposed to make the world of history possible are not a very poor substitute for the variable conditions of concrete selves located in history, which are apparently the only selves there are. Second, even though it may be true that Husserl's disregard for *(bracketing of)* existence may have been for the sake of understanding it, one wonders if something is not lost when existence is turned into an object to be gazed at from a detached point of view. If we are to follow Husserl's great motto: *to the things themselves,* must we not rather, in this case at least, find some way of penetrating into existence as it is lived from the inside? These reasons, among others, have led later phenomenologists, including Husserl's student Heidegger, to reject the idealistic notions of the transcendental ego and the transcendental reduction, which were taken from the idealistic tradition of German philosophy, and were certainly remote from the thought of William James. But if we cannot escape from the world to know it from a distance objectively, how then can we know it?

In working out a coherent answer to this question, later phenomenologists have not followed the idealistic way of Husserl. They have followed another way, first suggested by Descartes in his famous *cogito,* now known as reflexive analysis.[7] This French tradition has always been skeptical of any attempt to know the self as an object. Husserl was wrong in thinking that all consciousness is intentional and outwardly directed. This is only partially true, for there is another self-consciousness that knows itself, not objectively but in the very act. Thus I do not have to watch myself walking from an external point of view. There is a mode of awareness that dwells in my walking, and which gives me the feel of walking as I walk. It also stretches around me and beyond me to reveal the direction in which I am moving and how fast. It is true that, for the most part, this immediate consciousness is submerged and repressed by my awareness of objects. But it can be developed and made explicit by the right sort of phenomenological attention.

Hence it is possible for me to become clearly aware of myself and my whole situation in the world without any transcendental ego gazing at me from outside. I can do this from the inside by cultivating and developing the consciousness that inhabits my intentional acts as they reach out toward their objects. In fact, the living phe-

[7] For a clear account of this French tradition and its relation to contemporary phenomenology, cf. Thevenaz, *What Is Phenomenology?* ed. J. M. Edie (Chicago: Quadrangle Press, 1962), pp. 113–133.

nomenology of our time is precisely the disciplined cultivation of this type of awareness which dwells in our lived existence, attending to it, developing it, and clarifying it without objectifying it and placing it in an alien frame. This is what phenomenology means to Sartre and Merleau-Ponty; and even Heidegger, strongly influenced by the German, transcendental tradition, has abandoned the transcendental ego and the transcendental reduction. This reflexive analysis is, of course, much closer to the thought of Kierkegaard as well as of James. It has enabled phenomenology to unite with the existential stream of thought, stemming from Kierkegaard, in one of the most significant developments of our time. We, also, will follow this course and will interpret phenomenology as not opposed to existential philosophy, in the following manner.

Phenomenology Today: An Interpretation

In this volume, the term *phenomenology* will mean the revealing and clarifying of the phenomena; that is, anything which shows itself in any mode, shape, or manner. In choosing what to investigate, and in the early stages, the phenomenologist must be guided by ordinary language. This guidance has proved to be especially helpful insofar as a relevant word can be broken down into its component roots and its present meaning understood as one stage of a living history, rather than as a fixed and frozen form. This sense of the history of a meaning may reveal fertile ambiguities and hint of depths not yet explored. But in any one stage of its development, ordinary language is full of concealment and deception, and if followed without constant attention to the actual situations in which the language is used, it will turn out to be an unsafe guide. The original significance of a term may have been covered over and distorted by an incidental interpretation that clings to the surface and is incapable of growth. Even worse than this, the meaning of a basic term, like *being*, for example, may have become so dulled by habitual usage that it is lost in the veils of "the obvious," and becomes little more than a mere word with a syntactic function. The aim of phenomenology is to penetrate through all these disguises and concealments to the things themselves, to uncover them, and to discover what they really mean.

No recipes can be given for this activity of discovering; it cannot be reduced to fixed procedures in a mechanical routine. But in the practice of living phenomenologists, three steps may be clearly distinguished. The historical facts of the life-world, with which human-istic scholars are concerned, are already interpreted and carry a meaning of their own. In this respect, they differ radically from the uninterpreted facts of the physical sciences (cf. Chapter 5). Hence, once he has chosen the phenomenon he wishes to study, the investigator must first of all take examples of this phenomenon, and in each case try to grasp its meaning as it was lived through by the persons involved. This requires a capacity to play the role of another, which is closely related to the actor's art. If I am to understand the ceremonies of a primitive tribe, the art of an alien people, the problems of another person, or even my own past of a year ago, I must first perform what Husserl called an *epoché;* that is, I must hold my present attitudes and beliefs in abeyance (put them in *parentheses*), and then use my feeling, my imagination, every noetic power at my command to put myself into the position of the person involved, to enter into his attitudes until I learn to follow them, and to grasp their living sense.

This ability to follow through imaginatively the acts and attitudes of others is essential to every phase of phenomenological research. It is important in the study of history, anthropology, and now in psychiatry. Phenomenology has had influence on such studies and has, in turn, been influenced by them. It is important to realize that in placing myself in the position of another, it is not merely a matter of imagining myself to be performing his acts. I must be able to understand these acts as he does, from the inside. I must enter into his world of meaning, and not merely observe him as an object in my own. This grasping of a range of phenomena as they are lived through and understood by the different people involved is the first step in any disciplined investigation of human experience. The work of the novelist or literary artist is, of course, finished when he has created, lived through imaginatively, and finally expressed the world—or some aspect of the world—of a person. Some have held that the work of an historian or anthropologist is finished when he has grasped the world of an existing person or group, as it was understood by them. But, however it may be with them, the phenomenologist cannot stop here. He must proceed further to another *epoché*.

Just as before he gained a certain distance from himself by bracketing his own beliefs and prejudices, so he must gain a distance from the welter of conflicting fields of meaning which confront him. He must now ask, not what do these experiences mean for the people living them through, but what do they really mean for man in general and the world of man? If, for example, we are concerned with that vast array of phenomena classified by ordinary language as magic, we must first try to clarify the meaning of this ambiguous term. What is it that holds these varying manifestations under a single ideal structure, or type? If the type that is vaguely suggested by ordinary language is inadequate, what modifications must be introduced? Then we also need to ask: What is the meaning of this type?—for meanings always point beyond themselves. Is magic to be understood as a primitive form of science and technology, or as an aspect of religion still far from dead? A great phenomenological student of primitive religion has suggested that, while these must be recognized as subordinate aspects of magic, its original meaning must be understood as a first protest by man against the uncontrolled miseries and agonies of the existence into which he was thrown, a first despairing attempt to give meaning to life, to humanize the world.[8] This suggestion has not yet been confirmed. If it is, we may be able to make sense out of this puzzling array of phenomena and to give them a meaningful place in world history.

If they are found everywhere, these structures are clearly important. But they need not be universal to be significant. They may be found only in a certain stage of historical development, in a single culture, or even in a single person. But if so, they must carry a possible significance for all men. These types are not events, though events may carry them. They are meanings which can be repeatedly expressed and understood in intelligible discourse. They are neither causes nor laws of succession. The meaning of magic as a human protest tells us nothing of the alien antecedents that brought it into existence. It does not state a law. It is simply concerned with a set of events, and their place in the human world into which our different personal and tribal versions open. The existential structures discussed in the first part of this chapter—the lived body, anxiety, conscience, death, and choice—are types of this kind, which have been more clearly uncovered and revealed by the methods of phenomenology. Much more remains to be done, but it has been shown, I believe, that they have a lasting place in the world of man, and some further light has been shed on their real meaning in the world. But this is not the end. A third *epoché* is still before us.

[8] G. Van der Leeuw, "Myth and Magic," in *Einführung in die Phänomenologie der Religion*, 1st ed. (Tübingen, J. C. B. Mohr, 1925).

Just as individual and cultural versions open into the human world, so does this open into a wider horizon which we shall call *the world.* The human world encompasses the life space and the time of human history, as well as the extensions of these which we owe to science and technology (cf. Chapter 5), in fact, all the natural objects and artifacts that can be ordered around man as a center of meaning. What then leads us beyond this to a third horizon? The answer may be briefly suggested as follows. The very fact that every version of the world, as well as the human world itself, is a *horizon* shows that something lies beyond. This is confirmed by our sense of the limits of our knowledge. Even more significant is the fact that the human world is centered in man. But surely man is not the only possible center of meaning. What of other horizons centered around other beings? What sort of worlds would they be, or would they even be worlds at all?

Even a negative answer to the last question involves us in speculation concerning a final, all-encompassing horizon, which includes illusions, dreams, hallucinations, the human world together with all its versions, all beings lying beyond it, and all the other perspectives of radically different kinds. We shall call this last "horizon," if it is a horizon, *the world.* It has been, and always will be, the object of the most radical and far-reaching ontological or metaphysical speculations. We shall present a speculative argument of this kind in Chapter 11 of this book.

Since life is short, and since men have rightly felt that they need to direct their lives in the light of the broadest horizon to which they have access, they have usually started with questionable metaphysical assumptions, in view of which they have projected an interpretation of the human world, and have finally worked out their own versions accordingly. Since meaning always points beyond itself to ultimate things, this procedure is, perhaps, not completely unavoidable. But the evidence relevant to metaphysics that is immediately available to us is very tenuous. We have direct access only to our own versions of existence, and to those of others through communication. Hence a chief aim of phenomenology is to reverse this usual direction of thought by the use of an *epoché,* as we have suggested. It is possible for me to *bracket,* or to hold in suspension, my opinions about the human world, as I seek to understand one or more versions as they were lived in fact by existing peoples or persons. Then, by a careful study of these versions, it may be possible to sort out types that are lasting, universal, and meaningful from what is temporary, incidental, and insignificant, and on this factual basis, to arrive at founded insights concerning the human world. In pursuing this important task of exploring the human life-world, philosophy can proceed in a disciplined manner, and can cooperate with other human sciences which are beginning to recognize this need, and to use phenomenological methods, thus confirming Husserl's life-long conviction that philosophy could become a strict and intersubjectively responsible discipline.

Similarly, as I focus my attention on this human world, it is possible for me to bracket my ultimate metaphysical beliefs. Then, in the light of basic, existential patterns in the life-world, it may be possible to engage in modes of speculation concerning *the* world, which are founded on relevant evidence. No doubt there will always be room, at this final level, for different ultimate choices. But to anyone familiar with the relevant evidence, many choices will be seen to be ruled out by the facts. So the range of choice may be narrowed, and the difference between an informed and serious choice, on the one hand, and an arbitrary, temperamental preference, on the other, will become increasingly evident. Phenomenology has already stimulated original work in all these areas of philosophical endeavor. In certain cases, it has arrived at lasting results, confirmed by different investigators coming from very different backgrounds. Perhaps the most important of these is the discovery of the human life-world, called *Lebenswelt* by Husserl, and it is to this subject that we must now turn in the three succeeding chapters.

Part II

The Human Life-World

Chapter 3

Is There a World
of Ordinary Language?

Having recently spent seven months on the continent of Europe and
having conversed with philosophers in five different countries there,
I was surprised to find, under wide diversities and sharp disagreements, a well-marked current moving in a single direction. Apart
from members of traditional schools, the living thinkers of Western
Europe are basically concerned with the human life-world, or *Lebenswelt,* as Husserl called it in his last published work, *Die Krisis der
Europäischen Wissenschaften.* I am not suggesting that most European thinkers are now committed to any of the special methods and
doctrines which Husserl defended at different stages of his long and
constantly self-critical career. This is not true. Nevertheless his concern to achieve an accurate description of the concrete phenomena
of the *Lebenswelt,* as they are experienced and expressed in ordinary
language, is a constant theme of all his writings. And in this broad
sense the influence of phenomenology has spread far and wide.
There are, no doubt, other sources for this contemporary interest in
the *Lebenswelt.* But Husserl is perhaps the focal center of this new
empiricism and his influence the most widely recognized.

By *world* Husserl meant not a thing, not any set of objects, but
rather an ultimate horizon within which all such objects and the
individual person himself are actually understood in the "natural
attitude" of everyday life. This horizon of concrete experience is
sharply contrasted with the objective horizons of science which attend exclusively to objects via perspectives that are partial and

41

abstract. As over against these, the world horizon of human life is concrete, subjective, and relative to man. This analysis has now been very generally accepted, and most European philosophers would agree that the task of describing the phenomena of this life-world and of analyzing its structure is of primary importance for philosophy. The scientist, like the rest of us, lives and moves within this world, and in a sense it is presupposed in his investigations. But we cannot expect him to perform the task of analysis, since he is interested in special, abstract objects of his own. Furthermore we must recognize that, since the time of Plato, philosophers have disregarded the *Lebenswelt* as a subjective region of shadows, and have turned their attention rather to transcendent objects and problems.

On the Continent, there is now a widespread skepticism concerning such objects and problems, and a widespread recognition of the need for a more radical empiricism, now generally referred to as phenomenology. The aim of this discipline is to describe the phenomena of everyday life as they are lived in the horizon of the *Lebenswelt*, and the foreign visitor is struck at once by the many philosophical studies of such concrete phenomena as laughter and tears, imagination, sorrow, the feeling of guilt, personal encounter, and so forth. In these studies, abstract terms and technical language are avoided, for it is recognized that the many shades of meaning and the very ambiguities of ordinary language are themselves significant and much closer to the concrete. Each abstract horizon of science has its own special mode of abstract speech. But to deal with the inexhaustibly open and ever-changing phenomena of the *Lebenswelt*, a richer, more flexible, and more far-ranging mode of expression is required. What we call "ordinary language" develops and lives in the *Lebenswelt*. Hence this radical empiricism has brought forth a deep and widespread interest in the modes and structures of common speech. This is of course only a brief sketch but, I believe, a true characterization of what is going on now on the continent of Europe.

After returning to this country via England and Oxford, I was deeply impressed by certain apparent similarities between the living philosophy of the Continent and the linguistic analysis which is now proceeding so widely and so intensively in the Anglo-Saxon countries. Here, too, I noted a similar distrust of transcendent, unobservable objects, and of the artificial problems engendered by such assumptions. One also finds a similar urge toward empiricism, a respect for what is called *fact*, and finally a similar recognition of the depth and fertility of that ordinary language which is presupposed in all the artificial constructions and abstract modes of speech which grow out of it. These similarities led me to reflect on the mistrust and suspicion which is so openly expressed on both sides of the English Channel, and to wonder if this is not somehow based on avoidable misunderstandings and misconceptions. Is not the ordinary language of daily life correlated with the ordinary phenomena of the life-world? Is it not true that the careful study of the one must require the careful study of the other? Are not phenomenology (in the current broad sense) and linguistic analysis both approaching the same thing (concrete experience) from different angles? Are they, then, not so much severely opposed as mutually supplementary and fructifying?

I think that these questions need to be asked, and that an affirmative answer is possible. But before an affirmative answer can be given, certain difficulties must be cleared away. There are, of course, evident differences between these two movements of thought. Perhaps the most basic of these is a tendency on the part of analytic philosophers to identify the world of everyday experience with the objective universe, or with the facts revealed by different sciences, and thus to follow our tradition in slurring over the concrete and humanly relative phenomena of the *Lebenswelt* with which ordinary language is primarily concerned. In this chapter, I shall first of all give a concrete illustration of this failure to distinguish between what we may call abstract facts of science and concrete phenomena of the *Lebenswelt;* second, I shall try to clarify the meaning of this term *Lebenswelt;* third, defend the distinction between scientific facts and world facts; fourth, offer some criticism of two recent attempts to avoid it; and finally, fifth, raise a question for analytic philosophers concerning the need for a distinctive kind of empirical analysis which philosophers alone can perform.

A Reduction of Fact to Scientific Fact

The above tendency to merge all facts together under a scientific rubric is at present very widespread in England and America owing to the prestige of science, and might be illustrated from many different works. I shall choose a recent essay by G. J. Warnock entitled

"Analysis and Imagination," in the volume *Revolution in Philosophy*.[1]

Warnock is considering the different tasks which he believes need to be performed by philosophical analysis. The first is to exercise a therapeutic function in revealing "the distorted character" of certain general philosophical questions (p. 114) and "breaking down the cramping rigidities which generate some philosophical difficulties" (*ibid.*). No radical empiricist could possibly disagree with this recommendation, especially as the author points out that the only remedy for such misguided questions "is to put our concepts back to work again in actual examples, to observe how in concrete cases they do actually function" (*ibid.*). Next Warnock turns to "the 'systematic' work of analytic philosophy," which is to "examine language in the spirit of pure research, describing and ordering its features . . ." (p. 115). The phenomenologist can only applaud this aim.

After this, the "explanatory task of analysis" is considered. It is possible for the analyst to ask, "Why do we use language in this way? (p. 117). Why, for example, do we use the concept of cause as we do? In order to answer such questions, Warnock again recommends a procedure that is thoroughly empirical and phenomenological. "To explain our concept of causation," he says, "we need to trace its connections not only with other concepts that we employ, but also with empirical facts about the course of events in the world, and the ways in which we concern ourselves with these events" (p. 118). In this passage he seems to be speaking not merely about the objective facts of an abstract scientific horizon, but about concrete facts in the life-world with which we ourselves are concerned.

Finally Warnock turns to the "inventive" function of analysis: How can the analytic philosopher be original? We think at once of the array of divergent systems, and as soon as metaphysics enters into the picture, everything changes. The idea that philosophy has any empirical function to exercise fades away. The world of fact is the same for all of us. There are no philosophic problems here. A past metaphysician, like Berkeley, "saw the same world that the rest of us see, but saw it from a rather different angle" (p. 122). He may have invented a new "conceptual apparatus," but in claiming that he was "discovering something real" (*ibid.*) he was wholly mistaken. Real facts are the province of science. In this respect the logical positivists were quite correct. "It was precisely by making these claims, by pre-

---

[1] (New York: St. Martin's Press, 1957), pp. 111–126.

senting themselves as super-scientists, discoverers par excellence, that metaphysicians drew on their own heads the formidable bludgeon of Logical Positivism" (*ibid.*). In claiming any access to facts of any sort not thoroughly covered by some science, philosophy sets itself "on quite the wrong ground, ground from which it is liable to be destructively expelled" (p. 123).

After some reflection on these passages, the reader is led to ask, does philosophy exercise any factual function or does it not? Warnock seems to give a divided answer, and this ambiguity, I believe, is significant. In dealing with the therapeutic and systematic functions of philosophy, he recognizes that the analyst is not concerned with concepts alone but also with certain facts, recalling our attention to "the concrete and the familiar" (p. 115). Now science may begin with the concrete and the familiar but it does not end there. Indeed, to be in this condition is precisely the sign of imperfection and immaturity. Each science tries to move away from this, as soon as possible, to the abstract and the unfamiliar. To dwell on these familiar facts of concrete experience in the attempt to analyze them accurately and interpret them is not the function of science. If it is to be performed at all, it is the function of philosophy. If there are such *philosophic facts*, or world facts, as we may call them, not "covered" by any special science, then it is false to assert that philosophy is exclusively concerned with language alone, or with our "conceptual apparatus."

But then a few pages further on, after suggesting something of this kind, Warnock ridicules the whole idea that philosophers (now called metaphysicians) might be "discoverers" (p. 122), and asserts that any claim to factual evidence will bring them onto ground from which they are "liable to be destructively expelled," especially by Logical Positivists.

This, I believe, is a confusion, to which I desire to call the reader's attention. It is in essence the failure to recognize an important ambiguity in the English word "fact," which refers not only to scientific facts, such as that the boiling point of water at normal atmospheric pressure is 100° C., but also to *world facts*, as I shall call them, such as that the pencil I write with is on the table at my right. I shall maintain that these two senses of the same word "fact" are quite distinct, and that our constant tendency to reduce the second to the first leads to basic confusions concerning the nature of philosophy. Before turning to this distinction, however, I must first say a few words about the human world which has now emerged as one of the best confirmed discoveries of phenomenology. This is a term in ordinary usage which we have already used without special explanation. Now let us analyze it a little more carefully.

The Human World

The American philosopher William James played a vital role in this important discovery. In his *Principles of Psychology* (pp. 258, 281–82, and 471–72) he points out that the objects of experience are not insular impressions sharply separated from one another, as the British empiricists had supposed. This is a logical ideal of how we should experience them. In our actual perception, however, they are always surrounded by a field of meanings which refer them to other objects. These references are easily taken for granted, or forgotten, as we concentrate on the central object of our attention. But they play a vital role in all perception. James called them *fringes,* and the sections noted above were carefully read and annotated by Husserl.[2] They led Husserl to his notion of the *Lebenswelt,* the last horizon of meanings in what he called the natural attitude of our everyday existence.[3] After Husserl's investigations, this world horizon has been studied by many thinkers, including Sartre and Merleau-Ponty in France. One of the most thoroughgoing and disciplined analyses is that of Heidegger in his important work, *Sein und Zeit.* The chief results of these studies may be briefly summarized as follows.

The life-world is a horizon of meaning which, in some particular version, is always found with men. It includes all the persons, events, and things which we do or can encounter. When we wish to express the most far-ranging doubt concerning the location of anything in any region, we say, where in the world will you find it? This world includes not only spaces and places but things, persons, and modes of action. Hence when we seek to express the most far-reaching doubt concerning any of these categories, we use similar expressions, saying, What in the world is this thing? who in the world will do this for you? and how in the world will he do it? This horizon of meaning encompasses all that we can know by feeling, thought,

[2] Cf. Aron Gurwitsch, "Les 'fringes,' selon James" in *Théorie du champs de la conscience* (Paris: Desclée De Brouwer, 1957), pp. 246ff. for an account of Husserl's relation to James on this, as well as other matters.

[3] Cf. *Krisis der Europäischen Wissenschaften und die transcendentale Phänomenologie* (The Hague: Martinus Nijhoff, 1954), pp. 127ff.

imagination, and any natural power. Hence, to speak of another world, or of what lies beyond this world, is a reference to what transcends our experience in the widest sense of this word. Any person, event, or thing in the world presupposes this background of meaning, for something not in this world would not be intelligible and would no longer be a thing. Indeed, it would be doubtful whether we could meaningfully refer to it as a being, for what a thing really is, refers to its place in a final world horizon.

The world has a spatial aspect; though, as we have seen, the primordial space of the life-world is very different from any geometric space. These are later abstractions from it. Hence, when I think of myself or some other person as being in the world, I mean something more than mere spatial inclusion, as a cup is in the cupboard, or a shoe is in the box. I am in the world rather as in a field of care, as we speak of a woman as being in nursing, or a young man as in love. This world is divided into the different regions of my care, like the kitchen for cooking, the bedroom for sleeping, and the library for reading and study. The different utensils in these regions are for some use, and are either in or out of their proper places. This referential for-structure is usually taken for granted and hidden under the "obvious." But when something is lacking or out of place, it may suddenly loom into view. The tools of a given region have a bearing on one another; the chair bears on the desk, and the desk on the paper for writing. Whole regions bear on one another, as the procuring of raw materials bears on manufacturing, which is for distribution. All these different regions are finally for the use of man who orders them in different ways, depending on the ultimate objects of his devotion. Hence the world order, or cultural pattern, of one people will differ from that of another; and in those where personal freedom is respected, the world of one individual may differ radically from that of another.

When we first become aware of these differences in world horizons of meaning, which enter into everything that we do and say, we are apt to think of them as isolated islands, each enclosed within itself. But this is a mistake which leads to the influential view now known as *relativism*. It arises from a failure to understand the perspectival character of human awareness. Thus I can never see or grasp, for example, the whole of the table before me, except in a partial perspective from the left or the right, from above or below. But this does not mean that I cannot see the whole table in this way. As I look at the table from above and in front, I can see the bottom of a rear leg, and also the table top that keeps me from seeing the rest. In this and other ways, each perspective leads beyond itself to other parts that it sees itself not to see. Hence, unless it becomes pathologically fixed and frozen, a single perspective remains open to other perspectives revealing other parts of the object without interference. Thus in and through a partial perspective or, even better, through a number of these, I can grasp the style and pattern of the whole.

The same can happen to our versions of the human world of meaning, though there is here an even greater danger of partial fixation and dogmatism. If I become, even to a slight degree, critical of my world of meaning, I can recognize gaps and areas beyond my horizon, involving vast regions that I know I do not know. This enables me, as well as those around me, to distinguish between our versions of the world and the world into which all these versions open. It is a main task of philosophy to keep these versions flexible, so that individuals and groups living in entirely different versions of the world may be able to communicate and to keep on growing. In order to do this, we must recognize, however, that there is no world in itself apart from our human versions, which are all real as far as they go, and must be taken account of in any interpretation of the world which is not hopelessly abstract and partial. There is no world apart from our human versions, and these different versions, unless they become rigid and congealed, open into *the world* which has a place for them and yet transcends them all.

Our lived existence is made up of encounters with powers and persons absolutely independent of us. Meaning is the human answer to these encounters. Man is the responsible being who can respond in this way, gather things together into a world that makes sense of everything, and, therefore, really is. The meaning of the Battle of Waterloo must take account of the plans and the actions of the men who fought and died there, to the last detail. It is inseparable from the concrete events, precisely as they happened. And yet meaning is relational or referential in character, and always points beyond to something further. Thus the meaning of the battle involves the public policies of France, England, and Prussia, the future course of history, and the projects of those of us who are now alive and trying to interpret it. The world is the ultimate horizon of meaning which tries to do justice to all events of which we are aware, and to all other perspectives alien to our own, by ordering them around our ultimate hopes and aspirations. To find a place for something in such a version of the world, which we have reason to believe fairly closely approximates the world, is to find out what it really is.

We do not know what these alien agencies are before we meet them and struggle with them. We call them beings a priori, in the hope that we may find a meaning in them and thereby find out what they really are. But these independent agencies do not give themselves up without a struggle. They resist not only our acts but our noetic powers as well.[4] Meaning has to be snatched from their hidden depths and brought up into the light of truth bit by bit. But further depths always remain. Being is an ambiguous word, which stands both for this resistance on the part of real beings, as well as for the hope that we shall find their real being or meaning in the world. At first, we grasp only a minimal meaning in these independent beings, their approximate location in space and in time, and whether they seem alien or friendly. These scattered findings we call *facts.* They may be trustworthy and hold up in time, but they are only a beginning. We do not find out what they really mean until we are able to fit them together in ways that make sense in a total horizon of meaning.

This discovering of the sense of things involves two distinct aspects that are usually opposed. On the one hand, full justice must be done to the scattered facts, down to the last detail. Any failure here will jeopardize the most coherent system. But on the other hand, the isolated facts must be fitted together in an overarching world of meaning. Only then can we catch a glimpse of what these alien beings and we ourselves really are. Each way of knowing has its own horizon, some being wider and some less wide. But in each of these we find a division of labor between those who are chiefly concerned with the detailed facts and those who are concentrating on the broader systems of meaning, though these diverse functions are interdependent and often overlap. Thus in science, for example, we find a division of labor between the experimental and the theoretical physicist, and in the life-world there is a similar division of labor between the historian, on the one hand, and the philosophically oriented student on the other.

But are there two horizons of this kind—science and the life-world?

---

[4] For a fuller account of this noetic resistance, cf. my article "Contemporary Phenomenology and the Problem of Existence," *Phil. and Phen. Research,* Vol. XX, No. 2 (December 1959).

If so, these two ways of knowing must be concerned not only with different kinds of meaning but with different kinds of fact. We have noted how Warnock denies such a distinction. For him, there is only one kind of fact—the facts of science. There are no historical or, as we may say, no historical world facts. I believe that this reduction of fact to scientific fact is found not only in the thought of analysts, but also in that of many other philosophers at the present time. It has even begun to exert a marked influence on our ordinary language and our common sense. I have chosen Warnock's essay simply as a clear and fairly typical example of a tendency that is now widespread in English and American philosophy. Indeed, this tendency is firmly grounded in a traditional distrust of the supposedly confused and transitory data of immediate experience, which goes back to the origins of rational thought in the West. But I am not concerned here with this historical background. I am interested only in showing that there is an order of world fact which is bound up with ordinary language, and which is quite distinct from the different ranges and levels of scientific fact.

Two Kinds of Fact

Let us begin, in the first place, with the difference between the one as concrete, the other as abstract. Science certainly begins with individual world facts. But as we have pointed out, it moves as rapidly as possible to various abstract levels where it can formulate certain hypothetical laws of the type, "if A then B." As is well known, these laws do not attempt to describe the actual course of concrete events. They state rather what will happen in general under certain specified conditions. Thus, disregarding atmospheric resistance, a body will fall at such and such a rate, or at a certain pressure water will boil at such and such a temperature. These abstract generalizations are the facts of science. When a science has arrived at maturity, concrete occurrences come into the picture only insofar as they exemplify or conflict with such generalizations. The movement is away from the concrete toward the abstract. Let us now turn to a world fact such as: this yellow pencil is now on the table at my right. The pencil is now here before me as I face the world. Such facts as these are at least as certainly known and as well confirmed by critical observation and intersubjective testing as any scientific facts. But two differences need to be noted.

General terms, of course, like "pencil," "yellow," and "table," have to be used. Otherwise the fact would remain ineffable. But the fact is individual and concrete, as is indicated by the demonstrative words *this* and *my*. The universal terms are used not to express a universal connection, but to illumine an individual situation here and now which must constantly be recognized and held in mind, if this fact is to be properly analyzed and understood. Here the movement is not only from the concrete to the abstract and universal, but also from the abstract and universal back again to the concrete, which is always the center of attention. Such an entity, in its full concreteness, like this pencil or me, myself, is always envisaged in the world horizon, though this is often left unexpressed. Thus I do not normally think of myself as being in the solar system, or even in the Milky Way, though these statements are technically true and acceptable in certain artificial contexts. But the whole of my concrete being, to which I refer by the first person pronoun, is too rich and variegated to be included within such abstract horizons. So I say rather of myself in a concrete context that I am in the world.

In the second place, while a world fact may be illumined by universal terms and by hypothetical judgments involving special movements and conditions (if I looked at it from below, it would still look yellow), it does not necessarily involve such special conditions or abstractions. It is simply a concrete fact that has now emerged in world history. Of course one can analyze out certain conditions, like normal light, that do in fact hold. But these conditions hold after the fact and in it, not before. The fact is not dependent on adopting a certain abstraction or making certain arrangements. It simply happens in the world. Hence it is to be described in a categorical, not in a hypothetical or universal mode. These two differences, then, must be noted. The facts of science are abstract and partially dependent on special modes of observation. World facts are concrete and independent of any special mode of approach.

A third basic difference, clearly noted by Husserl, is that the various fields and regions of science are purely objective, and consciously removed from what is called *the subjective,* as something incidental and capricious. To observe something scientifically means to gain an attitude of impartial detachment, and to regard it as an object that is simply there before the mind. Whatever cannot be regarded in this way is dismissed as capricious and subjective. Nonliving things cannot be examined in any other way, and probably

not too much is lost in analyzing them. Every phase of human existence also can be regarded from the outside, even human thinking
and action once it is finished, in its deposits and results. But something is missed by such an objective procedure. This is the act as it
is proceeding, as lived and experienced from within. Thus it has now
been shown that it is one thing to analyze the finished results of
language from the standpoint of an external observer, and quite another to analyze it as it actually proceeds from the point of view of
the living speaker.[5]

These inner factors of lived experience may be ignored as subjective by the detached attitude which is normal for science, but
they are nevertheless important to living men and play an essential
role in the world horizon, which, as Husserl said, is relative to man
and subjective. This is certainly true in spite of the vast range of
this world horizon. Thus it is clear that the organs of the human
body map out a world pattern, and that the human infant, from the
time of birth and before, is open to a world that answers positively
or negatively to its needs. It is no wonder, then, that we speak of the
human world in contrast to the life-fields of other animals with
different organs and needs. We go even further than this and speak
of my world, and of the world of a given individual, x or y, whose
pattern is quite different. Such subjective factors have no place in
the objective perspectives of science. Hence we do not speak of my
galaxy nor of the Hindu solar system. It is perfectly natural, however, to speak of the Hindu world, for this horizon of concrete facts
involves not only objects but also subjective factors which are
normally omitted by science.

That this is no mere accident of speech, we can show by a brief
analysis of the world fact we have chosen: this yellow pencil now on
the table at my right. Physical space does not lie around a vital center, and is not oriented with respect to vital directions. Hence, while
the physicist may have to employ the notions of right and left in
manipulating the instruments of his experiment, they have no place
in the finished products of his analysis. But the space of the world is
an oriented space, and we would at once lose our bearings if we
could not distinguish in it the directions of right and left. Not only is
this true, but the notion of the pencil being *on* the table refers to a
subjective orientation that is wholly absent from physical space. It

[5] Cf. F. de Saussure, *Cours de linguistique générale* (Lausanne: Charles Bally
et Albert Sechehaye, 1916).

involves a category of above and below, which is derived from the relation of my body to external objects, which cannot be conveyed by any purely geometric or physical analysis. No matter how detailed such an analysis might be, unless it surreptitiously introduced "anthropomorphic" factors, I could not tell from it alone which of the extended objects was above or below, or whether they were merely side by side.[6]

The objectivist will no doubt wish to say that this is merely the introduction of a distorted and biased version of physical space. But this is also to express a bias. Without begging many questions it will perhaps be fairer to say, in the light of what is now known, that world space contains many human factors which are absent from any pure geometric or physical space. This should not be understood as implying that world space, or the world, is merely *subjective* in the usual sense of this confusing word. If we turn to ordinary language for guidance, we find it hard to imagine any situation in which it would be reasonable to say that space is in me, or that the extended things outside of me are in me, or that the world is in my head. The relativity of which we have been speaking makes no demand on us to accept any such absurdities. Neither does it necessarily imply that our experience is a distorted version of things as they are in themselves.

It does require that the things we know are in relation to us. But there is no reason for doubting that these relations are quite real; that we can know them, at least in part, as they are; and that by abstracting from these relations, science can give us some knowledge of what things are apart from them. The beings around us are quite independent. But we understand them and order them in a world horizon which is relative to us. This is a digression, however. The point we are concerned to make is that this relative world horizon is different from the more abstract perspectives of science, and that world facts, therefore, include relative factors which are absent from what we may call normal scientific facts. What are these relative factors?

I shall not attempt to draw up an exhaustive list, but now, as a fourth point, will make a few comments on one of the most important of these, namely, value.

These phenomena can, of course, be regarded from a detached

[6] M. Merleau-Ponty, *Phénoménologie de la perception* (Paris: Gallimard, 1945), pp. 117–118.

point of view as value facts. In this way they can be embraced within a scientific or objective framework. We can observe that such and such a person A has a desire for B, and that such and such a culture Y has a dislike for Z. But objective facts of this sort are quite different from values as they are directly experienced in the *Lebenswelt* and expressed in ordinary language. Hence the statement that science is neutral to value conveys a certain truth which needs to be spelled out. We shall take the time now briefly to note three differences.

First, we have inherited from our tradition a strong tendency to think of things as substances which are prior to their relations including value relations—a certain kind of accident. A thing must first be what it is before it can have a value. Thus for the objective analyst, the pencil is first of all an extended substance with a certain shape and point, a certain color, and so forth, which may be used for writing. Value predicates are later additions that things come to have in relation to human desire. In the *Lebenswelt*, however, values are original, and lie at the very core of things. Thus in ordinary conversation, we would never refer to the object at my right as a thing with certain properties adapting it to writing. We refer to it straight off as a pencil, which is not a neutral noun but a value term. This is not only true of artificial objects but of natural objects as well, like sunshine, storm, and fire. In the life-world, these objects are originally loaded with value meanings. To lose sight of these meanings is to fall into complete disorientation. In the *Lebenswelt*, value is not a later addition. It is constitutive of the thing.

Second, the realistic tradition has led us to make a similar analysis of the human agent or the human group. Good or evil desires and acts are later accidents which the agent may or may not "have." But the living agent is not separated from his acts in this way. He *is* a set of desires and aspirations. A human culture is not a neutral structure with approvals and disapprovals added on. It *is* a structure of approvals and disapprovals. To be committed to a value is very different from observing this from outside. When I actually hold to a value, it becomes essential to me, and affects my whole existence from the ground up. Thus in ordinary, moral discourse, as distinct from detached argumentation, we do not say that a friend of ours had courage on such an occasion. We say he was courageous. We do not speak of a person as developing attributes of slyness and greed. We say he is rapacious.

Third, we have already touched on a point which needs to be developed further. This is a tendency commonly found in objective analysis to regard value as a special kind of property, or genus, or region separate from other regions. One example of this would be the traditional way of distinguishing between value and fact. More specific illustrations would be Hartmann's realm of value, and even G. E. Moore's conception of value as a very peculiar, simple, and unanalyzable property. It is difficult, however, to find concrete illustrations of this restrictive character when one turns to the life-world. Here what we refer to by the term "value" refuses to let itself be confined within any special compartment or region but seems rather to run through various regions, even getting itself involved in whatever it is that enables us to distinguish between different regions, each of which is for some end. Thus the whole area of agriculture, farms, fields, storage plants, and slaughterhouses, is for food; that of medicine, sewers, food inspection, research laboratories, medical schools, and hospitals, is for health; and so on.

In the light of these facts, it would seem to be hard to maintain that value is confined only to a single, special region of its own. It would seem rather to pervade the whole life-world. This pervasive character is reflected, as we should expect, in ordinary language, where value is not expressed by any special words or forms but by all words and all forms, including the tone of voice.

I believe that this is sufficient to show that there is an ultimate world horizon correlated with ordinary language, which has certain features distinguishing it sharply from the objective horizons of traditional realistic thought and modern science. This world horizon is (1) concrete and (2) categorical. It also contains (3) certain "subjective" and relative factors, among the more important of which is (4) a pervasive "value" factor which cannot be understood (as it is) from the outside, but only as it is lived, so to speak, from the inside. As over against this, the horizons of realist philosophy and science are abstract and hypothetical. They also have no place for the lived experience of value and other experiences of this kind, whose pervasive character they try to restrict, and which they neglect and dismiss as private and subjective. Hence I believe that the distinction between world facts and scientific facts is justified. World facts are in the former horizon, scientific facts in the latter.

We have pointed out that the world horizon is characterized by a certain ultimacy, and that, for ordinary language at least, what lies beyond the world possesses an unqualified transcendence which certainly does not seem to belong to any facts of science. We have also suggested not that every scientific fact, but that every type of scientific fact, can be found as an abstract aspect of some world fact. In the context of ordinary discourse, we should certainly find the statement that science is out of this world as odd. These observations might seem to suggest that the various perspectives of science, or *the* perspective, if there is such a thing, should be regarded as an abstract horizon within the *Lebenswelt*. Such a view is, I think, defensible and certainly does not imply any traditional form of idealism. But it raises many basic issues which I have not touched upon. So I am not considering it here.[7] I am simply asserting that world facts belong to an independent world horizon quite distinct from the scientific universe, that this is the factual horizon of ordinary language, and that it deserves disciplined attention and study by philosophers. This is my thesis.

Two Ways of Reducing World Facts

As we have pointed out, the central tradition of Western philosophy has been predominately objectivist, and has been marked throughout its history by a strong tendency to restrict and depreciate world facts as relative and distorted versions of reality, and finally to absorb them into a purely objective perspective. I shall not try here to review the manifold phases of this prolonged attempt to discredit ordinary language and its world. I shall single out two recent versions of this attempt, now widely familiar, for a brief concluding comment. One of these uses the distinction "private vs. public," the other that of "subjective vs. objective." Both distinctions are now commonly employed as ways of restricting the world horizon of everyday speech to a very limited perspective which, in this reduced form, can be more readily fitted into the scientific universe—the last framework into which objectivist thought has crystallized.

Those who make the former distinction arbitrarily cut off the human person from his world horizon and enclose him within a private world of his own. Since the sensory equipment of each individual is different from that of every other, we can understand why the sensations that arise in him must be different from their objective causes, and also different from those of another. Each individual lives

---

[7] This view will be considered with some care in Chapter 5.

in a private world of his own which he directly experiences within himself. These private worlds, though different in quality, vary in correlation with objective stimuli. Hence, if properly interpreted, they may be biologically useful and may justify the inferences of science. They appear with the human organism as a late phase of biological evolution and, as such, they may be fitted into the great public world of objects, which includes them spatially as well as temporally, and which is always the same for all observers. Just as the private dwellings of individuals are tiny parts of the public town, so the private worlds of individual organisms are tiny parts of the public universe of science. Both Russell and Broad have used the terms "public" and "private" in a reductive argument of this kind.

Of this argument we need only note that, while every experience arises from a private center, it always opens into a public world horizon, from which it cannot be separated except by arbitrary abstraction. My world is never exclusively private. It is my private way of relating myself and my experiences to an ultimate horizon which is shared. In its very constitution it is a union of the private and the public, and, therefore, has room within it for both. As a matter of fact, both factors are always found, as is clearly witnessed by ordinary language; for do we not only say that I myself, my body, my innermost thoughts and desires are in the world, but that the public streets, the fields, the mountains, and the stars are in the world as well? Both public and private are factually in the world. As the British philosopher W. H. F. Barnes remarks at the close of his interesting essay "On Seeing and Hearing": "I have merely tried to bring out the simple and obvious feature about the senses which makes us feel rightly that each person is, by having senses, at once given access to a common world, and at the same time possessed of a private one."[8]

The distinction between subjective and objective has also been used to break down the integral structure of human existence in the world, and to discredit ordinary language for the sake of artificial constructions. Such attempts are subject to a similar criticism. Consciousness has a subjective center, but it is found to be always stretched out toward objects of some kind. These objects, and the way in which they are ordered, may differ from individual to individual and from culture to culture, but no self has ever been found

[8] *Contemporary British Philosophy*, Third Series (New York: Macmillan, 1956), pp. 63–83.

in an objectless state. As a matter of fact, our experience is neither exclusively subjective nor exclusively objective but a relational structure to which neither term alone does justice.

Concrete experience is private as well as public, subjective as well as objective. Neither can be separated from the other and reified without distorting the facts, for human existence is open to a world horizon. Man carries this "field" with him wherever he goes, and it is now clear that this is a necessary aspect of his existence. Without a world there can be no man, and without man there can be no world. Far from containing us within a special, mental region, it is precisely our lived subjectivity that opens us to an ultimate world horizon, and it is precisely this last objective horizon that requires a subjective center. In the light of these remarks, I shall now venture to suggest that the distinction of private vs. public, and subjective vs. objective, as they have been commonly used in traditional philosophy, are phases of an age-old effort to depreciate the world of lived experience as subjective and relative, and to discredit ordinary language as hopelessly vague and confused.

A Final Question Addressed to Analytic Philosophers

I began this chapter by noting the present sharp separation of those phenomenological studies of the world of direct experience which have had a revolutionary effect on the continent of Europe, from the method of linguistic analysis which is now exerting a marked effect on Anglo-Saxon thought. In the light of the close correlation between ordinary language and the empirical world, this mutual separation and distrust seems strange, and I suggested that a study of the reasons for this mistrust of philosophy on the Anglo-Saxon side, as in any sense an empirical discipline, might have something to do with the traditional tendency to disparage, or at least to restrict, the immediate data of experience as unstable and subjective.

I then examined a recent account of analytic philosophy, and showed that it was characterized by a certain ambiguity in its use of the term *fact* which easily leads to a reduction of world fact to scientific fact, and to a denial that philosophy has any empirical function to perform. After this, I made some comments directed toward the clarification of the notion of the human life-world, one of the most important discoveries of recent phenomenology. Then I offered four kinds of evidence to show that there are cogent reasons for making the distinction between world facts and scientific facts. Finally, I chose two types of argument, based on the distinctions private vs. public and subjective vs. objective, which have recently been used to restrict and discredit immediate experience as purely private and subjective. I showed that these arguments are subject to certain criticisms, and that our subjective experience, far from being reducible to a set of impressions, or inner sense data, actually opens into a world horizon which is markedly distinct from the objective perspectives of science and traditional philosophy. In the light of these observations, I should now like to raise the following questions which, it seems to me, are important for analytic philosophers.

Is it not true that ordinary language is concerned with facts of a different order from those of science? Is there not a world of ordinary language? Is it not likely that this world has a certain structure which is not the concern of any special science but is worthy of disciplined attention? Such a study has been inaugurated on the continent of Europe by the so-called phenomenologists. Is not such a study closely correlated with that of everyday discourse? Instead of being essentially opposed, are not these two approaches mutually supplementary and fructifying? In short, is there not a world of ordinary language, and is not the disciplined study of this world of interest to the analytic philosopher?

A number of analytic philosophers have shown an interest in these questions. But while we wait for a considered answer from them, let us now return to the life-world, and the new concepts and new methods that will be required for its disciplined exploration.

Chapter 4

The Exploration of the Life-World[1]

I am going to discuss a philosophical project that has opened up in the twentieth century and in which I believe that many of us are directly or indirectly participating. This is the exploration of the life-world, or *Lebenswelt* as it is called in Western Europe, following a usage of Husserl which can be found in his recently published *Krisis der Europäischen Wissenschaften.* This is the world of history into which we are born, in which we exist and engage ourselves in our chosen projects, and in which we die. It is the world of ordinary language with its wealth of concrete usage, its obscurities, and ambiguities. The exploration of this world and the non-technical language in which it is interpreted and expressed, though long neglected, is now proceeding throughout the Western world in different ways.

The disparagement of the *Lebenswelt*, in which we actually exist and work out our individual styles of life and thought, goes back, as we have noted, at least as far as Plato's warning against the Cave and its unstable confusions, and the advice he gave philosophers to leave the Cave in their disciplined reflections to find abstract and objective explanations. This advice was followed all too literally in ancient and medieval times. In the modern period, epistemological arguments absorbed the attention of philosophers, and served to discourage the

---

[1] The substance of this chapter was delivered as the presidential address before the Fifty-seventh Meeting of the Eastern Division of the American Philosophical Association at Yale University, December 27–29, 1960.

60

serious exploration of the world of our existence. Our knowledge of the things and persons around us was attacked as distorted and biased. This knowledge was finally whittled down and discredited to such a degree that doubts were raised as to whether there was any external *Lebenswelt* at all. As a result of this, philosophy became isolated from real life as a special academic discipline with restricted technical concerns of its own.

In their disparagement of the world of our lived existence, it is remarkable how close these thinkers are to Plato, who used such adjectives as shadowy, confused, and fleeting, and who discounted our knowledge of it as mere "opinion." I remember how once in a debate with a positivistically oriented philosopher, in defending what I took to be world facts as data deserving of disciplined attention, I was met with a reply of this kind. "Yes," he said, "there are such data, but these are sloppy data—too vague and confused to be subject to any exact form of measurement." Nevertheless, while they are not scientific facts, they are facts of some kind, forced upon us by constraining evidence. Let the reader now imagine that he was present at our 1960 Association meeting. If he had been present would he not now know that we were meeting together in New Haven in the month of December in the year 1960? If world facts of this kind are vague and confused, all the more need for disciplined attention and analysis.

We have already noted the world-wide effort at the end of the last century, and at the beginning of our own, shared by such disparate thinkers as Berdyaev in Russia, Ortega y Gasset in Spain, Husserl and Scheler in Germany, Bergson in France, to break through the barriers of traditional objectivism and the subjectivism which always attends it. In spite of their differences, these philosophers shared a profound dissatisfaction with central traditions of past philosophy as encouraging abstract constructions remote from life, and a profound concern to explore the neglected depths of what has been traditionally dismissed as the "subjective," thus bringing their thought into closer touch with human experience as it is lived in the concrete. The so-called *existential philosophy*, or *phenomenology*, of present-day Europe is a more recent, special manifestation of this world-wide trend.

It is often held that the healthier Anglo-Saxon countries have been free from morbid and exotic symptoms of this kind. But this, I think, is not the case, if we focus the general trend of which I have been speaking. Let us think for a moment of William James. In his Lowell Lectures, delivered in 1906, he expressed his profound dissatisfaction with the aloofness of traditional academic philosophy, and its remoteness from the primary philosophic process that actually goes on in every living man throughout the waking hours, and as we now know, often through the sleeping hours of his daily life. Thus at the very beginning of his first lecture on *The Present Dilemma in Philosophy,* James says:

> I know that you, Ladies and Gentlemen, have a philosophy, each and all of you, and that the most interesting and important thing about you is the way in which it determines the perspective in your several worlds. You know the same of me. And yet I confess to a certain tremor at the audacity of the enterprise which I am about to begin. For the philosophy which is so important in each of us is not a technical matter; it is our more or less dumb sense of what life honestly and deeply means. It is only partly got from books; it is our individual way of just seeing and feeling the total push and pressure of the cosmos. . . .[2]

In France, this primordial mode of reflection by which each person in a free society to some degree works out his own style of life and his own way of understanding the world, is now distinguished as *primary thinking* from what is called *secondary reflection,* that critical reflection on the former, to which we may devote a calm moment in life, and which has been judged important enough to be handed over to a special group, known as philosophers, for disciplined attention throughout a large part of our history.

Primary thought is spontaneous, always concerned and interested, often creative, but uncritical. It is to this type of thought that we owe the first original answers that have been given to the ambiguities and agonies of life. But when left to itself, without criticism, this style of reflection becomes provincial, fanatical, and closed to what is universally human. Secondary reflection, on the other hand, is reflective and disinterested, self-conscious, critical, and open to the universal. It is through this type of secondary reflection, when it is in touch with the former, that fanaticism is avoided, and our existence in the life-world is kept open and free. When left to itself, however, it becomes abstract, sterile, and uncreative. The original aim of academic philosophy was not to replace primary thought by developing special techniques of its own. As expressed in the ancient ideal of wisdom, it was rather to exercise a kind of therapy over the act

[2] *Pragmatism* (New York: Meridian, 1942), p. 28.

of primary reflection that constitutes an essential phase of human existence, warning it against serious errors, clarifying the basic meanings and issues, and thus helping it, so far as possible, to face those decisions between different global interpretations of the world which every free man must make. Insofar as it has actually exercised this therapeutic function, philosophy is properly regarded as the discipline of freedom, and I believe that by its pressing of basic questions in the face of political and theological tyranny, and by its maintenance of communication between radically divergent worlds, it has made an essential contribution to the life of free societies in the West.

But it is easy for special groups, set aside to perform a basic therapeutic function, to develop special aims and techniques of their own in its place. James had a keen sense for the needlessly abstract and academic, and hated it with all his heart and soul. He realized that the traditional philosophy of his time had become separated from the primary thinking of our lived existence. Instead of trying to clarify and criticize this vital process of the *Lebenswelt,* it was concerned with formulating special techniques and artificial constructions in a very different world of its own. There are many passages where James contrasts the pattern, the meaning, the very feeling of these different worlds. Thus a few pages further in the essay from which we have quoted, he says:

> *The world* of concrete personal experience to which the street belongs is multitudinous beyond imagination, tangled, muddy, painful, and perplexed. The world to which your philosophy professor introduces you is simple, clean, and noble. The contradictions of real life are absent from it. Its architecture is classic. Principles of reason trace its outline, logical necessities cement its parts. Purity and dignity are what it most expresses. It is a kind of temple shining on a hill.
>
> In point of fact, it is far less an account of this actual world than a clear addition built upon it, a classic sanctuary in which the rationalist fancy may take refuge from the intolerably confused and Gothic character which mere facts present. It is no explanation of our concrete universe; it is another thing altogether, a substitute for it, a remedy, a way of escape.
>
> Its temperament, if I may use the word *temperament* here, is utterly alien to the temperament of existence in the concrete. . . .

The two horizons and attitudes are entirely different. World facts are "confused," "concrete," and "sloppy" from a logical point of view. In contrast, scientific facts are simple and clean. The global meanings which we require for the interpretation of the world in which we live are not principles of reason. They are existential structures of a very different kind. The life-world has a different feeling tone, and must be understood, if it is to be understood at all, in a different way, which, as James saw, aims at a very different kind of truth.

James wanted to bridge this chasm, to bring the secondary reflection of official philosophy closer to the primary existential thinking of life. But in order to do this, he saw that a new approach to the life-world was necessary, quite different from that of traditional, so-called empiricism. He was always concerned with the world of concrete existence, as he called it, and ever groping for new ways of expressing its meanings. Since his time, this central core of James's teaching has been ignored in the Anglo-Saxon world until recently. But in Western Europe many of his novel suggestions soon bore rich fruit. As we noted in the last chapter, several insights of his great and still living text on "psychology," such as his luminous account of "fringes," were taken over and further developed by Husserl. His attack on the atomism of British empiricism, and his emphasis on the relational structure of our lived experience have both borne fruit in recent phenomenology. Indeed, it is not only fair but positively illuminating to think of phenomenology in general as a form of radical empiricism in James's sense of this phrase. By this discipline, he is trying to bring academic philosophy out of the ivory tower into the streets where it can criticize the thinking of living men, and keep it free from dogmatism and provincialism.

To those who are puzzled by the recent union in Western Europe of phenomenology and existential thought, the study of James can provide many clues, for, as a recent study has shown,[3] not only did he use the term *existence* constantly in the Kierkegaardian sense of "subjective" lived experience, but, in his own way, he worked out many interpretations of this experience, which are now regarded as peculiarly existential. For example, the notion that to be alive is to be concerned; that different ways of understanding the world are subject to choice; that these choices cannot be justified by rational demonstration but are subject to faith and risk; that we are confronted by forced options where not to choose is itself a form of choice; that man is radically free, and that the individual person is

[3] Cf. G. Clive, *The Romantic Enlightenment* (New York: Meridian, 1960), pp. 74ff.

the fragile but creative source of change in human history—all these ideas are now widely accepted as characteristic existential insights. If this is existentialism, we have had it right here in our very midst!

Like the thought of James and modern phenomenology, the philosophy of linguistic analysis has also developed from a critique of British empiricism. Hence it is not surprising that, in spite of substantial differences, there are also marked similarities which make it possible to bring at least the more recent manifestations of this movement in line with the general trend with which we are concerned. Here, too, we find a deep dissatisfaction with the pretentious system-building of the past, a lack of interest in wholesale explanation, and instead of this, a concern for the meanings enshrined in ordinary linguistic usage. Thus according to Wittgenstein: "Philosophy simply puts everything before us, and neither explains nor deduces anything."[4]

In both movements we find a trend away from the dominance of formal logic to actual use, a strong skepticism concerning sense data and other odd entities, and a deep respect for the richness, the openness, and, indeed, the very ambiguities of that ordinary language through which the life-world is interpreted and expressed. Other similarities might be mentioned. These may be sufficient to justify our suspicion that present-day English thought, such as that of Hampshire, for example, and that of the Continent are by no means separated by such a deep and unbridgeable chasm as our behavior at international philosophical conferences would seem to indicate.

This exploration of the life-world has, of course, only just begun. But already we can see how secondary reflection, to use the phenomenological phrase, is breaking away from its traditional isolation, and moving into closer touch with the spontaneous, primary thought of our lived existence. In making this important move, however, many traditional methods and concepts have been tested and found wanting. New methods and meanings have now emerged to take their place. Here again James's recognition of the radical differences between the world of our lived existence and the universe of rational and scientific discourse has been confirmed.

In fact, I believe that the best way to suggest the meaning of this new and more radical empiricism, now appearing under such names as phenomenology, existential philosophy, and situational analysis,

---

[4] *Philosophical Investigations* (Oxford: Blackwell Scientific Publications, Ltd., 1953), p. 126.

is briefly to contrast these two world horizons in five major respects which are implied in James's own thinking: I, World Facts vs. Scientific Facts; II, World Meanings vs. Scientific Meanings; III, World Understanding vs. Objective Understanding; IV, World Truth vs. Scientific Truth; and V, Two Distinct Horizons, the Life-World vs. the Objective Universe.

World Facts vs. Scientific Facts

As we noted in our discussion of Warnock's ideas, there is a widespread view at the present time in the Anglo-Saxon world that philosophy can no longer be understood as an empirical discipline. All facts belong to the province of some science. Hence philosophy has to be understood as a reflection on science and its methods, or, as is often said, the study of logic and language. This, I believe, is a serious mistake which has not only had an unfortunate effect on philosophy but has obstructed the investigation of vast regions of our lived experience. By *fact*, I mean any bit of evidence that is forced upon our attention, whether we will or no. The term refers primarily to such pieces of evidence while they are in a disordered and chaotic state. In this sense, facts are disparate and disorganized. But the term may also refer to such scattered information after it has been gathered together by meaningful theories which have been strongly confirmed. We may note the traditional saying that the theories of today are the facts of tomorrow. But, as we have already indicated, the word *fact* in our language is ambiguous, and covers two very distinct kinds, scientific and world facts, which I shall now try briefly to distinguish.

Take the fact of our Association meeting in New Haven in the month of December, 1960, to which I have already referred. This is a fact of some kind. It is not a scientific fact, though the data of all the different sciences can be found in it, and abstracted from it. Clock time was proceeding; the earth was turning on its axis and revolving around the sun (astronomy). Energy was radiating from the lights (physics). We were digesting our dinners (biochemistry and physiology). This meeting had economic aspects which I know too well, sociological and psychological aspects. There were what we call "subjective" factors as well. Many of us were feeling tired; many of us were bored. This meeting cannot be reduced to exclusively objective factors. It is a world fact—an historical fact, as we sometimes say.

World facts do not occur in the limited perspective of an abstract science, nor in that of all the objective sciences taken together. They occur on a different ground, the unlimited horizon of the world. Hence the name. They are already being interpreted in the light of some way of understanding this world. We may sometimes speak of an historic fact, like the Black Death, as though it were a purely objective process subject to detached observation and analysis. But this is false. The process cannot be really understood without a grasp of the way it is actually interpreted by those undergoing it, and these interpretations cannot be dismissed as mere "subjective" constructions. The aim of the historian is finally to understand human events in terms of their world horizon. He seeks first to give us a sense of the past world as it was lived from the inside, and then to find out its real meaning for us and for the future.

The attitude of detached observation has a more restricted horizon of its own. Hence when it turns to human events, it misses this lived, historic existence and its open world. For those who actually lived through the Black Death in a way of their choice, they were staking the whole of their existence on this venture. For them it was a unique project, risking the only existence they had. But the objective observer places this in an alien frame. For him, this interpretation is only one possibility among many. The lived experience is closed, fixed, and relativized, like a butterfly fixed on a museum frame.

We have already noted (pp. 41–42) that scientific facts are abstract; they reveal human existence and its global meanings only insofar as they can be objectified, and thus deprived of their ambiguities and openness. World facts, on the other hand, are temporal and existential—always open to the global world horizon which is beyond the range of objective reason and science. As soon as human sciences, such as psychiatry, become concerned with these dynamic structures of lived existence, as they are now beginning to be, they become phenomenological. This does not mean that they lose all discipline. They become disciplines of a different kind.

This is happening not only in psychiatry but in other disciplines as well. I have a friend in social science who, several years ago, was working on a large project involving 800 subjects and 30 variables. Then he experienced a sudden crisis. He felt, as he said, that *the people* were disappearing in these essences and variables. As a result, his whole procedure has changed. His students are no longer concerned with objective measurements and correlations. He now sends them to families in the area where they make no tests or detached observations. Instead they try to communicate and to participate, to some degree, in the life of the family, attempting to grasp the sense of some aspect of the family situation as it develops in time.

As we pointed out in the previous chapter, scientific facts are of a special order requiring distinctive modes of attention and special conditions for investigation, such as laboratory tools and instruments. They are expressed and interpreted by the technical languages of science which place them in the limited frame we may call the objective universe. World facts, on the other hand, simply occur in world history, and can be known to some degree of clarity by all men in pursuing their vital projects in the world, without special attitudes or special conditions for investigation. Thus every living person has an understanding, vague and erroneous though it be, of his own history and that of the public world in which he lives. These world facts are expressed and interpreted by ordinary language which is saturated with value, and which places them in a world horizon open to global interpretations of very different kinds.

Scientific vs. World Meanings

Man is neither a god who can soar over the facts nor an animal who can bury himself in them. He must, of course, pay attention to the facts. But then, unlike the animal, he may say "no" to the facts as they are given, and may seek for what they really are—for what they really mean. This meaning gathers the facts together in some way, and always points beyond to further meaning. Of every fact and every specific meaning the question may be raised: What does it really mean? According to traditional realism, meanings exist independently in nature, and are passively received by an empty mind. But this theory fails to recognize that man can control and develop meanings. Thus we ask a person to explain *his* meaning, but we do not speak in this way of *his* facts. According to certain schools of idealism, meanings are created *de novo* by the human mind. But this theory fails to recognize that meanings must be grounded in facts. Thus we speak of something as having a meaning, and of someone as finding the meaning of a set of facts. I shall reject both of these extreme views. Meaning is rather the result of a unique interchange between man and the independent things and persons around him. This interchange is not causal in character. It is more like a dialogue to which each partner makes an essential contribution. We are now interested in contrasting two very different types of meaning.

Scientific meanings are developed from a detached point of view and are concerned with objective, scientific facts. Here we are playing a much more active role in the dialogue. We are dealing with inarticulate things, and with reference to them we must set the questions and formulate meanings of our own which are true insofar as they correspond with external facts. It is widely held that facts are simply given; then meanings added on by us from the outside. In objective science, this familiar generalization is at least partially justified. The meanings of science are abstract essences or variables, laws, and theories under which the individual events of nature may be subsumed. These meanings are abstract and partial rather than global. If found by experiment to be grounded in the observed facts, they enable us to predict what will happen in the future, and thus to control the events of nature to some degree. The objective factor which we can change to exert such control is *the cause* of what regularly follows. In this way, reason and science are concerned with causal explanations and the genetic origins of things.

Now there is a very different kind of meaning, which we shall call *interpretation,* that is concerned with world facts. As we have seen, such facts are already interpreted and filled with a meaning of their own. In terms of our dialogue image, we are here dealing with a far more active and articulate partner who raises questions and gives answers of his own. The interpretation of such world facts must, therefore, fall into two distinct steps: first, finding out what these events meant to the persons involved in their lived existence; and second, searching for their real meaning.

Such an interpretation will not be exclusively concerned with objects. It must be concerned with "subjective," or better, with intentional factors as well. It will avoid the traditional concepts of *substance* and *subject,* and will recognize that human existence is always stretched out into a world field. It will not subsume historic events under laws of succession, and then place them in a neutral, objective frame. It will seek rather to discover types or structures of lived existence in the open horizon of the life-world. It is dealing with free beings capable of choosing styles of life and global world interpretations of their own. Hence it will aim not at prediction and causal control but simply at understanding. The truth of such a global interpretation will be checked not by explanatory power, but simply by fitting the world facts. Perhaps we may clarify this distinction by an example taken from the recent anthropological study of primitive burial customs.

It has been found that many primitive peoples in widely scattered areas buried their dead in a crouching position. Here is a wide array of similar facts. What is their real meaning? Many different explanations have been put forth, all subject to serious objection as not taking account of all the facts, or as being strained and forced. Then it was suggested by one investigator that this was the position of the infant in the womb. Burial in this position is an expression of the hope for regeneration. This interpretation takes account of the facts in terms of a lived experience shared in some way by all men, the anxiety concerning death. It is then open to further readings in terms of the ultimate meaning of life and death. I shall not say that this interpretation is proved. Meanings of this kind cannot be demonstrated by any mode of calculation or formal proof. But it is now widely accepted, and may be said to be the leading theory in the field. Let us assume for the moment that it gives us the real meaning of this ancient burial custom, and compare it with the objective type of meaning.

This interpretation has nothing to do with the causes or genetic origins of the facts. It does not subsume them under any law of uniform succession. It is not abstracted from the facts as a property or set of properties, nor is it derived from them as a likeness or copy. It is in the facts, but at the same time goes beyond them to give them a place in a wider field of meaning, the world in which we all struggle for life and face death with uncertainty, fear, and sometimes hope. I do not understand this world from an external point of observation where I make up theories about it, which may or may not correspond. I know it directly from within by living in it. This world is not just the alien world of a primitive people, nor is it just my present-day American world of the twentieth century. It is something else, *the world,* which has a place for each version and yet transcends both. This meaning gives us no control, no mastery over these corpses. It simply takes account of the facts and places them in a broader field of meaning, the outlines of which we at least dimly understand and seem to share in common.

An interpretation must, of course, fit these facts and take account of them. But this is more than merely to copy the facts or to repeat them. It is to interpret them, to place them in a global world con- text. Such interpretations are not defended primarily by inductive or deductive arguments, but by arguments of another kind which appeal directly to the facts, and which claim to show that one in- terpretation fits these facts more adequately than other alternative structures of meaning. In this way, we speak of a doctor as arguing for his diagnosis of a patient's illness, and of a lawyer as arguing out his case, that is, showing that his interpretation alone, against other alternatives, really fits the known world-facts and places them in the real world, so far as it is globally interpreted. Most serious argu- ments in the human sciences and in philosophy now are arguments of this kind. They are concerned with world-facts rather than scien- tific facts, and with world structures and meanings rather than with abstract variables and laws. They proceed according to a different mode of understanding to which we shall now turn.

Objective vs. World Understanding

If it is true as we have argued, that we are confronted with two kinds of facts, scientific and world-facts, and two kinds of meanings, it is clear that we are also confronted with two distinct ways of un- derstanding. Following our past procedure, we may call these *objective* as against *world* understanding. As we have already indi- cated, the latter attends our active engagement in the world. Now let us try to clarify these different modes with greater exactness.

With the coming of leisure, man learned to detach himself from striking physical objects like the stars, to observe them carefully, and to find laws in terms of which their future behavior could be pre- dicted. Later on he examined surrounding objects over which he could exert some control in this way, and thus developed science and technology. This objective mode of understanding involves a differ- ent horizon and a different mode of revealing. It has achieved to some degree that mastery over nature at which it aims. But this perspective has limits. It cannot adequately reveal to us either the world or our existence. To think about existence as an object is not the same as to live through this existence. The thinker can describe and interpret his existence. He cannot include himself within his own system of thought.

The objective perspective on things, when it is absolutized, leads to confusions of this kind. If we are to avoid them, we must recognize another mode of understanding, otherwise known as *phenomenology*, in a broad sense of this term. It is important to realize that it involves three distinct steps, or stages, to which we have referred. All must be carried through if subjectivism in some form is to be avoided.

The first lies in a certain capacity to play the role of another which is closely related to the art of the actor. If I am to understand the ceremonies of a primitive tribe, the literature of a foreign people, a philosophic view, the problems of another person, or even my own past of an hour ago, I must first learn to hold my present attitudes in abeyance, or, as the phenomenologist says, to place them in parentheses, and then to exercise my imagination in taking the position of another, not my present self, sympathetically reconstructing and then entering into his perspective, until I can actually follow him and thus get the feeling of his own actions as he lives in them. This capacity to follow through the attitudes and acts of others is a necessary phase of phenomenological study. It is important in understanding primitive societies and the public worlds of advanced civilizations in different periods of their history. It is also important in the study of creative personalities, the original thought of great philosophers, and, indeed, in every area of the humanistic disciplines, including psychiatry.

But this is only a first step. After having eliminated his own prejudices, so far as this is possible, the phenomenologist is then confronted with an array of scattered, lived phenomena which vary from individual to individual and from group to group. The aim of the literary artist or biographer is achieved when this point is reached. He has revealed the world of an existing person as it is lived from the inside. In a similar way, the historian may reveal the world of a past culture or of a historic person, as it was actually understood and lived. But this leaves us with the same relativism to which objectivism also leads. A second step must be taken. We may say, indeed, that the recognition of this need for a second step (a second *epoché*) sharply distinguishes phenomenology from what is commonly known as *existentialism*, which abandons the search for meaning too easily and too soon. It thus falls into a relativism of closed subjective worlds which is rightly judged to be meaningless and absurd. The phenomenologist must not yield to the temptation to accept these scattered facts in their immediacy. At this point, he should rather give heed to the words of the Buddha who once said that it might be wonderful to see all things, but terrible to be them. He must say "no" to these concrete phenomena in their senseless disarray, and ask for their real meaning in *the* world.

This second *epoché* will lead him toward those dynamic types or structures of existence we have considered. Such meaningful structures may be found in all the humanistic disciplines. The philosophical phenomenologist will be especially concerned with the clarification of those structures like time, history, freedom, death, and world itself, which seem to belong necessarily to human existence, and thus to make any human world version possible. Since they are not relative to any particular individual or group, they may finally provide us with valuable clues for tentative speculations concerning that single world which transcends our special versions.

This mode of existential understanding is worked out in the constant struggle of man with the alien forces around him, which constitutes his history. These meanings are neither found in the facts that are forced upon us nor are they subjectively contrived. They go beyond the given facts, and yet take account of them. They are neither exclusively "subjective" nor exclusively "objective," but both together in one. They seem to be the best sort of answer we can give in a ceaseless dialogue, an answer to beckonings that come from a world which envelops us, and also transcends us and all that we know. These answers do not simply repeat what is already there, as the realist still believes. They bring something new into a great expanse of darkness, new meanings that erupt in revealing realms of sheer fact, like the explosion of a rocket that suddenly lights up a night scene at sea. These meanings are brought forth by a creative factor in man, which takes account of the facts and yet goes on beyond them.

But a risk is always there. Many meanings fail to illumine all the facts and are soon replaced by others. The appearance of a genuine new interpretation is usually preceded by long preparation and study, and by many false attempts. But when it appears, then suddenly the gaping facts fall into their place in the world, and the hidden thing speaks to us. The dialogue has reached a turning point. The *sense* of the matter is clear. This is the climactic result of phenomenology, or what we have called world understanding. But no matter how well confirmed the meaning may be, it is always open to further questioning, clarification, deepening, and reinterpretation.

World Truth

Why do we not call world-interpretations of this sort true and false? We call them fantastic or factual, superficial or penetrating, narrow or wide in scope, trivial or profound, and closed or open. But when it comes to truth we hesitate. We reserve this magisterial term for objective propositions or judgments alone, though they depend on meanings for their intelligibility. Why then do we slur over this crucial distinction between sound and unsound interpretations, and accept all of them as "subjective" constructions (unless they can be objectively tested) and, therefore, on an equal plane? Why such indifference, or as we may say, this truthlessness of world meanings? It leaves us with the partial objective perspectives of science, which are true but lacking in global meaning, and a Babel of conflicting subjective worlds which are global but not even possibly true. This, I believe, is a basic source of the relativism and the sense of meaninglessness which is so widespread in our time.

I think that it is due to a widespread belief that the truth of objective reason and science is the only mode of truth. This belief has deep roots in our history, and many supporting reasons. Each simple objective judgment has a unity of its own so that it can be separated off from the rest and examined by itself. Interpretations, on the other hand, are not readily analyzable, since they fit together in wider contexts or fields. The truth of such world-interpretations, which lie beyond the range of any particular science, cannot take the form of a correspondence with something external, since we cannot get outside ourselves and the world in which we exist. We are in no position to make up propositional meanings and then to compare them with external facts. We must directly reveal the world facts as we live through them and then recognize them, *see them as* fitting into temporal patterns of global meaning. Since each of us works out such a world pattern by primary reflection, and since it is involved in all that he feels and thinks and says, its truth will depend in part, as James and Kierkegaard both recognized, on *how* we hold these patterns of meaning and *how* we live them through. We have something to do with determining the authenticity or the unauthenticity of our ways of life and understanding, though this is not the same as falling into a closed and untestable "subjectivism."

There are tests.

In a given humanistic area, interpretations that are superficial, narrow, closed, out of line with the facts, and ephemeral can be, and are, distinguished from those that are penetrating, wide in scope, open, factual, and lasting. When it comes to those global versions of the world that are the special concern of philosophy, they must, of course, fit the world facts. James did not sufficiently emphasize this in his pragmatic theory of truth. But he was correct in holding that in the humanistic disciplines the test cannot lie in any form of correspondence. It must rather take a temporal and historical form. Does this interpretation hold up in time? Is it fruitful? Does it call forth authentic existence in history?

The evidence to which we have access in the life-world will never be sufficient to demonstrate one single ontology to the exclusion of all other alternatives. It is, however, sufficient to rule out many. To use Wittgenstein's example at the end of his *Investigations*, there is a real ground for *seeing the world as x* or as *y*, but not as any interpretation would prescribe, just as there is ground for *seeing his trick picture as* a rabbit or a duck and in other ways—but not, perhaps, as a kangaroo. Certain discoveries have been made, and the history of philosophy cannot be dismissed as a mere succession of arbitrarily chosen and closed systems. Philosophers can and sometimes do communicate, and if we penetrate to the moving spirit of this history we can discern essential agreement on such points as: the world is one, and must be distinguished from its relative human versions; this world contains factors transcending the limits of our human knowledge; but as the history of our discipline shows, man has a freedom of constituting world-interpretations by primary and secondary reflection which, in the light of accessible evidence, may lead him toward or away from world truth. This is enough to justify that never-ending, philosophic dialectic which must always attend the exercise of human freedom. Philosophy is the discipline of freedom, and her first responsibility is to keep freedom alive. But this does not mean that all interpretations can be dismissed as subjective opinions on the same plane. Some express lasting types and structures of the world, and call forth authentic existence. Others are false to the world as it is. They enslave, disintegrate, and dehumanize man.

The Life-World vs. The Objective Universe

Every mode of knowing has its own perspective, or range, within which it places what it is able to know. The horizon of that original, revealing power which is expressed in our ordinary language is *the world.*

Objective reason and science have another perspective by which everything, including human history, can be observed in a certain way. In this perspective, things are seen as objects out there before the mind from a detached point of view. An attempt is made to abstract from bias and from "subjective" interest of every kind, the observer trying to see only what anyone would see, and to recognize only what could be verified by other impersonal observers of the same kind. What can be observed and analyzed in this way belongs to the horizon of nature, or the objective universe, as we may call it. Since man can be regarded from this point of view, it is often held that he himself and the whole of his existence can be eventually included within such a frame.

Those who defend this theory use the term *subjective* in referring to human existence and the human *Lebenswelt* as inner experiences, or impressions, not yet fully understood but eventually to be objectively analyzed as complex occurrences in the field of nature. This field has a spatio-temporal character, and the things of nature are in this geometric space as in a larger container, as water is in the glass. Things are in this objective time as an event is dated in what we call clock time. Before analysis, this objective field is called experience. After objective analysis, it is called the objective universe, or things as they really are. Ordinarily, the perspective is forgotten. Experience is simply the sum total of experiences; the universe simply what there is—all the things there are.

James's penetrating remarks about fringes have played a significant role in the criticism of this traditional omnibus concept of experience, and in the clarification of that world horizon which has now come to replace it. A human being is not an isolated subject which receives its experience in the form of atomic sensations or impressions. Such impressions are always surrounded by fringes; they are figures on a world field which always places them and gives them some meaning. This world, therefore, cannot be understood as a mere set of insular impressions or things. The world is more than all the things in the world. It is the horizon of meaning without which they can neither be nor be understood. Before any actual entity appears to me, world fringes are already there.

I am in this world not merely as an extended object is in a spatial container. I am in the world not only spatially but also temporally as in a field of care, as a child is *in* school or a soldier *in* the service. I am engaged in this world, and its structure varies with different forms of care which are subject to choice. Thus we speak of the businessman's world, the artist's world, and the disturbed worlds of those we call mentally ill, which have now been revealed by psychiatric analysis.

The different world views which have been worked out critically in the history of philosophy are an expression of this freedom of world constitution. But here we must distinguish between those which are merely secondary intellectual constructions and those primary modes in which the author has been able to live and to exist. For most of us, and I include myself, the primary world in which we actually exist is different in varying degrees from that which we consciously profess, and has been worked out uncritically, and largely subconsciously, by a primary mode of thinking under cultural control. The bringing to bear of disciplined self-conscious criticism (secondary reflection) on this spontaneous process of world-formation is a basic need of our time, as indeed of all times. But it will now be realized only through the development of more concrete, phenomenological modes of philosophizing.

The world is the horizon of that way of understanding which belongs to our daily existence and to our common speech. Science also has its background, or horizon, but this has a distinctive character of its own. For me to understand something for myself in the concrete means for me to give it a place in that order of meaning, not necessarily an organic whole, which constitutes my version of the world. The field of nature which underlies the objects of science may be neutral to value, but the life-world is pervaded by meaning and value, as is our ordinary speech.

The world horizon is spatial as well as temporal, though it has now been shown that its modes of space and time are different from those of an objective perspective. Lived time is not the same as the clock time by which it can be measured, and the oriented space of the life-world is not the same as geometric space. I myself, including not only my observable acts and utterances, but my innermost thoughts and feelings as well, am in this world, which has a place for what we call the subjective as well as the objective. Indeed, this world-field is knit together by such overarching meanings as being, knowing, history, and meaning itself, which embrace both poles of this distinction.

But it is not an organic whole, or absolute. It includes conflicts, contradictions, and the radical diversity of different world versions, which are so different that they do not even contradict. As the German biologist Von Uexküll showed in the nineteen twenties in his criticism of the traditional theory of one environment that is the same for all species, no species can be understood apart from its own special environment. Similarly, it has now been shown that no man or group of men can exist apart from the human world. From the limited point of view of a scientist calculating about his objects, being may be the value of a variable. But prior to this, and even as he calculates, the scientist is a man; and for a man to be, is to be in the open horizon of the world.

I have argued that the philosophy of our time is mistrustful of objective systems and absolutes, that it is searching for ways of thought that will reveal and clarify existence as it is lived in the concrete. I have suggested that in this search it has discovered the life-world of man, which is quite distinct from the more limited horizons of objective reason and science. This world is known in a different way, is constituted by a different style of fact and meaning, and is revealed in a different mode of truth.

Since James's revolutionary investigations in the field of what he called the *philosophy of pure experience,* and Husserl's related discoveries in the field of what he called *phenomenology,* I believe that many important advances have been made. The disciplined exploration of the life-world has actually been inaugurated; a really radical empiricism is now under way. On this basis, there is reason to hope for further developments of which there are already significant indications. In the first place, it is now possible to hope for the coming of that foundational discipline for the human sciences of which Dilthey dreamed in the last century, though the name "philosophical anthropology" would seem more appropriate to this discipline than what he suggested—a descriptive and typological psychology.[5]

In the second place, we must remember that the divergent worlds of different tribes, peoples, and individuals open into *the*

5 We shall return to this subject in our concluding Chapter 12.

world, which includes all these versions and their histories, all the hidden aspects of things and persons we know that we do not know, and mysteries that we know we can never comprehend. Traditional thought was mistaken in thinking that it could pass directly from the objective study of things to the world. Such an objective path leads to the very subjectivism it is trying to avoid. We cannot escape our subjectivity by simply forgetting it, or by placing it as the "subjective" in an objective frame. This way is no longer possible for us. The only way to what was called metaphysics is through anthropology—the only way to the world as it is, is through man. A primary task of philosophy is to keep our minds open to this world by tentative speculation in the light of such evidence as there is (and there is relevant evidence) together with a constant critique of all forms of ontological dogmatism.

Finally, in the third place, we may hope for this radical empiricism that it may help professional philosophy, as it is already beginning to do in our time, to escape from its narrow confinement in special technical procedures, and once again to get into closer touch with the actual philosophic process which is always proceeding in the lives of living men. In this way, it may once again achieve vital contacts with art, literature, and religion, and with the other living institutions of our culture. This does not mean the abandonment of all discipline, nor of the most arduous Socratic discipline, which must be renewed with each oncoming generation, of stimulating, clarifying, and purifying the spontaneous, primary reflection of living men, and in thus helping to keep human freedom alive.

The life-world is a distinct horizon with an order of its own. This can no more be reduced to the abstract perspectives of science than can the open structures and meanings of ordinary language be reduced to the abstract grammar of an ideal language or logic. The two worlds are quite different. But which world is prior and more inclusive? Which is less inclusive and derived? These questions concern a conflict of attitudes, a war of the worlds, as we may call it, which is now proceeding, and which, I believe, confronts us with a most basic philosophical issue of our time. It is to this issue that we shall now turn.

Chapter 5

The War of the Worlds

As long ago as 1893, in his lively and illuminating text *The Principles of Psychology*,[1] William James concluded a careful and sympathetic discussion of the scientific method and its perspective on things with the following words. "Science, however, must be constantly reminded that her purposes are not the only purposes, and that the order of uniform causation which she has use for, and is, therefore, right in postulating, may be enveloped in a wider order on which she has no claims at all." Some forty years after, in the last work that he prepared for publication, the German philosopher Husserl argued that this *Lebenswelt,* as he called it, is the widest, richest, and most original horizon to which we have access, and that the objective perspectives of the different sciences, even when added together, are narrower, more abstract, and derived from the former.[2] Most phenomenologists and existential thinkers would now agree with their judgment. But it would be vigorously challenged by positivistically and naturalistically oriented philosophers who argue that it is objective science which gives us the wider and more basic horizon, and that the *Lebenswelt* is only a derived, subjective version of this objective universe.

This war of the worlds, as we may call it, has been proceeding in different forms throughout the whole history of our Western culture since its origins in ancient Greece. It was involved in the struggle between what Nietzsche called the Apollonian and Dionysian ele-

---

[1] Vol. II (New York: Holt, 1893), p. 576.
[2] *Die Krisis der Europäischen Wissenschaften und die Transzendentale Phänomenologie* (The Hague: Nijhoff, 1954), Sections 34–38.

ments in Greek culture, in the conflict between the Aristotelian and Augustinian traditions of the Middle Ages, and in the long debate of modern thought between realism and idealism. In our own time, this issue has been raised again with peculiar sharpness by the rapid advance of objective science and technology, on the one hand, and by the coming of phenomenology and its discovery of the life-world, on the other. In an open society where there is some respect for personal freedom but where, at the same time, our thought and action are deeply affected by the style of the mass apparatus in the midst of which we labor, and of the depersonalized communications of the mass media to which we are constantly exposed, this conflict is directly experienced by those who feel a thirst for freedom. In philosophy, we find a worldwide debate with positivists, many naturalists, and logical empiricists, on the one hand, and phenomenologists, existential philosophers, and many analysts of ordinary language, on the other. This is not merely a struggle between two technical theories or points of view. It is a war of two worlds, each claiming to include and envelop the other.

Which world is the broader horizon?

Which of these claims is nearer the truth?

Any one of us who thinks for himself must face these questions and answer them as best he can. Out of these answers will come the decision of our Western culture which must also give its answer in the end. On this answer will depend the future course of our way of life, our way of understanding, and many other things. In the history of Western thought as a whole, objectivism has been on the winning side of this struggle. Modern positivism and scientism are the last expression of a most ancient and influential tradition. Their defense of the overarching claims of the scientific universe is very strong. But before considering the arguments of each side, let us first briefly compare and contrast these two horizons as they face each other today, remembering what we may have learned from the discussion of preceding chapters. In the light of this comparison, we may then be in a better position to judge between their opposing claims.

The Two Worlds

A world involves three factors: (1) independent beings and agencies; (2) the understanding of these beings and agencies in such a

way that (3) they are gathered together and given meaning in relation to us and to one another. Since our human ways of understanding are all finite, every world is limited by a horizon referring beyond
itself to what is not yet known. The meaning of a thing is its place
in a world in relation to other things of that world. We also refer to
this place of the thing as *what it really is*—its being. We are now concerned with two worlds of meaning, the scientific universe and the
human life-world, which make conflicting claims. We have dealt
with them extensively in the preceding pages. Let us now try briefly
to summarize their chief distinguishing traits and the major issues in
conflict between them.

The scientific universe is a world of objects from which we can
become detached; the life-world, one of existing persons and objects
in which we are actively engaged. While the scientific attitude must
involve such detachment and, as is sometimes said, pure curiosity
simply for the sake of knowing, it is also aware that objective knowledge of this kind is power. Hovering in the background of pure science, there is always some form of technology, as in the background
of detached observation and calculation there is always the will to
power. Science seeks laws and uniformities by which it can predict
the future. Then, by making a slight change, it can produce a desir-
able result in the future and thus control the course of events. To
subsume an object, or some aspect of an object, under a causal net-
work of this kind is to explain it—a very useful and a very special
mode of understanding. Since it is ultimately governed by the urge
to mastery, science seeks always to explain. The philosophical understanding of the life-world, on the other hand, seeks only to understand, to find the order of meaning that will make sense out of life.
Objective reason and science are outwardly directed. They abstract
from the lived existence which they call "subjective." Their motto is
to know all objects, even the self as an object. World understanding,
on the other hand, is, first, inwardly directed, and only then toward
objects. Its motto is to *know thyself*.

As we have seen, objective space is an order of abstract extension
with no natural center in which all points are alike. The space of
the life-world is an oriented space which stretches out around the
lived body as its center. The objective time of the universe is a now
succession in which the present alone is real, the past and the future
being reduced and dismissed as unreal. Lived time, on the other
hand, involves all the ecstasies of time—future, past, and present. It

temporalizes itself through a present decision which takes over the past that it now has been, and devotes it to an ultimate future it now has to be. As William James said, "the most important phase of a living person is his perspective on the world."[3] Similarly, we may say that the most important thing about a people or a culture is its primary philosophy, the way in which it understands itself and the world of its lived existence.

This philosophy by which we live is not an artificial product worked out by experts in a laboratory. It is a necessary part of human life, worked out sometimes consciously and sometimes subconsciously as we walk about the streets and do our work in schools, in offices, and in our homes, pursuing our different projects by day and dreaming of them by night. The objective scientist, or analyst, can postpone such existential interpretations and decisions, in order to concentrate on special, abstract objects. From his point of view, these basic questions seem unanswerable by his methods, and, therefore, avoidable. Hence they can wait.

As James also pointed out, we are here confronted by a forced, global option where even not to choose means a drifting way of life that is itself the expression of a choice that is diluted and unauthentic.[4] The world of the street, as James called it, is the world into which we are born, in which we exist and pursue our chosen projects, and in which we face death. As we have seen, all the original data of the different sciences are found within it. This world and the ordinary language by which we express it are rich beyond description, filled with ambiguity, and surrounded by mystery. The scientific universe, on the other hand, is abstract and has to be expressed by artificial, technical languages. Their principles and laws, once formulated, are precise and clear. This universe confronts us with no mysteries in which we ourselves are involved, but only with problems external to our existence which we may hope to solve.

This must serve as a brief summary of the contrast between the two worlds, two modes of understanding, and two types of meaning about which we have been thinking in the preceding chapters. The issues between them are clearly marked in our colleges and universities, where for many years now we have been witnessing the grad-

---

[3] William James, *Pragmatism* (New York: Meridian, 1959), p. 17.
[4] William James, *The Will to Believe and Other Essays* (New York: Longmans, Green, 1897), pp. 22 ff.

ual encroachments of the sciences into the so-called humanistic disciplines. Here again it is a question of the one world attempting to surround and to assimilate the other. With no world and no responsible procedures of their own, we find humanists more and more adapting themselves to the scientific world and its methods. But since the human world with which they are really concerned cannot be approached in this way without serious reduction and distortion, we find their situation growing ever more precarious. Some humanists now proceed in the "scientific" manner, filling endless library shelves with objective and statistical researches in their ever more separate fields. But these investigations are trivial and lifeless. Others cling desperately to the human things to which they are devoted, without trying to reduce them, but admitting that they have no place anywhere and that they are, in the last analysis, absurd. This may be courageous. But it is a counsel of despair which leads to ultimate defeat. Others, finally, go on as if nothing at all had happened. They continue to express their faith in the values of human freedom and dabble in personal philosophy. But they lack a solid foundation for cogent answers to the charges of irresponsible subjectivism and random speculation that are raised against them. After reading some timid endeavor of this kind, one sometimes wonders whether the author really believes what he says—or whether he is anything more than a humanist by profession. Here the war of the worlds is going on with one side close to victory.

In what we may call our general culture, the situation is perhaps not so far advanced, but nevertheless analogous. Pure science and the daring advances of technology are, of course, great endeavors of man which, in any case, we cannot now live without. Unless we are both ignorant and fanatical, we owe them our unqualified respect. But their popular versions, and the effects these have had on the mass culture of our time, are a different matter. They have recently been studied from a phenomenological point of view by a German author.[5] The many millions of persons who work in the mass apparatus of our time tend to think of themselves objectively in terms of the functions they perform. Personal idiosyncrasies are discouraged and conversation is streamlined. During the time of the existentialist fad in the early postwar years, there was a mild re-

[5] Günther Anders, *Die Antiquiertheit des Menschen*, 2nd ed. (München: C. H. Beck, 1956).

bellion against these pressures toward a technological mass conformism. Men felt that they were being dehumanized by the machine.

Now in certain centers of advanced technology, a new stage seems
to have been reached. Instead of resentment, there is a kind of envy
toward the machine which, in its mechanical operations and logical
calculations, is now far more exact and efficient than the human
brain. Airplane instructors tell their students that the human organism is a deficient construction, and when confronted with the
precise, inerrant mechanism of his power lathe, the worker has been
seen to hide his little chubby hands behind his back in shame. As
Anders points out, this sense of shame before our artifacts is a new
development in the revealing history of human feelings which has
not yet been written, but which we now so badly need. The objective attitudes and methods of science have done nothing to counter-
act these dehumanizing tendencies. In fact, it probably strengthened
them.

The same may be said of the constant flow of pictures and verbal
clichés which reduce the audiences of our mass media of communication to the role of passive recipients, *never able to talk back,* during regular intervals in the day. There is no doubt that this is one
of the basic reasons for that wearing out and deadening of the living
language which is so evident in advanced technological cultures.
Instead of the expression of vital meaning, speech is becoming
rather the mere transmission of factual information, or the pouring
out of word-bundles that call for no reply. Genuine dialogue is on
the wane. In tending the repetitive operations of the machine, which
go on endlessly, the human future loses its meaning, or, as we say:
the future will take care of itself. As Anders suggests, this may be
partly responsible for that strange indifference to atomic destruction which future historians, if there are any, will note as one of
the characteristic symptoms of our time. In all these ways, we see
personal existence and its historical world leveled down, and gradually absorbed into a great public world of common ideas and objects
that merges with the objective universe of science.

Of course there is another side: heroic struggles for authentic
existence on the part of individuals and minority groups, personal
sacrifices for lost causes. There are noteworthy attempts to regain
our respect for the ordinary language by which we express our free
existence in the human world, to recapture a sense of its original

meanings and their illuminating history, and to employ it in small primary groups as a field of dialogue for the creation of new meanings. Those who are intelligently engaged in such ventures do not dream of returning to a pretechnological age. This is sheer fantasy. They are moved by the hope that it may become possible somehow to use these tools for the sake of authentic existence, or, in other words, somehow to humanize the scientific, objective universe, and to absorb it into the life-world of man. Yes! This war of the worlds is proceeding within us and around us in every region of our culture, and on its final outcome a great deal will depend. So let us now return to the basic issue. Which of these worlds is the broader horizon? Which of them can encompass the other with the least reduction and distortion? Let us listen to both sides of the argument, and as we listen, think for ourselves and decide.

The Case for the Scientific Universe

Scientific rationalism, or scientism, as we may call it (not science), has no interest in the life-world as it is immediately presented. This rich world of everyday life, in which we actually exist, is dismissed as a jumbled realm of confusion. Positivists think of it as a world of "sloppy data" where nothing is clear, and where mythical interpretation is rampant. The first step of any disciplined scientist, therefore, who wishes to find out the objective truth, is to retire to the laboratory and shut the door. Here he may detach himself from his human prejudices, think, and work in peace. Of course he has to return after a while to the life-world. This, it is granted, is unfortunately true at present, but it need not last.

Time after time, the rationalist will point out, human prejudices, active in the life-world, like the central position of the earth, have been revealed as unfounded delusions, and put out of circulation. Why, then, can we not conceive of a time to come when most of these delusions have been eliminated and replaced by objective interpretations; when, in other words, we shall no longer see and think of things subjectively, but objectively, as they really are? The exactly measured universe is already fermenting within the life-world, and transforming huge chunks of it. Why, then, can we not work for a time when all this dough of confusion will be evenly raised into an ordered mass of information ready to become the bread that will nourish a rational human life? The modern rationalist is interested in the life-world from one point of view only—so far as he can hope to replace it by the scientific universe.

We may summarize the case for the priority of the scientific universe in the following way. Those who defend this view will say, first of all, that it is only by objective measurement and logical analysis that the objective facts may be revealed, and the light of clarity may come to dawn in the darkness of ambiguity and confusion. Second, it is only through checking the experiments of one observer by those of others that objective truth and agreement may be attained. Without this, we are left at the mercy of subjective feeling and bias. The third argument is even more impressive. The scientific method has now given us access to vast ranges of observable fact far beyond the narrow limits of the life-world. Consider the microscopic and submicroscopic regions known only through the telescope and undreamed of in the life-world. In addition, there is the information we now possess concerning the earth and the stellar universe during vast ranges of time before the human species existed. The life-world is certainly relative to man. Hence this perspective cannot extend beyond the limits of human history except by myth and fantasy. But the physical and biological sciences can tell us about the objective universe as it was before the coming of man and his life-world, as it will be long after his extinction, and as it now really is. Surely, therefore, this is the broader and more inclusive horizon.

It is also said that to understand a phenomenon of the life-world is to *explain* it in terms of its invisible causes, that is, the laws of those component parts which are subject to human influence. Only such explanatory theories of science enable us to predict what will happen in the future and to control the course of ongoing events. All other explanations are merely irresponsible myth and fancy, which give us no power over things and cannot be verified.

Finally, in conclusion, it is said that what we have been calling the *Lebenswelt* is nothing but a series of private events within the individual subject. This subjective region is the field of psychology, and when this science develops further, these subjective experiences can be fitted into the scientific universe as aspects of individual behavior. The whole *Lebenswelt*, as it is now called, is nothing but a distorted, subjective view of things in the brain of an ignorant individual. These views and biases are now very prevalent. But we may hope that, with the advance of science, they may be replaced by reliable scientific views and more orderly and intelligent modes of action governed by real knowledge. In this way, the *Lebenswelt* will be explained and brought within the objective universe of reason and science.

Such, in brief, is the case that can be made for the scientific universe as the broader and more ultimate horizon which will eventually replace the subjective perspectives of untrained and ignorant men. Now it may be thought that this point of view is restricted to a few positivistic philosophers living apart in ivory towers and scientific institutes who have little or no appreciable effect on our everyday life and thought. So it may be worthwhile to indicate certain ways in which this argument has widely penetrated into our common-sense reflections, and has exerted an appreciable influence not only in our universities but in our public thought as well.

Have you ever been told that such a concrete object as this yellow pencil before me (a world fact) is really not solid because it is made up of invisible moving particles with empty space between, and is really not yellow because molecules have no color? The thrust of this argument goes far beyond the particular implement in question. The pencil here and now refers to the paper on which it can write, and the paper involves the table on which it is now lying. So if the pencil is reduced to molecules, these also must be reduced. And not only this. The table has its place in the region of this room which is in the building, which has its place in the town, which is in the country, on the earth, and finally in the world. Familiar statements of this sort show that a decision has been made, at least implicitly, on the war of the worlds.

It is not just the yellow pencil that is being reduced. The whole concrete life-world in which I exist, and my existence itself, is being dismissed as a subjective appearance in favor of the objective universe of science with which all of us alive today are to some degree familiar. Of course, as long as men exist they will be perceiving and dealing with implements like the pencil. This is true of even the most thoroughgoing analyst and positivist. Nevertheless, our concern with such arguments tends to weaken the sense of our own existence, and may lead us to basic confusion. It is important to recognize that the life-world is not merely being absorbed, as it stands, into another horizon. It is being negated, reduced to the status of an illusion.

Once again, has it ever seemed to you that our modern experience confronts us with a vast array of scientific facts that are largely meaningless, and a plethora of relative, conflicting worlds, the Eastern world and the Western world, the Chinese world and the African world; and here at home the different worlds of Susan, Jane, and Jones? This relativism is also a result of *Lebenswelt* reduction in the war of the worlds. From an objective point of view, we are confronted with the facts of science which have a restricted sense of their own, but which lack the open, global meaning which is beyond the scope of any particular science. The world in which we exist is splintered into a vast number of closed and relative versions which can be objectively pictured side by side, contrasted, and leveled down. Since the false cannot be simply eliminated and forgotten, as in science, the false exists just as vigorously as the true. Under these confusing conditions each seems to be as relative and as deficient as the rest. Hence they are readily reduced and absorbed into the objective universe of science as subjective delusions. This objectivistic relativism is now very widespread. It is largely responsible for that sense of meaninglessness which is so characteristic of the mental *malaise* of our time.

Another result of this conquest of objectivism in the war of the worlds is the separation of academic philosophy, as it is still called, from that actual philosophic process which is a necessary aspect of human existence, and is constantly proceeding in every free person who is struggling to work out his own style of thinking and living. Academic philosophy, as we can see in the Platonic portrait of Socrates, was first conceived as a therapeutic discipline which should try to clarify and to purify this process of primary thinking that constantly goes on in every man. But in our history, the two have become separated, and now the anti-intellectualism of the common man is equaled only by the scorn of the technical philosopher for popular thought. But this divorce has had an unfortunate effect on both. For without disciplined criticism, primary reflection is apt to become closed, fanatical, and open to the charge of relativism. And when pursued without any reference to existence as it is actually lived, technical philosophy becomes a mere game that is abstract, provincial, and academic in the worst sense of the term. This open antagonism is itself a clear-cut manifestation of the war of the worlds, and, in particular, of those objectivist claims which isolate our careful thinking from the world we live in, and which we have just reviewed.

A last way in which world reduction is now widely manifested is the theory of determinism. Too many of those who attempt to defend human freedom have learned from certain objectivist trends in the history of Western thought to restrict it to what is still called *freedom of the will*. But as this history clearly shows, this is a fatal concession. In an objective universe, in which all else is already fixed and determined, the indeterminacy of a single human faculty is an unwelcome and doomed intruder. Hence in this age-old debate, the determinists have had the better of the argument. But the issue cannot be restricted to a single factor in the world; it concerns the whole world horizon. If man is really free, he exists in a world that is freely constituted—that is pervaded from beginning to end by freedom.

As a matter of fact, there is evidence to show that man has a certain control over the interpretation of his life-world, over its global meaning and order. This is clearly indicated by the radical diversity of the worlds of different peoples and individual persons. In a free society, I am able to choose and to work out my own style of life and my own global meanings, which pervade all that I think and do. This is the source of our human freedom. If these choices are conditioned by "analytic molecular traits," as a well-known philosopher of our time calls them,[6] biological and genetic traits, the tension of neural synapses, and stimuli supplied by the environment, we are involved once again in a war of the worlds. A decision has been made for the scientific universe as the prior and more inclusive horizon. Of course we go on choosing and struggling over questions of global meaning. But our sense of responsibility is dulled and diminished. Our sense of the future is diluted, and we look at ourselves after the fact as an object already there and finished. We tend to postpone the choices still open to us with a greater sense of fatigue and helplessness. Freedom also is an illusion. Once again the life-world has been negated and reduced.

I cannot accept these claims. In my opinion, the concrete world of everyday life and of what is now called *ordinary language* is the broader and prior horizon. The living philosophers of our time who are trying to formulate a new philosophy of the *Lebenswelt* seem to me to be closer to the truth and to the real needs of our situation in

[6] Ernest Nagel, "Determinism in History," *Phenomenology and Phenomenological Research*, XX (1960), p. 305.

history. Such a philosophy as yet has never been thoroughly worked out. Hence I shall now try to show you what such a philosophy would be like. I shall do this not in the hope of saying the last word and thus of ending the argument, but rather in the hope of stimulating further serious reflection. Let me now try to show how the case for objectivism, just reviewed, may be answered.

The Case for the Life-World

Scientific facts are determined by objective measurement and logical analysis. But as we have already suggested, there are facts of another kind which we have referred to as world-facts, like your reading this book, let us say, in the evening, in your living room, by
• the light of an electric lamp.[7] The special objective facts of all the different sciences can be found in such a situation, but these historical facts also contain qualitative and subjective factors to which science, as such, has no access, like your disinterest or interest in the book and what it means to you.

Our lives, as we live them, are made up of world-facts of this kind. It is true that they are inaccessible to quantitative measurement and to logical analysis in the traditional sense of these phrases. To understand such historical facts we need a logic of individuals rather than classes, of historical change rather than of fixed essences, that is dialectical rather than rigidly systematic. These lived facts occur in a world horizon of their own. To the objectivist mind, they seem to be a chaos of confusion. It is true that they require a distinctive mode of understanding. But when approached in the right way, these facts may be found to bear a different kind of meaning, and to be open to a different kind of truth, as we have seen. They do not fall into any purely objective order. They are pervaded by ambiguity and surrounded by mystery. But they occur in an open, historic life-world with a structure and an order of its own.

We cannot get outside this world of our lived existence to gaze at it from a detached point of view. We must understand it or misunderstand it directly as we live it from within. Hence the different global interpretations of the world that have been worked out in the course of human history cannot be checked, as in science, by any external facts, and the false ones then eliminated. This elimination of false views, as soon as they are discredited by the evidence,

7 Cf. pp. 66–67.

greatly simplifies the task of science. In the life-world, where interpretation is an essential part of life, we cannot eliminate a false view without eliminating the person and his group as well. This is harder to do. So we must live with falsity and error both in ourselves and others, and bear with them, even though they have been shown to be inhuman and unauthentic. But this does not mean that they cannot be checked at all. As James saw, they are subject to a historical check, which is open to a different kind of truth. In a given humanistic area, as we have pointed out, interpretations that are superficial, narrow, closed, out of line with the world facts, and transitory can be distinguished from those that are penetrating, wide in scope, open, factual, and lasting.

Philosophy is the discipline of that freedom of understanding which lies at the root of all our other freedoms. But this does not mean that all interpretations can be dismissed as mere subjective feelings or opinions on the same plane. Some express lasting types and structures of the world, and call forth authentic existence.[8] Others are unauthentic and false to the world as it really is. They enslave, disunify, and dehumanize man. The scientific truth, which lies in the correspondence of meanings with objective fact, is an important type of truth. But the world-truth, for which James was seeking, is more fundamental. No one would continue to pursue science unless there was evidence to show that it furthers certain basic values, and offers hope for the humanization of the world of man.

The objectivist argues that his perspective is more basic, richer, and wider, and that the life-world is derived and less inclusive. But these assertions are open to question. Objective logic and science are special modes of knowing derived from a more basic revealing power that belongs to man, and opens up the *Lebenswelt* to him. As the history of philosophy clearly shows, the objective methods of reason and science cannot explain this basic revealing power. All explanation presupposes it. If we are ever to understand this mysterious openness, and the freedom with which it is so closely connected,[9] it will not be by the restricted methods of objective anal-

---

[8] Since the false interpretations often exist just as vigorously, if not more so, than the true, terms like *authentic* and *unauthentic* are more fit to express this mode of existential truth. Cf. pp. 164–165.

[9] We shall consider some of the basic questions concerning freedom in our next three chapters.

ysis. It will be rather by one of those global interpretations which guide our different styles of life, and that belong to the all-encompassing world horizon in which we actually exist. While we do science, we can postpone such global decisions concerning the total meaning of life. But as James saw, we cannot live without them. In the *Lebenswelt* they are forced options, and we must either work out our own style of understanding or accept such a world interpretation from others.

The abstract perspectives of science are neutral to global meaning and value. They can be fitted into the Nazi world, the world of the East, and the world of the West. Science evades or by-passes mystery and transcendence. In existence, they must be faced. It is this mystery and ambiguity of the *Lebenswelt* that calls forth those most basic global meanings, like time, space, being, nothingness, freedom, and meaning itself, which underlie the more restricted perspectives of science. These perspectives may be very rich and very vast. But the horizon of the life-world is richer and vaster. There is room in this horizon for all the objects of science and much more, without reduction or distortion. Its very ambiguity and openness is a sign of its wider range. This is the world of freedom.

For the rationalistic observer, reality is whatever can be gazed at out there from a detached point of view. This gives us a useful perspective on things, and on certain aspects of ourselves. But a great deal is always omitted—ourselves as the centers of freedom; all-pervasive meanings, like world, being, truth, and meaning itself. It is at this point that the detached observer brings the confused term "subjective" into play. All these global meanings are nothing but private, "subjective" feelings and opinions within the brain of the individual subject. As yet they are not clearly understood. But eventually they will be scientifically explained, and thus absorbed within the objective perspective. This strange term, "subjective," now plays a crucial role in the strategy of the objective thinker, enabling him to win an easy victory in the war of the worlds. It (the "subjective") is really an objectivist term that has worked its way into our common discourse and has influenced our common sense. But we should now be careful about its use, for it is compounded of many confusions.

Man is never locked up within a "subjective," mental container. When we speak in this way, we are playing the objectivist game, and forgetting ourselves and the world in which we exist. As we have tried to show, from infancy to maturity man is always stretched out into a field of care, and open to a world-horizon. His most private thoughts and feelings are ways of being-in-the-world which convey meanings and references to what is beyond. It is true that the intentions of a living person may become eccentric and distorted. But then, as the psychiatrists are now telling us, his world also becomes eccentric and distorted. Man and the world belong together, and the one cannot be understood without the other. Man, we can say, is a living version of the world in which he exists. This world is neither exclusively subjective nor exclusively objective, but if we cannot find better language, both together in one.

If we are to understand any world, whether it be the public world of a group or the personal world of a single person, we must understand not only the objects with which it is concerned, but its inner intentions, and the modes of concern by which it is ordered. This world of our lived existence cannot be subjectively reduced and absorbed into the universe of science without grave misunderstanding and distortion. But once we have learned to speak of it adequately and to understand it, we can see that there is room within it for all the perspectives of love, hope, joy, and despair, and every perspective of science *without reduction or diminution.* It is the life-world that is the prior and richer horizon.

The vast city of science belongs within this life-world, having grown out of it and within it by a long historical development which is now fairly well known. Scientists inhabit the very same world with the rest of us. They are born in our hospitals, educated in our schools, walk our streets, and participate in our common life. Their buildings, laboratories, and machines are well-marked regions and places in our living space. Their theories, experiments, and operations occur in our lived time, for science certainly has a past and a future.

The so-called scientific universe, which is constantly being confirmed and reconstructed within these regions, is not an ultimate horizon. It is rather a very important but abstract perspective on things in the *Lebenswelt*. It regards all entities within the world, including man himself, from a detached point of view. Then by its peculiar hypothetico-deductive method, it discovers the scientific facts about all these entities, even the facts about human meanings, after they have been formed and can be brought before the mind as objects. This perspective has a very accurate and wide-ranging revealing power. There is nothing, indeed, on which it cannot shed a certain kind of light.

The development of this objective perspective has been a vitally important phase of our Western cultural history which has transformed the human world and our whole way of life. It has given us a remarkable mastery over concrete objects of the life-world, and has also enormously extended and refined the hazy knowledge of objective detail to which our unaided powers are limited. But the concrete world of our existence can never be fitted into this objective universe without reduction. It is precisely the contrary which is true. It is this entire universe, its constitutive acts, together with all its objects, which may be fitted without reduction into the *Lebenswelt*. Like art and culture, which are also universal in scope, objective reason—or science, as we now prefer to call it—is a certain perspective on things in the world, and must itself be included within this ultimate world-horizon.

Its very openness and ambiguity shows that it is the wider horizon. Thus when I am told that this solid yellow pencil before me (a world fact)[10] is really not solid, since it is made up of invisible moving particles with mostly empty space between, and that it is not really yellow, since molecules have no color, there is an answer! Familiar statements of this sort show that a decision has been made on the war of the worlds. The concrete *Lebenswelt* is being reduced to a fixed delusion, and absorbed within the objective universe.

But this decision is unjustified, since it fails to take account of the perspectival character, and the ever-present openness of actual perception. I do see the whole of this yellow pencil, but only through partial, ambiguous perspectives. Each of these leaves the way open for an indefinite number of further aspects to be revealed by different points of view. The concrete object of direct perception is infinitely rich. There is no reason, therefore, why it should not have room for the submicroscopic perspectives of the physicist, and the further aspects revealed to him through his special techniques and instruments. In the open field of the *Lebenswelt*, there is room for all these aspects, and for many more as well. The abstract perspectives of science and reason are less open and less rich.

A similar reply can be given to the point about prehuman and posthuman time. How can these vast periods be included within the tiny expanse of human history? So runs the argument. But the

10 Cf. Chapter 3, pp. 50ff.

Lebenswelt is not a fixed "expanse." It is a moving, historical world that is open at either end. Science has extended these borders and given us information concerning its prehuman and posthuman history. But these important discoveries do not discredit or replace the time of the *Lebenswelt*. They are rather developments and extensions of the primordial historicity in which we directly participate. It is from this lived temporality that we gain our original sense of the meaning of time, and it is from this that other modes, like clock time, are derived.

When we look at this world from a detached point of view, it splinters into a manifold of relative versions. There is the growing world of Africa and the world of the West, the world of Jones and the world of Smith. While we gaze at them as objects there before us, comparing them and noting the peculiar properties of each, they become fixed and enclosed within themselves. Instead of an open, developing, living version, each becomes a total and finished world in itself. My own way of understanding my existence is often threatened by a freezing process of this sort, which may lead to the bigotry and fanaticism of a rigid version, incapable of growth. But this does not need to happen. As long as our existence remains authentic, we have a sense of the mystery which transcends even our most exhaustive and far-ranging interpretations.

It is this sense of transcendence which enables us to distinguish between my version of the world and the world itself that includes mine as well as other versions, and yet lies beyond them all. Those who maintain this sense of mystery know that they are not living merely in a relative, makeshift world-construction of their own, alongside other possibilities. They are living the one and only existence to which they will ever have access, in the one and only world there is. Such an existing person will live according to the best interpretation he can find, but he will recognize it as only a human version, and will keep it ever open to revision and correction.

Let me remark in concluding that I am, of course, making no claim to have finally settled this war of the worlds with which we have been concerned. I have tried to state clearly the strong case that can be made out for the priority and the greater inclusiveness of the life-world, as against the similar claims now being widely made for the objective universe.

If the exploration of this world now continues with the same vigor that has already marked its beginning, we may hope for some bridging of the deep chasm which has so long separated the secondary reflection of academic philosophy from the spontaneous, primary thinking of daily life that forms and orders our versions of the world. A critical purification and clarification of this primary philosophic process might help to elicit authentic existence at every level, and in every walk of life. For in this sense, every human being, as long as he lives, is engaged in the project of philosophy.

It is true that human freedom does not belong in a realm of things bound together by objective, causal relations. During most of our Western past, it has been regarded in this way. In any such perspective, an eccentric and isolated freedom of the will is sure to be gradually watered down and finally eliminated, as the history of Western philosophy clearly shows. As Kant pointed out, if freedom exists, it must exist in a different world horizon of its own, and as we now know, there is such a world, the human *Lebenswelt.*

The exploration of this world has led to a basic rethinking of the mystery we call freedom; and to a new sense of its importance, not only in human action but in what we call human consciousness as well. As we have indicated, the objectively oriented philosophy of the past has not been able to do justice to this central aspect of our existence in the world. Therefore we shall introduce this discussion of human freedom, with which we shall be occupied through the next three chapters, by a criticism of the classical, objectivist view.

Part III

Freedom and
Responsibility

Chapter 6

The Traditional View
of Freedom: A Criticism

In this chapter I wish to examine and to criticize a pre-Kantian objectivist view of freedom which originated in the classical Greek philosophy of Aristotle, was further developed in Aquinas and the central tradition of medieval thought, and is still very influential both in naturalistic as well as in analytic discussions of "free will vs. determinism." Professor Ernest Nagel has recently given a cogent statement of this point of view in his article "Determinism in History";[1] and in the second part of this chapter I shall refer to it as an example of the position I am criticizing. According to this conception, freedom is restricted to deliberate acts of the will which can be observed by introspection, or by some mode of objective apprehension, and fitted into an external world that is constituted by chains of causes and effects, or networks of interdependent variables which are quite independent of human choice, intention, and meaning.

In the discussion here, I shall first comment on the phenomenological approach to philosophy, and how it differs from certain forms of contemporary analysis. Second, I shall outline certain basic aspects of the view I am criticizing, with special reference to Mr. Nagel's article. Third, I shall initiate the criticism by some phenomenological remarks on the relation of freedom to consciousness.

---

[1] *Phenomenology and Phenomenological Research*, XX (1960), pp. 291–317. Further references to this article are inserted in the text.

And fourth, I shall complete it by some comments on the nature of scientific law and its relation to the world of men.

Phenomenology and Analysis

The aim of the phenomenologist is to reveal the phenomenon (whatever shows itself to us in any way) as it is, avoiding a priori predilection and bias, so far as this is possible. This resolution to let the evidence decide without any alien intrusion is, of course, shared by British empiricism, and it is possible to think of phenomenology as a new development of empiricism, a *radical empiricism,* to use the phrase of William James. But the qualifying adjectives are necessary, and certain important differences resulting from the investigations of Husserl and his followers must now be held in mind. Two of these are especially important.

The first is the discovery of the relational or intentional character of our lived experience which grew out of the penetrating critique of British empiricism inaugurated by Brentano and Husserl at the end of the nineteenth century. This lived experience cannot be adequately analyzed into atomic ideas, or impressions, enclosed within a subjective container. It is rather to be understood as a set of intentions radiating outward from an active center in different ways toward different ranges of objects of various kinds.

This discovery of intentionality has led to another related insight also missed by past versions of empiricism, which we have considered in the last three chapters. The human individual cannot be rightly understood as a subject or substance isolated from an external world. His existence from the very beginning is ecstatic or relational in character. He is stretched out into the past and the future and into a spatial field, or world horizon, which he carries with him wherever he goes. This world field is constituted in part by an element of "thrownness," or factuality, coming from independent things and agencies. Thus every situation in which I find myself involves facts which are simply given and for which I am in no sense responsible, like my birth. But it is also constituted by a factor of global meaning which pervades it as a whole, and over which I have some control. Man cannot be separated from this world-horizon. He *is* the world in which he lives, and knows, and exists. This conception of the human *Lebenswelt,* first sharply focused by Husserl in his *Krisis der Europäischen Wissenschaften,* is not only widely accepted by living phenomenologists, but has already exerted a marked influence on anthropology, clinical psychology, psychiatry, and other human disciplines.

These discoveries have now led to a new phenomenological method quite distinct from introspection and other modes of approach associated with traditional forms of empiricism. To regard a lived experience as an inner "object," from a detached point of view, is to place it in an alien frame, and to miss the world horizon which is essential to it. As the French phenomenologist Merleau-Ponty puts it, "As soon as I look inward into my lived experience, I am immediately thrown out into the world again. Even the private experience of pain occurs in a situation with objective elements of which I am at least dimly aware." We have been trying to suggest some of the new light which, I think, is now beginning to be shed on our human being-in-the-world, and on such basic ways of existing as dying, human time, oriented space, and, finally, freedom with which we are to be primarily concerned in this and the two succeeding chapters.

The phenomenological approach to philosophy, as I have described it (pp. 30–38), has much in common with that of recent, so-called linguistic analysis. Both movements share a distrust of those great cosmic systems which have claimed to explain our concrete lived experience, and have usually generated paradoxical conflicts with ordinary modes of speech. Both agree that many of the traditional so-called "problems" of epistemology, for example the relation of sense data to physical objects, and the existence of an external world, are artificial and based on corrigible misunderstandings. Finally, both share a deep respect for the usages of ordinary language. These points of agreement are important. But there are differences as well. We have already noted in Chapter 3 the tendency among analysts to confuse world facts with scientific facts, and to discount the empirical, revealing function of philosophy. There are also other differences which now need to be mentioned.

In the first place, while the phenomenologist is deeply concerned with the disciplined analysis of ordinary language, he is not content to rest with this. He does not believe that an ordinary use can be understood without an understanding of the whole situation in which it occurs. For him, the analysis of language is not an end in itself. It is rather an important aspect of a wider project, the clarification of human existence as it is lived and its more basic meanings, some of which are certainly not linguistic. Thus the bottle means something to the baby, and a scowl means something in a personal conversation.[2]

Second, the phenomenologist is disappointed in the "minute philosophy" which so far seems to be characteristic of the analytic movement. He is, of course, far from denying that a detailed analysis, for instance, of the distinction between "seeming to see an object" and "seeing a seeming object" may prove to be illuminating. But it may lose itself in a verbal morass. It can hardly become significant without a careful analysis of the basic distinction, also found in ordinary language, between seeming and being. But analysts so far have been very hesitant about such basic ontological investigations, and have failed, for example, to examine the global meaning of the term "world" as it is used in ordinary discourse. This distrust of far-ranging "theories" is probably due to a distrust of "metaphysics" and to a desire to appear technically exact and scientific in their procedures. But exactitude is not the same as triviality. And it is now clear that the richer, primordial language of the *Lebenswelt* is not to be confused with the abstract and derived technical languages of the special sciences. The exploration of this world of lived existence requires a radically different method which is open to structures neither wholly subjective nor wholly objective, but both together in one. There is no "science" of the world. I am not saying that this analytic hesitancy about world structures may not eventually be overcome. But so far it has led to difficulties which are subject to the third and fourth criticisms.

The third is directed against that detachment from the actual concerns of everyday life in which many analysts seem to take great pride. Thus they are not so much concerned with ethics, the making of value judgments, as with meta-ethics, the objective analysis (in itself neutral) of the meaning of such judgments. But can the meaning of these judgments be dissociated from the active engagement through which they are made and its total world horizon? Can they be regarded as objects in another world without distortion? The phenomenologist doubts that these questions can be answered with a confident affirmative. As we have seen, he understands that the *Lebenswelt*, and the ordinary language by which it is expressed, are pervaded by value. He believes that it is possible to understand

---

[2] Cf. H. P. Rickman, "Philosophical Anthropology and the Problem of Meaning," *Philosophical Quarterly*, X (1960), pp. 16–17.

these structures as they are lived, without imposing our own values on them. The phenomenologist is trying to reveal human existence as it is. But while this requires arduous discipline and self-restraint, it is no mere academic game. It is rather an attempt to follow the suggestion of Dilthey in working out in each generation a growing body of disciplined knowledge, founded on lasting truth, which may provide a firm basis for humanistic studies, and which may become relevant to the situation of each age, capable of helping free people maintain their freedom in the varying situations of their different times (cf. Chapter 12).

Finally, there is a fourth criticism to which the minute analysis of our time is subject. This is connected with the global character of meaning which constantly expands from more restricted manifestations to ever wider circles, until an ultimate world-horizon is reached on which all the rest depends. The minute analyst, in concentrating exclusively on what he takes to be isolated and restricted expressions, is apt to be forgetful of presuppositions, ingrained in the structure of his language, which he never subjects to careful criticism. Thus he may become trapped by ancient assumptions of a most dubious character, belonging to systematic world views which he officially repudiates. This, I think, has happened in the case of many recent analyses of freedom-language, which instead of giving us anything really new, have simply given us the modulation of an ancient theme derived from traditional realistic philosophy. It is this theme, the realistic or objectivist conception of human freedom, which I now wish briefly to explain, and then to criticize.

Freedom as Reduced to Freedom of the Will

The basic assumptions still underlying naturalistic and analytic discussions of the issue between so-called free will and determinism were first laid down in ancient Greece. They are found in the philosophy of Aristotle and his followers, including Aquinas and his school. They are also found in naturalistic discussions of this problem, including the recent article by Ernest Nagel entitled "Determinism in History," to which I have referred. Three of these basic assumptions are worthy of comment.

In the first place, no distinction is made between the concrete human life-world and the objective perspective of reason and science. As a result of this, it is assumed that if freedom exists at all, it must be envisaged as an objective event of some kind within the realm of determinate objects which are normally related to one another as cause and effect, or as interdependent variables. Thus in writing on the soul and on the events of human history, Aristotle uses the same method he employs in his *Physics*. These events may be more complex. They may have a different causal structure. But they have no world of their own; they belong to the same objective cosmic order, and must be regarded as objects in the same objective way. Similarly for Nagel (pp. 304–05 of the article cited), historical events are more complex and, in contrast to the strict objects of physics which possess "analytic molecular characteristics," are said to possess "common-sense molar characteristics." Freedom has no world of its own. If it exists at all, it must be found within the objective universe of science and examined in the very same way.

In the second place, according to Aristotle and the whole classical tradition, freedom, insofar as it exists at all, is never conceived as a basic ontological factor pervading the whole world of man, not even the whole of human nature. It is definitely restricted to one particular faculty, the will, and to the voluntary choices made by this faculty. Such choices are preceded by a certain process known as *deliberation* in which reason and desire work together. Two things need to be noted about this process. First, it occurs subjectively within the limits of the human organism where it determines the direction of my practical attitudes and acts. Second, it operates within the framework of an objective universe with whose real structure it has nothing to do, except, perhaps, when malfunctioning, to introduce subjective distortions and misunderstandings.

Similarly, for Nagel (p. 313) the whole issue between freedom and determinism is concerned with the interpretation not of the whole world in which we live and think, but with certain "deliberative choices" in which "men often do deliberate and decide between alternatives." This classical restriction is epitomized in a standard philosophical phrase, "freedom of the will," or "freedom of choice," which has even found its way into the precincts of ordinary language. I could mention many recent analyses of freedom-talk which accept this basic assumption without question, and allow it to determine the whole scope of their discussion.

Finally, there is no freedom in the proper functioning of either feeling or reason since, according to classical thought, these faculties are wholly determined by their formal objects. If I am to understand a thing, or a world from which I am detached, I must simply see it out there as it is. I have no free control over the global meanings which constitute my world. Hence there is no proper sense in which the scientist and the philosopher have choices to make. The vast history of different worlds of different peoples, different philosophers, and even of different ordinary individuals in the "same" culture have to be explained as unfortunate, subjective deviations due to ignorance. Thus we find Professor Nagel, for example (p. 309), dismissing different forms of indeterminism as "but a name for our *de facto* ignorance."

Unfortunately, many of the most acute defenders of "human freedom" have accepted these assumptions, and have restricted themselves to the dubious effort of trying to show that, in a universe where all is fixed, the human will at least is free. But in such an objective frame, the exercise of subjective choice is an alien intruder which obviously does not belong. It is a strange subjective object, an uncaused cause, an indeterminate determinant, a whimsical and irresponsible responsibility. It is not surprising that under these conditions, in this pre-Kantian way of putting the question, the determinists should have had the better of the argument. Mr. Nagel (p. 314), of course, has no difficulty in showing that the difference between what we call "a freely chosen act" and "a determined one" reduces to "the distinction between acts over which a man does have control, and those over which he does not . . ."; or as an Aristotelian would put it, between those acts whose causes lie within ourselves and those whose causes lie outside. To be free is simply to have the honor of being fitted into a nexus of causal determinations.

Thus the philosopher of science himself will be absorbed into his system with no remainder, as Queen Elizabeth, according to Mr. Nagel (p. 305), will be eventually "explained" in terms of her "analytic molecular characteristics" which will include "mention of, say, her detailed biological and genetic traits, the condition of her neural synapses, and the specific physical stimuli supplied by her environment . . ." Mr. Nagel (p. 316) goes out of his way to assure the linguistic analysts that "our ordinary moral language with its associated customary meanings will survive at least partially . . ." This seems reassuring until we are reminded by the final qualification of what is really going on. Yes! ordinary language will be allowed to survive as a vague but permissible pragmatic tool for those incapable of rigorous determinist analysis. The human life-world, or *Lebenswelt*, the world of ordinary language in which we may live and freely participate, is being absorbed into the objective perspective of reason and science where all is fixed and determined, including the perspective itself, by objective networks of variables apart from all human meaning and choice.

Like other determinists before him, Mr. Nagel spends little or no time in focusing and defining the basic pre-Kantian assumptions which underlie his argument. Three of these we have pointed out: (1) that we exist in a world of abstract objects; (2) that our freedom is restricted to voluntary choices of the will; and (3) that it plays no role in science, philosophy, and the constitution of the world of man. On the ground of these assumptions, Mr. Nagel's argument is quite correct, and I would not think of questioning it. At this point, though, I want to raise the discussion to another plane and question these assumptions. The questioning may seem a lapse into irrationalism and subjectivism. But we shall see. I believe that these assumptions may be questioned from a phenomenological position quite distinct from any traditional form of idealism or subjectivism. In the following parts of this chapter, I shall try to offer some evidence for this position, first of all by some reflections on the relation of freedom to consciousness, and second, by some comments on the abstract nature of scientific law and its relation to the world of man.

Freedom of Consciousness

We say that an act is indeterminate if it might have been otherwise. But if we ignore the awareness dwelling in every human act, and place this act within an objective, causal frame, such a statement fails to fit the frame, and seems to be impossible. We all know the way in which recent analysts have argued that it can mean: this act might have been otherwise *if the situation had been different*. With the *if* clause, freedom here vanishes into a normal, objective, causal sequence. Those of us who have studied the long history of this controversy also know the way similar moves have been used in the past by determinists who, in my opinion, have had, on the whole, by far the better of such arguments. When restricted to an isolated act of will, which is placed in an objective perspective of this sort, freedom has little chance.

But perhaps freedom is something far more basic. Perhaps it cannot be restricted to a specific kind of act which can be regarded objectively in this way. Perhaps, as Kant realized, it belongs in a world of its own, the *Lebenswelt* of our daily life, which lies beyond the objective perspectives of science and of objective thought in general, and which Kant, therefore, still a rationalist in this respect, mistakenly regarded as *noumenal*. Perhaps it cannot be properly understood as any object or set of objects *in* the *Lebenswelt* but rather as a necessary phase of this world-consciousness itself. Let us try to make these statements plausible by suggesting a contrast with which we are all in some degree familiar.

There is a mode of immediate experience, as we sometimes call it, in which we gain no distance from the so-called object. We pay no attention to *what it is*. Our whole attention is directed rather to changing it, and mastering it for the satisfaction of some desire. We have little self-awareness. As we sometimes say, we are lost in our pursuit. At the same time, our field of awareness narrows to the immediate situation determined by our need. We lose our sense of the world as a whole, of the past as well as the future. Our immediate experience here and now simply carries us along.

This, of course, describes an ideal limit which can only be approximated by men. It is a reasonable guess, however, that it applies fairly accurately to the experience of animals where language, in the strict sense of this term, is lacking. Such experience is pragmatically determined. Hence we do not call it *free*. We say of persons in such a condition that they are obsessed and have lost their sense of reality. When we talk to them, we feel that they are not wholly present to themselves (not themselves) and not wholly present to us. Let us now contrast this condition with the more authentic order of awareness from which it is, in man, a deviation.

This mode of awareness is not content merely to follow the immediate flux of pragmatically determined experience. It has accepted another standard, the standard of reality, to judge its thoughts and actions. I am not content with the given data. I become aware of *things* confronting me, and I want to know *what they really are*. I am present to myself, and I wish to know and to become what I really am, not merely on the background of my familiar needs and attitudes, but on the background of a broader horizon which encompasses all that is, and to which we refer sometimes as *being* and sometimes as *the world*. Let us now ask ourselves what lies at the root of these distinctive traits of human consciousness.

I believe that if we raise this question seriously, we shall find that this is a self-negation or self-transcendence, only one partial aspect of which has been inadequately expressed by the notion of indeterminism. Man is the being who can say *no* not only to others but to himself. This is the root from which our freedom and responsibility grow. Let us see if we can clarify this by a few brief indications.

First of all, if my awareness is to free itself from the biological determinism of animal experience, it must be able to achieve a distance from what is given, to get away from the drives that glue it to this given, and to confront it as a real thing in the world. This is a basic fact of our human awareness, which is ecstatic or outside itself, always giving itself up to what is other than itself. But in order to do this, it must first gain a distance from itself that is missing in the animal. It can identify itself with what we call *an object* only from this distance. Our awareness actively confronts the beings it knows. It irrupts into them and makes them present as real things, or to use the ancient analogy, it brings them out of the darkness into the light.

But in order to become other and to identify with them in this way, our consciousness must first free itself from what it is already. Only by gaining this distance from the given, can it win that openness to what is other than itself, which is the heart and core of what we mean by freedom. This being-open-to-otherness (freedom) is found in every basic manifestation of human consciousness. Thus the animal can understand a sign which is manifestly related to its "signatum." But it cannot take an arbitrary element of its experience as a way of regarding something else that is absent. Hence language in the strict sense is beyond its capacity. Our imagination enables us to take any given experience as related to something with which it is not related, and to see it as what it is *not*.

The question *why* lies at the root of our efforts to gain intellectual understanding. *Why*, we ask, is it this way and not some other? It is only by first separating ourselves from our original experience that things may be revealed as they *are*, in their being, and brought into the light. It is only by first becoming absent from him that I can truly become present to another.

The same holds true of my presence to myself. As our language indicates, this is a self-relatedness based on a prior self-separation, of which the animal is incapable. It simply is what it is. Man, on the other hand, is never just what he is but always other, so that he can be present to himself, thinking with himself as *con-scious* or as *con-science*. This primordial, *thinking with,* does not originally mean staring at myself in an objective perspective. This is a special and later derivation. Originally it means a lived awareness of my whole being-in-the-world of which I am the center, for I am not an isolated thing at an instant, here and now.

I *am* my lived body. But I am also outside this body *in* the various regions of my concern—in the book that I am reading, in the work that I am doing, in its tools and in its objects. I am also the past that I have been, and the projects I have projected into my future ahead of me. Of all this, during my waking moments and in certain ways even during sleep, I am dimly aware in a pre-thematic way, within the broad horizon of my life-world, the *Lebenswelt.* All these things, past and present, and I myself, are in this world-horizon that belongs essentially to my lived awareness. What can we say of this horizon as against other backgrounds, such as what is now called the *life-field* of an animal?

It is interesting to note that this biological concept of the life-field is similar to that of the human life-world, and that they were both worked out at approximately the same time. The discoveries of J. von Uexküll, the German biologist, and his school from 1920 to 1930 were particularly important in breaking down the traditional conception of a single material environment which remains the same for all species and all individual organisms. Von Uexküll showed that this is an abstract construction which has no real importance in understanding the life of a given species.[3] What is important here is the life-field (*Umwelt*) into which the animal's action radiates, and where it can be present. The nature of this life-field is correlated with the projects of the animal and grounded on the peculiar anatomy of each species, which thus has an environment of its own. Each individual member of the species lives in its own field, and is sensitive to any invasion of this field by alien forces. Such invasions will lead to a life-and-death struggle.

In this country, George H. Mead developed similar conceptions of the mutual interdependence of the living animal and its environment.[4] No living organism can be adequately understood without an understanding of its life-field. The inner cycles of its bodily life de-

[3] *Theoretische Biologie* (Berlin: 1928).
[4] *Mind, Self, and Society* (Chicago: University of Chicago Press, 1934), pp. 125–134.

fine an objective territory with certain traits which are necessary to its existence. This existence depends on the field which conditions it. But the field depends on the type of organism which carves it out and gives it vital meaning. This is a strange *sui generis* relationship in which each factor is conditioned by the other, and which cannot be understood in terms of cause and effect. To live is to radiate. Hence each individual plant and animal not only has, but must have, a vital field into which its existence is projected.

The human being is no exception to this rule. He also has his vital field, or habitat, where he knows his way and where his presence is radiated. He has the house and the family where he is at home; the carpenter has his shop where he works; the scholar his library where he studies and the classroom where he argues and teaches; the farmer his field and barns where he lives on the land. The individual becomes attached to his vital field and cannot be separated from it without becoming displaced and disoriented, as the city man in the country or the peasant who gropes for his way in the city. Without roots in a vital field of this kind, the normal person can do nothing.

But this human world differs from the animal field in the two vital respects we have suggested. In the first place, unlike the animal, man can get at a distance from his field, reveal it as it is, and thus become open to a being other than his own. The radical freedom of awareness has enabled different *cultures,* as we call them, to order different meaningful horizons, and different individuals, even in the same culture, to work out radically different styles of life and different horizons of their own. There is a freedom of world-formation, closely connected with what we call philosophy. This is the first difference.

But the second is equally important. Our awareness is free. It can negate itself, and out of this nothingness reveal the being of what confronts it as it is. But this freedom is finite. It is limited by the situation into which it has been thrown and by the special projects to which it has access. It cannot escape from history, which, at any given time, makes certain things more accessible and conceals others.

What is revealed is understood in perspective, always ambiguous in certain respects. Hence while we shed some light around us, this light fades into shadow. The truth we reveal is always partial and necessarily mixed with error. Though this has sometimes been denied by dogmatic philosophers, it is known to the pre-thematic and primordial understanding of men. Hence, though I may be living in a world of my own quite different from that of Jones, we are both able to make an important distinction between *my* world, or *my version of the world,* and what we call *the world* as it really is, which includes all that we see truly as we see it, all that we see falsely but not as we see it, our false seeing, and much more. It is this openness to the radical otherness of transcendence, as we may call it, which makes communication between different styles of life, and even different schools of philosophy, always possible. In fact, this possibility of communication between radically divergent worlds and styles of life is one of the most important disciplines to be learned from the study of philosophy, the discipline which pushes our awareness to its farthest limits and even beyond, and, is there-fore, in a peculiarly appropriate sense the discipline of freedom, for it is our human awareness that is, as such, self-transcendent and free.

This, of course, is only a brief sketch, which we shall develop further in the next chapter. If, as I believe, it is on the whole sound, freedom is not a mere derivative trait founded on reason. Rather, that which is most essentially human about our consciousness, in-cluding what we call "reason," is founded on freedom. In order to understand anything, not merely as it fits our needs, but *as it really is,* we must negate our ever-present pragmatic attitudes to win dis-tance from it. This requires intensive discipline and struggle. Only by emptying ourselves in this way can we achieve that openness to other being, that ability to conceive things otherwise, sometimes called imagination, which is the source of freedom.

It is only through the exercise of this conscious negativity that we can transcend the utilitarianism which rules the animal kingdom and a great part of our human life. Out of this nothingness, being can be revealed, and we can gain some access not merely to things as they are in *my* world for me, but to things as they are in *the world.* Then instead of using them or mastering them, we may have the courage to respect them and to *let them be* as they are.

The Laws of Science and the Life-World

It is in actively living my life and pursuing my projects in the *Lebenswelt* that I encounter those friendly and inimical powers which aid me or threaten me with death. These powers can be an-alyzed into causes or into abstract functional relationships, from a detached, objective point of view. But as I directly meet them in living through my world, they are active forces pervaded with positive or negative value. The stone that breaks my window is not just a body of such and such a mass, moving with a momentum that exceeds the resistance of the glass. It is an alien force, disturbing my peace and making my room uninhabitable. The dandelion in my garden is not just a plant of the genus *Taraxacum*, following its predictable cycle of germination and growth. It is a weed that is killing my flowers. The thin air into which I climb at the top of the mountain is not just a mass of gas expanding as the pressure decreases in accordance with Boyle's law: $pv = C$. It is a power that thins my breath and ebbs away my strength.

When I fall into the attitude of detached observation, I abstract so far as possible from my active engagement in the world. From this attitude, I gain an objective perspective on things which is blind to the actual exercise of power. From this point of view, I see the objective uniformities, or functional relationships, expressed in laws. But it is only in and through my active engagement in the *Lebenswelt* that I am directly open to the exercise of alien or friendly powers. I must myself be exercising my feeble forces to feel the forces around me. These are two radically different perspectives, opening into two radically different horizons; first the *Lebenswelt,* and second, the objective realm of science. The former is the richer of the two, and the primordial source from which the other is derived by abstraction.

Hume glimpsed this truth at the end of his *Treatise* where, after having shown with penetrating clarity that there is no place for power or influence in the abstract perspective of science and reason, he cries out in the famous passage: "Where am I or what? From what causes do I derive my existence and to what condition shall I return? Whose favour shall I court, and whose anger must I dread? What beings surround me? And on whom have I any influence or who have any influence on me? I am confounded with all these questions and begin to fancy myself in the most deplorable condition imaginable, inviron'd with the deepest darkness, and utterly depriv'd of the use of every member and faculty."[5]

This is a classic description of the experience, familiar in some degree to all intellectuals, of passing abruptly from the abstract

[5] Hume, *A Treatise of Human Nature,* ed. Selby-Bigge (Oxford: Clarendon Press, 1958), pp. 268–269.

regions of objective reflection into the so-called "subjective" world of our human existence where all is confused, dynamic, and indeterminate. Confronted with this clash of two warring worlds, Hume could not decide which was richer than and prior to the other. The one was for him irrational and subjective; the other so abstract and remote from existence that he could not live in it. Hence he remained a skeptic. All through the ages, the rationalist mind has taken the position that the objective realm of reason is prior to and more inclusive than the *Lebenswelt*. Plato gave a classical expression to this rationalist view in his image of the Cave. The world of our existence is not a world at all. It is a mere restricted chamber, or Cave, in the great wide world of reason and science which ultimately surrounds it and absorbs it as a confused, subjective part of itself. The philosophic theory of determinism, inspired by the successes of modern science, is a special development of this rationalistic point of view.

According to this theory, no clear distinction is made between the objective perspectives of science and the human life-world. Scientific laws are then interpreted as applying directly to the latter, and scientific predictions are expressed in the so-called "causal" form: *if this happens, then that will happen*. That is, for every concrete event in the world, there is thought to be another event which some scientific laws (perhaps as yet undiscovered) will reliably predict to follow the first event, and another to follow that, and so on *ad infinitum*. Such predictions are being increasingly verified, and the number of laws on which they are based is constantly growing. The relations expressed by these laws, such as Boyle's law, $pv = C$, are certainly set and unchangeable by any human wish, or will, or any human act. Hence on the tacit assumption that these laws apply, with no qualification, to the life-world of our existence, then it would seem that the concrete sequence of events in this world, including our own acts, are set by scientific law, and that there is no point in our doing or attempting to do anything to make the course of the events in the life-world different from what scientific law determines them to be. Hence the notion of free will in the ordinary sense is an illusion.

This is simply an example of what must follow from that consistent attempt on the part of objectivist thinkers to reduce the *Lebenswelt* and absorb it into their abstract perspectives, which is part of the war of the worlds we considered in the previous chapter. These perspectives are blind to freedom, and to power, which must be approached in another (phenomenological) way if they are to be understood. Determinism is not just one theory opposed to a contrary theory of freedom. As we noted, it is part of a more far-reaching strategy, deeply embedded in our intellectual tradition, to discredit the world of our lived existence as "confused," "ephemeral," and "subjective," and to absorb it into the abstract perspectives of reason and science.

Let me now offer some further evidence in opposition to this thesis, by pointing out what seems to me to be an error that is made by determinists in their equivocal conception of scientific law, which applies directly to abstract aspects of the life-world and only with certain qualifications to this entire world in its full concreteness.

Let us take our example of Boyle's law: $pv = C$, the pressure and volume of a gas vary inversely in relation to a constant C. The determinist wishes to think of this law as though it might eventually, in combination with other laws, apply directly, and with no qualification, to concrete pressures and volumes in the *Lebenswelt*. Thus for Nagel (*op. cit.*, p. 305), it is precisely the concrete events of history with their "common-sense molar characteristics" which can be explained by a scientific analysis of their "determinate conditions," consisting in part of "analytic molecular characteristics." The substitution of particular values in a general equation gives a concrete event in world history. Is this really possible? The answer is definitely No!

Why not? Because something else has been forgotten which is essential to the meaning of scientific law—lack of interference by external factors; or stated affirmatively, that certain conditions of human observation must obtain. It is now known that Boyle's law will not hold exactly if the temperature varies. Hence this condition must be introduced. Other more complex laws may be formulated to take care of this temperature factor. But even these will hold only under certain conditions. Any predictions based on such laws would certainly break down, for example, if a nuclear explosion occurred in the vicinity. This is enough to show that scientific laws are abstract, and can never be used by themselves alone without significant qualification as a basis for predictions as to what will happen in the concrete course of historical events.

In order to illustrate the same point, let me take an example from the work of Professor A. F. Anderson, formerly of Lincoln Univer-

not always work. Dean interrupt it.

sity.[6] Galileo is said to have tested and verified the law of falling bodies in his famous experiment at the tower of Pisa. On the basis of a certain formula he accepted as a hypothesis, he predicted that if two bodies of different size and weight are dropped simultaneously from the same height they will strike the ground simultaneously. This seems to be a prediction of one concrete event as following another in the world of lived experience, and is so taken by determinists. But let us imagine that you and I had been present, and that being of an impulsive nature, as the two bodies were falling, you had stepped out and caught the smaller one in your hands. In this case we are tempted to say that the prediction would not have been verified, and the law left unconfirmed. But such is not the case. Galileo, no doubt, would have been very much annoyed, and the next experiment would have been conducted under heavy guard. But the interrupted trial would have been dismissed as no trial at all, since the necessary conditions of no active interference were not maintained.

Science is applicable to the rich and complex course of events in the *Lebenswelt* only under this condition. This life-world is jammed with interference. The pure scientist deals only with certain abstract variables, observed under special conditions. The dialectical philosopher of history, the clairvoyant, and the prophet may attempt to predict the future history of the *Lebenswelt*. But the strict scientist does not attempt this. He does not work directly in the *Lebenswelt*, but only in a special region, under special conditions of his own, which abstract from chance and human freedom.

Having once confirmed abstract laws, however, they offer us certain choices which follow from their universal meaning. Take our example again: $pv = C$ under the conditions of constant temperature and no interference. This law now offers us an indefinite number of choices; first, of different constant temperatures, and then of different values of p or v. It tells us nothing of what constant temperatures or what specific values of p or v will actually obtain at a given time and place in world history. It expresses only a universal, unalterable relation between these variables, whatever they may be. If then we are able, by our own free intervention, to set up certain conditions, and determine a value of p, we may reliably predict the value of v. To make these free choices is the task of applied scientists and engineers, who bring science back into the wider horizons

[6] *Uncovering a Gross Misconception About Science,* unpublished MS.

of the *Lebenswelt* for the realization of human projects. But this always involves a struggle with alien powers that is attended with risk.

If this analysis is sound, the determinist has committed an error which violates the meaning of science and the scientific attitude. He has forgotten that scientific laws are verified not by actual events, but only by observations carried on under certain conditions in an abstract region of their own; or to put it another way, he has confused the instance of a universal law with a whole happening of world history. Stated more basically, he has tried to absorb the wider and richer horizon of the *Lebenswelt,* the world of freedom, into the more abstract and derived horizon of objective determination. But if he were to succeed in this attempt, we must point out to him that not only would freedom be destroyed, which he does not mind, but that science also would be destroyed, which presumably he does mind. For as Karl Popper has remarked: science is not prophecy. Like other special projects of man, it grows by free choice out of the *Lebenswelt.* It gives us a precious and deeply illuminating perspective on objects of this life-world. But it cannot take this world over and digest it into itself. When absolutized in this way, it ceases to be science and becomes another one of those delusions of world conquest and assimilation so familiar in the past.

There is no science of *the world,* and there never will be. This does not mean, however, that it is a mere jumble of confusion opaque to any disciplined mode of understanding. We do not need to accept the *hubris* of Greek rationalism, which believed that the existing thinker and his world could be absorbed into the system of his thought. This dogmatism has been undermined for us by the critical questions of Hume and Kant, who glimpsed our existence as a murky region wholly opaque to traditional reason and, therefore, as they thought, to any mode of disciplined analysis.

Today a third alternative has opened up. We need not try to include ourselves in great systems of science or reason. Neither should we leave the two side by side, the one as an impenetrable mystery, the other as a realm of light and clarity, entirely remote from life. Man is not a thing, or substance, to be included in an objective horizon. He is a free being who exists in an open world. This is the broadest and richest horizon to which we have access, from which our basic meanings and values are derived. Reason and science are subhorizons, not worlds in themselves. Ultimately they are to be understood only in terms of the global meanings of the *Lebenswelt*. As we have suggested, following certain penetrating hints in Kant: this is the world of freedom. If this is true, and if the task of philosophy is freely to clarify and interpret this life-world from within, then a very intimate relation between philosophy and freedom would seem to be indicated.

Is it also true to say, as we have said, that philosophy is the discipline of freedom? It is to the consideration of this question that we shall now turn in the following chapter.

Chapter 7

Philosophy and Freedom

In the central tradition of Western thought, philosophy has usually been regarded as a purely theoretical or scientific discipline, whose function is to understand the basic structure of the objective universe as it is in itself, apart from human desire and prejudice. Conceived in this way as a rational discipline, or super-science, philosophy as such has nothing to do with freedom; for reason, as an apprehending faculty, is strictly determined by its formal object. Freedom belongs to a quite different faculty, for it is concerned with action, not truth. In the light of this sharp separation of freedom from understanding, practice from theory, Western thought has oscillated between two opposed extremes—that of voluntarism, on the one hand, in which reason is held to be the slave of passion, and rationalism, on the other, in which true freedom is held to be acting in accordance with reason. On the whole, it is the latter view which has been more influential in our history.

In this chapter, I am going to challenge this whole point of view, and more especially the separation of freedom (and action) from the understanding which lies at its root. As against this traditional doctrine, I shall try to show that while there is good reason for opposing freedom to one specialized mode of objective understanding, there is no good reason for opposing it to that more primordial world-understanding with which philosophy is concerned. I shall argue that this mode of understanding is an expression of freedom. Both, in fact, are derived from a common root which I shall call "being-open-to-otherness." If we consider this openness from the

120

standpoint of its stable results, that into which it opens—this is knowledge. If, on the other hand, we consider it from the standpoint of its originating source, the opening itself, that is what we mean by freedom. Philosophy is concerned with this original opening of man to the world. Its primary function is not to establish an objective science of being. It is rather to elicit and to strengthen that original freedom of mind, as we sometimes call it, which is a distinguishing feature of human existence in the world.

As we have seen, this world horizon into which we are born, in which we pursue our chosen projects, and in which we suffer and face death, is not the same as the derived perspectives of the different sciences. It is constituted by a different kind of fact and meaning. World facts are commonly referred to as historical facts. They require a distinctive mode of understanding which we shall refer to as phenomenological, and are open to another mode of truth, world-truth. The disciplined exploration of this life-world has been pursued throughout the history of philosophy in the West, though this investigation has been obstructed by the confusion of scientific facts with world facts. Significant advances have been made recently by the resolution of this confusion and the development of what is now called the phenomenological method.

It has been learned, for example, that while man is surrounded by absolutely independent things and persons over which he exerts only a modicum of control, he is able to work out global interpretations of the world in which these things and persons exist, over which he has a high degree of control. The scientist, as such, is not directly concerned with such interpretations. In performing his professional duties, he may indefinitely postpone any decision concerning them. But, as James pointed out, in living his life as a human being, he must make such decisions, either working out an interpretation of his own or accepting one from his tradition. In the life-world, such global interpretations are a forced option. We cannot live a human life without making, or accepting, such a free, philosophical choice. We are learning that this freedom of world-constitution, as we may call it, lies at the root of human freedom which belongs in a far more intensive degree, and with a much wider range, to the individual person than to the human group.[1]

Furthermore, by the phenomenological method we have discovered the cognitive importance of what has been traditionally

[1] This topic will be considered in detail in Chapter 10.

disparaged by the term "feeling" as a mere inner, subjective disturbance of the viscera. Feeling may be of little use in the natural sciences. But without it we would be absolutely lost in the life-world —unable to distinguish between a friend and an enemy; unable to find our way home. Many feelings, like anxiety and joy, for example, have now been closely studied, and some revealing light has at last been shed on these obscure phenomena, long consigned to that convenient wastebasket of the objectivist mind, the loose and confused notion of the "subjective."

What we now commonly refer to as the transcendent is also not an objective structure open to the methods of normal science. Recent investigations, like those of Van der Leeuw and Eliade, have shown rather that it is a phenomenon of the life-world. As such, it is open to the different methods of phenomenology which try to reveal it not as a mere object, but as it is lived through by the existing agent. In the *Lebenswelt*, we are confronted with alien powers that are sometimes friendly and often dangerous. It is filled with uncertainty and surrounded by mystery. Religion is a *fact* of this world, not a fact of the sciences, and it is only in this world horizon that religion, as it has been actually lived and practiced, can be adequately understood without reduction and distortion. As against the objective structures of science, those of the life-world are global in character and freely constituted.

World Understanding as Free

These meaningful structures of the world are closed to any perspective of detached observation. Since they have been freely constituted and not merely produced by force, they require a free method of active participation and interpretation, if they are to be understood. This method has always been used, at least half-consciously, by the best practitioners of the human disciplines, but recently it has been further refined and clarified by Husserl and his followers. As we have observed, in order to understand any human phenomenon, like the magic and myths of a primitive people, a critical decision on the part of a living person, or even a past experience of his own, the phenomenologist must first free himself from his present biases and preferences bracketing them, as is said, or putting them out of action so far as this is possible. Only by exercising this free act of self-negation or *epoché*, as it is called, do we gain access to the phenomenon as it was lived and understood by the agents themselves. But this is not the whole story. After this, another *epoché* is necessary. Once again we must try to free ourselves from the limitations of these different versions by gaining a distance from them, and by asking the question: what do they really mean? Only in this way can we finally open ourselves to the sense of the phenomenon as it really is in *the* world. We cannot understand the free acts of men without ourselves participating in this same freedom.

I believe that this exercise of free understanding is the peculiar characteristic of philosophy among the other academic sciences and subjects. Many of them are concerned with the construction of pure theories which should correspond with the objective facts. Others, more practical and technological, are concerned with the control over nature. But philosophy is concerned with the life-world of man and its free constitution. It is, in a special sense, the discipline of freedom. Making use of the phenomenological method we have just described, we see that it attempts to understand this world of man, its common structures, its varying modes, and its multiple manifestations.

In a complex culture, it is important to maintain a sense of unity in the public way of life, and to avoid chaos and disintegration. This requires an understanding of the relation between special perspectives and the ultimate horizon of the life-world. How are the particular projects of the fine arts, for example, related to the way of life in the whole community? Such questions belong to an important field to which we now refer as the *philosophy* of art. Indeed, there is no special project which can be understood without placing it in the horizon of the life-world by a *philosophy* of investigation of this sort. Such reflections are widely prevalent in our time. Is this, perhaps, due to a growing sense of disunity in our culture? Are we, perhaps, spending our energies in many vast projects without any clear understanding of what they really mean? Can we hope to attain this much-needed understanding without first clarifying the order of the world in which we exist? Is this not presupposed by a comprehension of the meaning of any human endeavor, and is this not primarily a phenomenological and philosophic task?

We must not forget that the other human arts and disciplines employ the same phenomenological method, each in its own special way. The philosopher can certainly learn much from them, and we may say that they are all engaged in a single cooperative inquiry—to understand the world horizon of human existence and its relations to more restricted perspectives. They are all exploring the human life-world in its manifold aspects and manifestations in human history.

The literary artist, in creating the persons of his drama, must create their divergent worlds at the same time. By enabling us to grasp these individual styles of life, he broadens and enriches our understanding of freedom. The psychiatrist is now discovering that he should no longer classify and treat a disturbed person as a mere object; he must first of all try to understand him, and in order to understand, he must listen to him and try to grasp the disturbed world in which he lives. The historian is concerned with reconstructing and reinterpreting the world of the past events or persons in whom he is interested; the anthropologist, with the whole cultural pattern, or world, of a primitive culture. He is not concerned with the world merely as an object to be gazed at from the outside, but as it is actually lived and understood by the people themselves from the inside. In order to gain this intimate insight, it is not enough merely to read books or to examine artifacts. It is essential to meet the people face to face, to talk to them, and to live with them—at least in imagination.

As we have already indicated, the philosopher has much to learn from all of these, and perhaps something to give. He is trying to understand not scientific facts but world facts, and the world to which they belong. Hence he is interested in any mode, or concrete manifestation, of this *Lebenswelt*. But he is especially concerned with the process of free understanding by which these world-versions are constituted, and by the common conditions such as life-space, human time, history, death, meaning, and existence itself, under which this freedom is exercised. By gaining some light on these common conditions, which are found in every version, he will hope to catch glimpses of that single human world which excludes no one of these historical versions, yet transcends them all. Finally, the philosopher is not concerned with this world as an object from which he can detach himself. In fact, he cannot detach himself from it, for this is the world in which he is inescapably existing and facing death. He desires to understand this world freely and independently for himself, to communicate this to other free men, and to learn from their criticism. This is the discipline of freedom.

In our discussions of truth, we often assume ourselves to be in a detached attitude from which we are looking at external objects out there in the range of vision. For this perspective, truth is rightly analyzed as a correspondence between mental propositions and objective facts. Here our lived experiences (the forming of propositions) is of no importance in and for itself. It can be disregarded, except insofar as it agrees or disagrees with external things. Our attention is outwardly directed away from ourselves. This is an important mode of truth, but not the only mode. As we have noted, it presupposes another type, *world-truth,* which is more fundamental. This is the truth of our own existence in the open and ultimate world horizon. We cannot become detached from this existence to gaze at it as an external object, because we are living it as we think. It involves not only objective factors but intentional (subjective) factors as well. Here the truth must be directly revealed out of our lived experience as we live it. This truth is prior to the truth of correspondence, for we must know our meanings directly in this way, before we can decide whether they agree or do not agree with the external facts.

We have presented evidence to show that the objective understanding of science, and its technical discourse, is a special development from this more primordial mode of world-understanding and ordinary language which it presupposes. The objective perspective is outwardly directed toward external things and structures, and abstracts from intentional attitudes and acts which it discounts and disregards as "subjective." It aims at formulating propositions which will agree with the objective facts as they already are and have been determined to be. In this sense, it is externally determined and passive. World-understanding, on the other hand, is concerned with revealing and clarifying the world directly from our lived existence in it, and with the ordinary language in which this is expressed. Hence it must grapple with situational facts and meanings of the world which involve not only objective factors but so-called "subjective" factors as well. It is open to the indeterminate future, and aims at a living truth which will sustain and integrate our human existence in history. This truth is not externally determined, passive, and closed. It is spontaneous, active, and open, or, in other words, free.

The world-understanding of which we have been speaking is not found merely in books or in college classrooms. It is an essential part of the living of life with which every man and woman is engaged. This primary thinking, as we have called it, does not occur merely at isolated moments of conscious reflection. It occurs throughout our waking hours as we eat, work, play, converse with others, and feel our way through life. Academic philosophy was conceived by Plato as a therapeutic discipline to care for this vital process by which free men work out their styles of life, and to protect it against error and confusion as expressed in the ancient ideal of wisdom, which encompassed the whole of life. To some degree, we find this ideal approximated in the history of professional philosophy in the West, with its divergent systems and styles of thought. The greatest of these are not merely different theories but different worlds, each with its own characteristic structure of meaning, in which leading thinkers of our tradition have been able to live. But as we have seen, this discipline has often been weakened and obstructed in the exercise of its proper therapeutic functions by the influence of objectivism, and other deformations that follow in its train.

It is this influence which still leads us to think of philosophy, like science, as sharply opposed to freedom of the will, as freedom has come to be called by the traditional, objectivist thought which now deeply pervades our common sense and discourse. We have had to refer to freedom in the preceding pages in a rather loose way, and it is now time for us to examine it more carefully. What do we mean by freedom? Insofar as we can penetrate to some degree into this mystery, do we find that it is basically opposed to philosophy, or to what we have been calling world-understanding? Let us now turn to these questions.

The Separation of Philosophy from Freedom

In the rationalistic tradition of Western thought, as we noted in the preceding chapter, reason has been conceived along objectivist lines, as externally determined by its formal object rather than spontaneous and independent, as passive and assimilative rather than active, and finally as receptive of what is already determined rather than as open to the ambiguous and indeterminate. Now, in virtue of three distinctive features which clearly belong to it and mark it off from any passive receptivity of this sort, freedom is sharply opposed to *this* mode of understanding.

The first of these we may call *spontaneity*. A free act must be independent and self-originating within the agent. Insofar as I am following some urge unknown to me, or the hidden will of another, I am not free. If I am to will a free act, this act must arise within me spontaneously, and I must know what I am doing.

The second mark of freedom is *activity* as opposed to the passive and receptive. Insofar as I am pushed about by alien forces, I am not free. Any obstacle, in fact, that impedes my action also restricts my freedom. Thus obsessions that force me to think of one thing only, as well as physical imprisonment, which restricts my movements, interfere with my freedom. I become free only by acting in some way.

Finally, a free act is indeterminate. There must be other alternatives, ambiguities which are really open. I have not freely performed an act, unless it can be truly said that I might have done otherwise—with no *ifs* involved. This belongs essentially to the meaning of freedom, which is always open to otherness. Indeed, we are here approaching what lies at the root of all these distinctive marks. Freedom is an act of self-transcendence, or as we may say, an active-being-open-to-what-is-other. The agent himself must *be* open himself, from himself spontaneously. He must actively achieve this in and for himself. Finally, what is achieved must not only be other than what was before; it must be achieved in a radically indeterminate way. It is only out of this openness that it can discover what has to be. Freedom is this openness to what is other.

Now it is quite clear that freedom, in this sense, is opposed to that mode of objective understanding which is determined solely by its external objects, and is, therefore, neither spontaneous, active, nor indeterminate. But traditional rationalism has not clearly distinguished this mode from the primordial world-understanding which it presupposes. Hence it has denied that there is any real sense in which our human awareness and, therefore, our human philosophy, is free. It has excluded freedom generally from the life of thought, and has restricted it, since Augustine, to a special choice-making faculty known as *the human will*. Let us now examine this doctrine more carefully. It is true that the world-understanding, which is expressed in the activities of philosophy, both at the basic level of primary thinking and at the derived level of secondary reflection, is basically determined by its objects and, therefore, is not spontaneous but receptive? Is it separated from life and action? Finally, is it fixed or determinate, or is it indeterminate and ambiguous? Let us now try to answer these questions.

Rationalistic thought has opposed freedom to understanding as the self-originating and spontaneous to the externally determined and fixed. Meanings have been supposed to be already established in objective nature as fixed structures or essences which then float into an empty mind without the slightest change or alternation. Each of these suppositions is subject to doubt. The world in which we exist is ordered by structures of human meaning which are open to criticism and reformation. Some of these structures turn out to be lasting. But they are always subject to reinterpretation. Far from being passive and receptive, the human mind is capable of developing new interpretations which constantly arise in history with the coming of new projects to meet new situations. This does not mean that no lasting meanings are ever found. But these are always pervaded by ambiguities which call for revision. At the basic levels, at least, the human mind is active and creative in working out its meanings. In confronting critical situations, the mind must make decisions at every level of understanding, and new meanings must be found. This much may be learned from the history of post-Kantian philosophy. The mind is not merely an empty receiver of fixed meanings coming in from the outside. It is born with a certain map of the world outlined by its physical organs, and as long as it lives, short of breakdown, it is guided by some revision or reformulation of this original map. Here again the distinction between free action, as spontaneous and creative, over against thinking, as passive and receptive, proves to be untenable. This suggests that freedom and understanding are derived from a common root. Both require spontaneity and independence. Both are weakened by sluggish passivity and loss of autonomy.

The unmediated, traditional dichotomy between theory, as a detached gazing at necessary truth, and action, as the biased embracing of a contingent alternative, needs re-examination. Perhaps these contraries are also derived from a common source which is to be found in our vital projects as we live them through from the inside. My decision to pursue such a project is not neatly divided into theoretical and practical portions. It takes account of everything that I know through reading, thinking, feeling, and many semiconscious and even subconscious sources. It does not occur at any well-marked interval of rational deliberation, but grows up gradually as I meet the changing situations of my daily life, and even as I sleep. There is no sharp divorce between objective gazing and subjective choosing and acting. In my very act, to some degree of clarity, I know what I am doing; and in my thinking and knowing, I am choosing and preparing to act. Neither the action nor the thought is locked up within a subjective mind-container. Both occur in a world horizon that I am struggling to understand and to face by the free exercise of every power at my command, whether it be conscious or unconscious. In this primordial field of my lived existence, theory and practice fuse into one. Pure theory is a special affair, derived from this primordial life project, which has its special uses.

Traditional rationalism, still alive in the common sense of our time, has not only maintained that understanding is nonspontaneous and divorced from action; it has also held that our human awareness is directed toward an objective universe that is already fixed in its essential structure. It has, therefore, maintained that philosophy is an objective discipline concerned with the acquisition of timeless truth rather than primarily with action and freedom. If this were so, philosophy, so far as it is realized, should manifest itself as a single all-encompassing system of truth with which different philosophers in different cultures should increasingly agree. From this point of view, basic differences between the different philosophies, guiding different cultures and different individual thinkers, are a sign of special prejudices producing confusions and mistakes of various kinds. In the course of the ages, at least, such disagreements should be mitigated to some degree, and overcome in a gradual advance towards systematic unity and concord.

If the human mind has access to immutable truths of an overarching order, we should expect the assimilation of such truth to be much slower in the untutored reflections of human groups and untrained individuals where subjective biases are bound to interfere. But some signs of progress should be discernible. In the case of disciplined philosophers, specially trained for the discovery of philosophical truths about the universe as a whole, and for the ordering of such truths into a coherent, logical system, a far more rapid advance might be expected. Here, through the centuries, we should be able to observe a progressive ironing out of difficulties, with the gradual emergence of a single, systematic structure of truth, at least in outline. What then are the actual facts? Do they bear out this rationalistic, objectivist conception of philosophy?

It is now evident, it seems to me, that they do not! So we shall be very brief in making the necessary points we have in mind. At the present time, most of us are aware of many cultures on the earth whose styles of life and ways of understanding the world differ totally from one another. Our present situation in history is dominated by a conflict between two different worlds of the East and of the West, as we say. This conflict cannot be broken down into a disagreement concerning specific, objective problems which now await solution. It goes deeper than this. The difference is of a philosophic order, involving divergent conceptions of man, human history, and of the world itself, which underlie everything else that we say and do. The issues between these different worlds involve action and freedom, as well as theory, and they will never be resolved by the solution of specific, objective problems, for they involve different styles of life and different interpretations of the meaning of such problems and of their solutions. If these overarching issues are to be settled in such a way as to avoid global conflict, they must be settled through that strange sort of existential communication which sometimes happens between philosophers inhabiting different worlds, and through that humility which alone makes such communication between free men possible.

It is true that modern science and technology have introduced certain patterns of life and thought that are spreading rapidly over the earth and introducing a definite uniformity into certain cultural areas. But marked diversities still remain at the deeper levels. Both the Eastern world and the Western world are committed to the development of technology. But they are far from any basic agreement. Furthermore, even in the East, we can note a wide variety of different individual styles of life which, in the West, is far more evident. It is difficult to suppress this individual freedom by the strictest use of social controls. The rationalist may, of course, discount this variety as the mere result of chance and ignorance. The trained mind, he may say, will be led beyond this chaos toward the single order of truth. But this judgment is hardly borne out by any careful reference to the history of philosophy, where we find an even more striking diversity of opposed systems and world views in which great minds have been able to think and *sometimes to exist*. Those who have defended some versions of the so-called perennial philosophy have been able to do so only by forgetting large sections of this history of world-formation. The world of Democritus is not that of Plato, nor is the world of Hegel that of Kierkegaard.

When studied with some care, this record looks not so much like the emergence of a great super-science of the universe as an expression of the basic, noetic freedom of man, refusing to be locked up permanently in any fixed frame, and constantly striving in an ambiguous world to achieve a unity it never perfectly attains. We shall return later on, in Chapter 11, to the continuous struggle for unity. We need only note now that at the basic level, freedom and understanding, far from being opposed, seem to be joined together in a single enterprise. So far as it succeeds to a degree which is never final, it is properly called insight or understanding. But so far as it has to recognize always that more lies beyond, it is properly termed freedom of mind. If this is true, we may be on the right track in suggesting that both freedom and what we call understanding are rooted in a power of self-transcendence, or as we shall call it, an openness-to-what-is-other that is perhaps the most distinctive trait of man.

Freedom as The Source of Understanding

Traditional thought has always recognized a close connection between freedom and understanding in the form of a dependence of the former (freedom) on the latter (reason). Indeed, it is evident that our action is not free, if we do not know what we are doing. Would anyone call the acts of one under hypnosis, or those of a sleepwalker, free? But because of its exclusive attention to objective modes of apprehension, it has failed to recognize the ways in which our primary understanding of the world in which we exist is dependent upon freedom. This primordial understanding has been regarded as the assimilation of an objective structure, or order of nature, that is already fixed and finished. As a result of this, freedom of the will, as it is called, has been restricted to action alone, and has been interpreted as acting in agreement with this fixed order of reason and nature. In my opinion, this is a basic misconception which has tended through the ages to gravely weaken and hamper our human freedom of thought and action. Hence I wish to argue here for an opposite emphasis. It is, indeed, true that freedom involves understanding. But it is also true that world-understanding involves freedom. Let me try to make this clear by recalling a significant contrast between the obsessive consciousness of an animal and the normal, open consciousness of man which we have already noted.[2]

The animal achieves a certain self-transcendence which opens it to a field of objects surrounding it in space and time. But animal awareness, like that of an obsessed person, stops at this point, and goes no further. This type of consciousness is wholly given over to the objects which attract or repel it, and cannot say "No." Human awareness, on the other hand, as we have observed, is always able to withdraw, and to gain a distance from its vital situation. This awareness can say "No" not only to interesting objects but to its drives and urges as well. Man is the creature who can say "No"; from this negative distance, he can take a second look at himself and at things, in order to grasp what we call their *meaning*. Sometimes stable meanings are grasped in what we call acts of insight, or understanding, though these are always subject to further questioning and revision. But this process of self-understanding takes its origin in a free act of negation, which sets me at a distance.

If I am to understand myself, I must first get away from what I am, and divide myself from myself. Having gained this distance, I may see myself in the light of other possible alternatives, and raise the basic question as to why I am this way and not otherwise, which inaugurates the quest for meaning. This is the prototype for every act of understanding, which begins with a transcending or what is given, a being open to otherness, which lies at the heart of what we mean by freedom. Insofar as this dynamic self-negation comes to rest in stable structures, we call it understanding. But we can never bring it finally to rest. No matter what is given, or what has been said, man can always ask, Why is it not otherwise?, and seek for further meaning. The process begins and ends with the negative self-transcendence we call freedom. The two are interconnected. But freedom is the source of this dialectic of awareness. Understanding is its preliminary result.

This freedom of self-transcendence is not restricted to a single human faculty, like the so-called will. It is a distinctive character of man, and it, or its absence, pervades the whole of our human existence. It overflows into what we call free action. But it begins with that primary thinking by which we work out our own ways of understanding the world, and our own styles of life, for, as the great poet

[2] Cf. p. 109.

Heine once said, "thought precedes action as lightning precedes thunder." Philosophy is concerned with this first source of our human freedom, as we attempt to gain a distance from ourselves and the world in which we exist, in order to understand. This process must be renewed with each coming generation as long as man remains man. It is quite distinct from the rational and scientific investigation of objects, for, as we have seen, it is spontaneous, active, and indeterminate at its source. Academic philosophy is the attempt to care for this primary process, which goes on in every living man, in a careful and responsible way. It is rightly conceived, I think, as the guardian of mental freedom.

The Discipline of Freedom

Let me now try to illustrate and to confirm this thesis by examining three special functions of academic philosophy with reference to their bearing upon human freedom. Let us turn, first of all, to its systematic and speculative function; second, to its logical and linguistic function; and third, to the critical function of philosophy, as they have been revealed in our Western history.

The free man is independent and stands on his own feet, accepting nothing unexamined from the outside. He works out his own version of the world, and his own style of life in and through himself alone. To think and to exist in a frame, of which he is unconscious, is to lose his independence and freedom of mind. The complete mastery of a special region will not protect him against this danger, if he has inadvertently accepted alien assumptions which another has thought through. He will then be living and thinking in a world that is not his own. *Everything* must be lifted out of the murky depths of darkness, and brought up into the light. Otherwise he will be at the mercy of unknown powers. Hence the sensitiveness of the philosopher to hidden assumptions and presuppositions both in his own thought and in the thought of others. To be guided all the time by a hidden presupposition unknown to himself is to lose his independence. It is to live in an alien frame.

To be unaware of details known to be there is a lesser evil. But to exist unwittingly in the world-frame of another is unbearable. It is to become a mental slave. It is the whole world pattern that matters, for this gives order and direction to life. To find that one's whole version of the world is a mere fragment included within the wider horizon of another is to be framed. Time after time through sad experience we discover that what we regarded as the universe · was only a piecemeal fragment, with no place at all for regions discovered later. This undreamed-of ignorance, not knowing we do not know, is the worst of all, for it leads to tyranny and slavery of mind. If we know or suspect that we do not know, this is bad enough. But it is not so bad, for the general outline may still be correct. Hence the speculative urge for wholeness and totality at the expense of minor detail that is found in the great thinkers of our tradition.

Thus we find in Plato the aspiration to become the spectator of all time and all existence, and in Aristotle the concern for being *qua* being, which pervades and yet transcends all the categories, and thus omits nothing from its range. Spinoza's God includes infinite attributes, and the infinite modes of each attribute. This type of speculative philosopher, of course, must do justice to the evidence, to all that is known. But he must also try to do justice to the infinite reaches of what lies beyond. Hence he is seeking the most comprehensive vision, the most far-reaching horizon of all.

To think of these diverse systems merely in terms of the different things that they said leads only to chaos and confusion. To think of them as approximations to a single final truth, mistaken in varying degrees, leads to dogmatism. This is to think of philosophy as a great super-science of the world, which, in the end, makes little sense. But perhaps this is a great mistake. Philosophy is not an objective science. It is rather the guardian of human integrity and independence. When understood in this way, the history of philosophy appears neither as a mere chaos of conflicting views nor as a procession of unrivaled dogmatisms. It is rather a perpetual search for world-understanding, and that personal freedom of mind on which such understanding depends.

As we shall soon suggest (Chapter 10), the thinking of the individual person is more flexible and far-ranging than the shared reflection of the group. He is the source of new ideas, the spearhead of social change, and in the last analysis, the first bearer of human freedom. Hence it is not surprising that the history of philosophy is centered around the names of individual thinkers who have pushed their reflections to the farthest limits, and have worked out coherent world interpretations of their own. As soon as this independent thinking is taken over by a group, or a school of disciples, it is apt to become standardized and oppressive, and ready for the criticism of individual rebels who eventually appear. Public opinion is concerned with action. It does not worry over hidden assumptions and presuppositions, and is always ready to postpone and evade the discussion of basic issues. Hence as Plato says[3]—"the many will never become philosophical." It is always a single individual who raises the original questions, makes the basic criticisms, and works out his own version of the world in and for himself alone. It is with him that freedom originates.

But this fluidity and dynamism has its dangers. It is here that the gravest distortions and the most fantastic errors occur, for that which is capable of the best is also capable of the worst—*corruptio melioris pejor*, as the ancient saying has it. The individual person may develop peculiar meanings of his own which separate him from the public world of the community in which he lives. This may be due to insight and originality. It may mark a turning point in history. On the other hand, it may be due to egotism and eccentricity. In this case, the individual becomes locked up in a solipsistic world of his own which cuts him off from his fellows, so that genuine communication at the deeper levels is impossible. This obstructs freedom in two ways. In the first place, it blocks the openness to the worlds of others which is an essential aspect of liberty. It keeps us from that widening and deepening of vital meaning which comes only with genuine communication. In the second place, we must recognize that man cannot act in a human way without the free cooperation of others, and that such cooperation depends on communication. This is an even more serious obstruction. Unless he can communicate, the individual is immobilized and cannot act. But freedom expresses itself only through action. A man who is content to imprison himself in an eccentric world of his own making is no longer free. This danger is always a threat to a society in which there is any respect for individual independence.

So there is another special type of philosophizing which has devoted itself to this aspect of freedom. We may call it our openness to others. From Greek times, this discipline has been concerned with language and logic, the tools of communication, and the common, objective meanings of public discourse that make it possible. Logicians and philosophers of language are now primarily concerned with this essential aspect of freedom. In the past, these

[3] *Republic*, VI, 494A.

studies have been closely associated with the objective attitudes that are characteristic of social life, and have made important contributions to the closely related perspectives of science and technology, in helping to develop their instruments of communication.

But philosophers have always been concerned with the more formidable difficulties of communicating between one total world order and another whose basic, global meaning is quite different. In such cases, everything that is said by one conveys a different meaning, understood in a different context, from that of the other. In spite of the seemingly insuperable obstacles, history has shown that with proper discipline and humility, intelligible argument is possible. Philosophers can communicate, and what they have learned is relevant to the similar difficulties faced by psychiatrists in trying to understand the eccentric worlds of disturbed persons, and by phenomenologists and anthropologists in studying languages and cultural patterns quite alien to their own. The discipline required for such studies is arduous. A high degree of self-restraint and unusual flexibility of the imagination are demanded. But something has been learned which is of great importance for the life of a democratic society, where individuals are able to work out styles of life and world versions of their own.

No other discipline of limited scope can help us in those *strange conversations* where we suddenly find that every word we say is being interpreted in a different way, and that we are confronting a whole world that is ordered quite differently from our own. Unless we can find ways of bridging these philosophic chasms, we cannot hope really to act and live together. The only alternative is conformism produced by propaganda and the threat of force. The existence of a free society depends on communication in depth by free men. The difficulties here are basically of a philosophical order. Of all the different academic disciplines, philosophy is in the most favorable position to give us aid. Once again these facts suggest that philosophy is the discipline of freedom.

Its basic task is to grasp the life-world by an act of understanding that is spontaneous, active, indeterminate, and therefore free. If it is to be spontaneous, independent, and self-originating, it must be open to the whole of being, not merely a fragment. Hence there is an all-transcending, speculative phase of philosophy which tries to come to terms not only with the facts we know, but with what we know that we do not know, as well. We are not only surrounded by things; we are also surrounded by persons. Without the cooperation of these persons, we cannot act; and without communication, we cannot cooperate with them. If the mind is to be really and actively free, it must be open to other persons and their alien worlds. Hence there is a phase of philosophy which is concerned with language and communication between the differently ordered worlds of free men.

All of these phases are threatened by an ever-present tendency toward rigidity and dogmatism which closes them to the open dialectic of freedom. Thus it is easy for us, in our everyday reflections, to confuse our life-world and its contingent accidents with *the* life-world; and even for first-rank philosophers, like Heidegger, in his book *Sein und Zeit* at certain points, to confuse his version of the world, as a modern German intellectual, with *the Lebenswelt* itself. It has also happened to well-known philosophers that, unaware of certain hidden assumptions, they have speculated a mere fragment of existence into a spurious and truncated version of the whole. Finally, those concerned with communication have sometimes confused their own special instruments, useful for certain purposes, or their own language, effective in its own province, with the Adamic language for all mankind, capable of expressing all possible truth.

The philosopher must be ever on guard against such rigid provincialisms, hidden assumptions, and absolutes of every kind, which freeze our thought and prematurely close it to the dialectic of freedom. Hence there is a third special phase of philosophy, well marked in our history, which questions every concealed presupposition, every manifestation of dogmatism, in order to keep this dialectic open and free. Socrates and Kant were critical thinkers of this kind. All genuine philosophers have something of this spirit in them. They accept nothing without raising questions; they are loyal to nothing without prying into the assumptions on which it rests—which is why they are regarded as uncertain allies and as unreliable enemies.

Indeed, there is no fixed value, or absolute, with which philosophy can be naturally or permanently associated—even that of absolute truth. When used in the Middle Ages as the handmaid and support of organized religion, it ended by fostering liberalism and skepticism. When employed by Hegel to defend his version of the Incarnation, God as the Absolute Spirit becoming man, it turned into Feuerbach's doctrine of man becoming God. Recently used by existentialists to support their version of radical humanism, it has led many toward radical transcendence. It is not at home with any fixed doctrine or dogma. It cannot be identified with any final value or norm. Indeed, it cannot be justified in terms of any human construction, system, or institution. From their point of view, it is useless. And this is true! It represents neither life, nor truth, nor goodness, nor beauty; nothing, indeed, but the spirit of freedom on earth, the self-transcendence of man.

But the time has now come to say emphatically that the noetic freedom of which I have been speaking does not mean irresponsible choice, or believing anything we please, irrespective of the evidence. At each of the levels to which we have referred, there is evidence against which our chosen interpretations must be checked. The life-world is not a chaos of arbitrary constructions. It is marked by lasting structures of existence, like lived time and space, feeling, language, death, and worldliness itself, which condition and limit our choices. We do not become free by ignoring these conditions. We become enslaved by our own eccentric fancies, and cease to act. At the level of speculation where the whole meaning of life is at stake, there is not sufficient evidence to prove one ontology to the exclusion of all alternatives. But there is enough to rule out many, and we ignore this evidence at our peril.

Here, too, discipline is needed, if self-delusion is to be avoided. We have already referred to the arduous self-restraint and flexibility of imagination that are required for existential communication. Here the checks are evident. Failure at this level results in misunderstanding between individuals and groups, conflict, and ultimately in the outbreak of force and tyranny. As philosophers soon learn when they reflect on their arguments, sound criticism does not mean an indiscriminate attack on every interpretation put forth. It means rather the exercise of a delicate art of discrimination between what is true and what is false in the view expounded, asking precisely the relevant question, getting precisely at the concealed assumption, opening up the issue in the right direction. Such criticism requires serious discipline and what Pascal called the spirit of *finesse*.

Here again we can see the close relation between freedom and understanding, both of which belong to a process of opening toward the world that lies near the root of our human history. The relation between man and the independent things and persons around him is a peculiar *sui generis* relation which cannot be adequately interpreted in causal terms. Each contributes something to the world of human meaning that develops and declines in history. This historical dialectic, we can say, begins with a self-transcending act which reaches out toward what lies beyond the facts already known, and which is closer to what we now call *freedom*. It comes to a provisional rest in the verified interpretations which are known as the facts, and which are closer to what we call the attainment of understanding. But each involves the other.

Every exegesis is the interpretation of some fact already understood. And every fact is a verified interpretation. Each plays a vital role in the process as a whole. Without painstaking care for checking in the light of the evidence, free interpretation loses itself in a thousand solipsistic centers, each imprisoned within itself and incapable of communication and action. Without freedom, the known facts crystallize into a rigid structure that soon becomes a breeding ground for dogmas and fanaticism. Without disciplined criticism, the primary thinking of our daily lives is constantly threatened by these dangers. A basic function of academic philosophy, as I see it, is to care for freedom by exercising this necessary criticism.

In our consideration of freedom, we have so far been mainly concerned with negative self-transcendence and criticism. These are the initiating phases of human freedom, which the word in our language primarily suggests. To become free, we must get free from the concepts and attitudes that hold us in inflexible and immobile frames. But to become really free, we must also become free for something, and, to use a word that we now often oppose to freedom, responsible. No examination of the former can be adequate without an investigation of this latter meaning, with which freedom is inextricably intertwined. So it is to this affirmative aspect of freedom, which is often forgotten, that we shall turn in the next chapter.

Chapter 8

Responsibility

In the two preceding chapters, I have pointed out inadequacies in
the traditional concept of freedom which opposes it to understanding, and have shown how it originates in a philosophical way of
thinking that is comprehensive, open, and self-critical. Let us now
turn to a wider, existential structure known as *responsibility,* to
which what we have been calling freedom belongs as a component
part. The fact that this term occurs in ordinary discourse shows that
we already possess a dim and pre-thematic understanding of it. But,
as is true of other existentials, this understanding is vague, confused,
and often distorted by one-sided interpretations that have become
frozen in fixed traditions. The meaning of such terms often seems
"obvious" at first, but when carefully examined, this obviousness
dissolves away and many inadequacies appear. Phenomenology is a
disciplined attempt to penetrate through these barriers of prejudice
and tradition and to interpret basic meanings in the light of the original, lived experiences on which they are founded. Responsibility is
an "obvious" meaning of this kind. In this chapter I shall examine it
from a phenomenological point of view. My aim will be to reveal as
clearly as I can the meaning of this phenomenon as it is lived
through by individuals existing in the life-world of our time, and its
relation to human freedom.

First, I shall state certain accepted assumptions concerning responsibility which identify it with causation, and oppose it to freedom, as this term is employed in current usage to indicate what is
spontaneous and uncaused. Second, in the main part of the chapter,
I shall try to work out a phenomenological interpretation of this ex-

perience, using ordinary language as a guide. Third, I shall confirm this interpretation by referring to a firsthand account of the experience as it was lived through by certain prisoners in the concentration camp at Auschwitz. Finally, fourth, I shall show, in the light of this examination, that the assumptions stated are false, that responsibility is quite different from causation, and that it is not opposed to freedom.

Three Traditional Assumptions

In arguments concerning the traditional problem of free will and determinism, I find both parties commonly taking for granted, first of all, that (a) responsibility is to be identified with a certain type of causation which we may call, following Aristotle, internal causation. I am responsible for an act, and for its consequences, when this act is caused by factors within me. If it is caused by factors external to me, then I am not responsible for it. Thus in a recent article,[1] the California Associates, like Mr. Nagel,[2] have accepted the traditional distinction between a free act and one that is compelled. Both types of act are objectively determined and predictable. But there is no reason why we should not preserve the word "freedom," purified of its indeterministic associations, and apply it to acts that are proximately determined by factors within the agent. Acts over which we have no internal control, which are forced upon us by external causes, are unfree. In this way, the traditional use can be preserved without accepting any irrational breach in the causal principle that underlies all scientific and rational procedure.

Those who defend the traditional conception of "free will" accept a similar notion of responsibility. They deny that a free choice is caused by reasons, motives, and other influences. Such a choice arises spontaneously within the agent as an indeterminate and unpredictable factor. But once it has arisen, it produces its effects like any other cause. The agent might have chosen otherwise. But once he chooses, he is solely responsible for the act and its consequences; i.e., he is its exclusive cause. Thus in his defense of "free will," Campbell says: ". . . a man can be said to exercise free will in a morally significant sense only insofar as his chosen act is one of

---

[1] "Freedom of the Will," *Readings in Philosophical Analysis,* Feigl and Sellars (New York: Appleton, 1949), pp. 594 ff.

[2] Cf. Chapter 6, p. 101.

which he is the sole cause or author. . . ."[3] The free choice is an uncaused cause without normal antecedents but with fully determined consequences. Otherwise a free act would never be responsible; i.e., be the cause of anything. For both parties, to be responsible for X is the same as to be the cause of X. This is the first common assumption we shall consider.

Both parties also assume, in the second place, that (b) freedom and responsibility are concerned primarily with acts rather than with insights and meanings. In common usage, we find the phrase *freedom of thought* as well as the phrase *freedom of the will*. But philosophic argument has focused, almost exclusively, on the latter. Both parties seem to have accepted the notion that the mind, insofar as it functions properly, must be determined by the objective facts. The mind is not responsible for these facts. It can only recognize them as they already are. Hence questions concerning our philosophic freedom of interpretation, our choices to constitute different worlds of meaning, have not been seriously raised, except by idealists, and have played only a very minor role in traditional debates on freedom. The basic issue is concerned with freedom of action—freedom of the will, as it has come to be called. Man may be responsible for his acts. At least this is a serious issue. But is he responsible for the meaning of these acts? This question has not been sharply focused.

Finally, in the third place (c), both parties have ordinarily assumed that the free and responsible act, if it occurs, must occur in the same field of meaning as objective, causal sequences. It is true that Kant spoke of a world of freedom quite distinct from the phenomenal world of causal determination. But owing to difficulties in his distinction between the phenomenal and the noumenal (especially the latter notion), this suggestion has been dropped. At least it has played a role of little or no importance in recent discussions of free will. If it happens at all, a free and responsible act simply happens in the very same world where causal laws obtain. No change of perspective is involved. In connection with this, we may note that little attention has been paid to what is meant when we speak of the responsible agent as accepting or taking over his responsibilities. In the first place, what is taken over? And in the sec-

---

[3] C. A. Campbell, *On Selfhood and Godhood* (New York: Macmillan, 1957), p. 164.

ond place, into what? These questions, so far as I know, have seldom
been raised.

Now, with these assumptions in mind, but nevertheless held in
parenthesis and put out of action so far as this is possible, let us turn
to the phenomena of responsibility as they are revealed by ordinary
language, the language of the life-world, and in our lived existence
in this world.

These Assumptions in the Light of Living Linguistic Usage

We shall focus our attention here on the three traditional assumptions we have just considered (A, B, and C).

A. TO BE RESPONSIBLE IS NOT THE SAME AS TO BE A CAUSE

First of all, we must note the derivation of this term (responsibility) from the Latin *respondeo*—I answer or respond. This is a
relative term which presupposes a question that has been put, or at
least an ambiguous situation which challenges an agent who is consciously engaged. Such a response may be given in a routine manner
without preparation or forethought. Thus we speak of thoughtless
and even of irresponsible answers, which brings us to the second
part of the term (respons-*ible*). What is the difference between a
mere response and an ability to respond?

Here two factors may be noted. First of all, the center has shifted
from the external stimulus to the agent. The responsible answer
comes from the speaker himself in such a way as to take account of
the question, and not simply as being caused or elicited by it. In
the second place, the ability to respond, as against a mere response,
indicates a certain distance from which different answers may or
may not be given. A response may just happen as the result of external and internal causes. A responsible act, on the other hand, comes
from a distance beyond, or, as we say, free from such influences.
From this distance, the responsible agent can gain a new orientation
of his own, and instead of being taken over by habitual pressures, he
can now take the situation over and fill it with new meaning. A responsible act is, therefore, a breakthrough, an eruption of free existence into regions of cause and effect, and frozen cultural patterns
which are taken up into a new world of meaning.

At this point, we must take note of a linguistic usage which reveals a second aspect of responsibility sharply distinguishing it from a causal effect or raw response. Such a response is to an external stimulus of some kind. I respond to a tap on the knee with a knee jerk, to a slap on the face with an angry gesture. I do not respond *for* something *to* something. But in cases of responsibility, this *for-to* structure is always found. The child is responsible *for* his public behavior *to* his parents; the Secretary of Defense is responsible *for* the acts of his Department *to* the President, who is responsible *for* the global administration of national policy *to* the nation as a whole, including those citizens living today and their descendants. The mature person is responsible *for* his acts *to* his conscience, or as we say, *to* himself.

This usage clearly indicates two different answers that are involved in the structure of responsibility. First, there is the active answer to external things or persons of which we have already spoken. This is an act, or piece of behavior, for which the agent is responsible. Thus the child is responsible for proper and polite behavior in public. His active responses to social situations should agree with certain norms which constitute a meaningful pattern. His acts should never sink to the level of mere reactions or blind causal effects. They should rather be answers bearing a meaning, at least partially understood by the child, which brings us now to the second answer underlying the first. In becoming responsible *for* this first, active answer, the agent also becomes answerable *to* something, or someone, more remote from the act, or even from his present self. Thus insofar as he is responsible (*able to* respond) the child should be able to give an account of his acts *to* those who can judge it in terms of a wider and deeper field of meaning. In a similar way, the Department head is answerable *to* his Chief of State, the Chief of State *to* the historic judgment of the nation, and the adult person *to* the true self that he is able to be.

This usage suggests two basic factors which sharply distinguish a responsible act from a mere reaction, or causal effect. First of all, it comes from a source that lies at a distance from the original stimulus. In the case of responsible social action, this ultimate source lies in the ideal figure of the nation as interpreted by the head of an executive hierarchy. In the case of the responsible individual, it lies in the real, projected self, as interpreted by the existing person in his situation. We may note in this connection how, as responsibility increases, we become responsible *for* what we were previously responsible *to,* and how the latter expands in range of meaning. Thus when a Department head becomes Chief Executive, he now becomes responsible *for* that determination of general policy *to* which he was previously accountable; and when a child becomes mature, he becomes responsible *for* the interpretation and maintenance of those social norms *to* which he was previously answerable.

B. THE UNION OF ACTION AND MEANING

In the second place, we must note the peculiar way in which action and meaning are united in the structure of responsible existence. Thus as we have pointed out, responsibility requires overt action in the public world. The inactive dreamer is not responsible. But at the same time, and even more essentially, this overt action must bear a meaning which the agent who is responsible for it must himself be able to understand and to give an account of in terms of a broader world of meaning. A senseless act is not responsible. Hence it is fair to say that responsibility is meaningful action. This union of action and meaning is sufficiently important to deserve a brief, further comment.

It is clearly indicated by the phrase *responsible action* which is in common use, and which involves thinking of the act itself as an answer or response that carries meaning. Hence an automatic reaction, or a thoughtless response, is not responsible. To be responsible, the act must be thought out. It must come from a reflective distance, and bear with it a place in a field of meaning. Thus before we can assume our responsibilities and carry them out, we must first understand them, and so we speak of someone as facing his responsibilities, feeling them, and seeing more exactly what they are. In his own way, Aristotle was aware of this noetic element in responsibility, and went to some trouble to show how certain forms of ignorance detract from our responsibility.[4] But his view of reason as a passive, receptive faculty prevented him from recognizing the union of thought, as such, with action, and that noetic freedom, as we may call it, which, as we have observed,[5] lies at the root of our human freedom, and greatly expands its depth and range.

We are thrown into a world of nature and culture which is already prepared for us, and which starts to assimilate us into its various orders and processes as soon as we are born. We interact causally

---

[4] *Nicomachean Ethics,* Book III, Chap. 1.
[5] Cf. Chapter 7, pp. 137–138.

with the things of nature in regular and predictable ways as long as we stay alive. Thus we imbibe and digest our food, and grow older with the seasons. In the world of culture, strange meanings must be learned. But here, too, our first participation is largely passive in the Aristotelian manner. We simply learn meanings that are already fixed in the patterns of our society. We learn the language of our people, and the various roles we are called upon to play, like those of son and daughter, playmate and pupil. This process is continuous, regular, and subject to general prediction.

But the world into which it assimilates us is still unfinished. It sometimes presents us with ambiguities, questions, and challenges. For the most part, we simply ignore them and respond in the expected manner, going about our business in the public world. But from that reflective distance where responsibility originates, and of which we have spoken, these challenges can be noticed. From this distance, an ambiguity will strike our attention, an appeal will touch our hearts, or a challenge will arouse our passion. It may soon pass away. But if we maintain our distance, it may become a center of meaning, and around it a new version of the world may begin to form. This is the heart of our human freedom which Aristotle failed to recognize, the forming of a new world of meaning around a chosen project. Instead of merely responding, we are now able to respond (*respons*ible), and ready for responsible acts.

A responsible act is one that makes sense to the agent, and can be explained to others as bearing a meaning. I am responsible not only for my act but for its meaning which is, of course, part of the act. If I kill a man, meaning to kill him, this is first-degree murder. I am held responsible not only for the act but for this meaning, and am punished for it by the state. We sometimes think of the world of meaning—the world as it is for me, as though it could be analyzed into separate units or particles of sense. But this is an error. Each meaning points beyond to others on which its significance depends. To understand the meaning of an act, or an event, we must place it in a total world order. A murderous act comes out of a murderous world which has been ordered by the agent in a murderous way, and for this way of thinking-acting he is held responsible.

The child is born into a public world that is already ordered in certain accepted patterns which he assimilates into his thought and action as he learns his mother tongue. This learning takes time, and, as it proceeds, the child becomes more and more responsible. At first, as we have indicated, his understanding of the whole world order in which he exists is very dim. But with certain limited regions, like that of the household, he soon becomes familiar, and for certain special acts within such a limited region he is held responsible *to* others, like his parents, who possess a clearer grasp of the whole. As yet, he is neither able to think and act for himself, nor, therefore, fully responsible (answerable) to himself. He cannot answer for the final significance of his acts, but only for a limited, regional significance. He is not yet existing in and for himself in a world that he has worked out for himself. He is existing in a public world of others that they have worked out for themselves and for him.

Hence he is not yet fully *able to* respond (responsible).

This may never happen; it may happen only very gradually; or it may emerge suddenly after lengthy preparation at a time of crisis. When it does happen, the agent may have accepted the world of his tradition and the roles assigned to him in this world, or he may have reinterpreted this world and worked out projects of his own. But in either case, he will have thought his way through an understanding of himself and the world to some degree of clarity (more clear in the latter than in the former), and will have decided for himself. He has recognized and opened himself to an opportunity. We speak of one who has reached this existential turning point as ready to take his life into his own hands. He has recognized his responsibilities, and is ready to meet them. He is able to answer for himself (to be responsible) in a world that makes sense for him.

C. TAKING OVER THE SITUATION

After a reflective distance has been gained, and a meaningful project formed to meet an opportunity, a third critical step remains to be taken. The opportunity must be seized. In ordinary language we refer to this as the accepting, the assuming, or the taking over of a responsibility. First of all, it is clear that when we speak in this way we are referring in the active voice to an act that is to be performed, a deed that is to be done. Second, like human behavior in general, this act bears a meaning; it occupies a place in an ordered world. By this specific act, a situation, in which the agent is already involved, is taken over as it stands, and lifted up into a new field of meaning. What is actively taken over, or accepted, is the concrete situation just as it is. What it is taken over into by this specific act is a world of meaning worked out and understood by the agent himself.

As we have indicated, the agent who acts without thought is merely responding in an irresponsible manner. He can act. But he cannot answer for it. On the other hand, we are all familiar with the agent who becomes absorbed in dream worlds of meaning, without acting. He also is irresponsible. He can answer, indeed, but not for any act. The responsible agent must accept the situation into which he has been thrown. He must recognize the facts precisely as they are. Otherwise he cannot act in the given situation. At the same time, he must be able to take them over into a world that makes sense to him. This ability to give a creative response within the strict limits of a given situation is the essence of human freedom. It is also that flexible style of action, supported by a coherent world of meaning, which is ready to answer any contingency, and which we call *responsible*.

To attain it, the three stages we have considered must be lived through. First, a break must be made with the continuous chain of causal reactions and responses into which we have been thrown. At this distance, we are *able* to respond. Then, from this distance, opportunities must be recognized and a meaningful answer prepared. Finally, third, an opportunity must be seized by an act which faces the situation as it stands, which meets it, and yet answers it by taking it over intact into a coherent world which gives it genuine sense. This is a responsible act.

It is important to emphasize the way in which the situation is taken over *intact*, precisely as it is, with all its causal pressures, tendencies, and motives, as they stand. Otherwise the act will be misguided and will fail, for it is in this particular situation that the responsible act must be performed. The determinist, seeing that all remains factually as it was, with no interruption of regular causal sequences, and no law being broken, infers that nothing new is happening, and that the responsible act itself is caused. But this is a mistake. As the analysts now recognize, reasons are not the same as causes. The indeterminist, seeing novelty arising, insists that this novelty pertains exclusively to the act as an uncaused violation of the whole natural order. But this also is mistaken. The novelty lies not in the act alone but rather in the whole world of meaning which sustains it. This world reaches beyond the causal laws and tendencies which belong to the situation. But it does not violate or break them.

It takes them over, precisely as they are, intact, and lifts them into a new field of meaning, which gives them a different sense. It is freely thought through and carried out in a free world of its own.

Let us now turn to a concrete example of the struggle to become responsible under the harsh conditions imposed on prisoners in a Nazi extermination camp as recorded firsthand by a prisoner, Viktor Frankl, who survived.[6]

The Struggle for Meaning

There is no need to dwell on the degrading conditions to which these prisoners were subjected. They lived in a world where forced labor, starvation, disease, and torture were the rule. This world "no longer recognized the value of human life and human dignity." It "had robbed man of his will, and made him an object to be exterminated. . . ."[7]

Human time became deformed. "In camp, a small time unit of a day, for example, filled with hourly tortures and fatigue, appeared endless," and the prisoner "ceased living for the future" (p. 70). If he allowed himself to be absorbed into this degraded world, he also came to despise life "as something of no consequence" (p. 72). He simply preferred to close his eyes and "to live in the past" (p. 72). "Life for such people became meaningless" (*ibid.*). "If the man in the concentration camp did not struggle against this in a last effort to save his self-respect, he lost the feeling of being an individual, a being with a mind, with inner freedom and personal value" (p. 49). Some prisoners engaged in this struggle for responsibility, and Frankl describes it firsthand from his own experience. In his description, the three phases we have noted in our analysis are clearly marked.

A. THE GAINING OF DISTANCE *above camp life*

He notes the deeply felt need "for privacy and for solitude" in order to reflect (p. 50). Disgusted with the daily pressures that were forcing him to think only of food, warmth, and his chances of survival, the prisoner finally forced his "thoughts to turn to another subject" until he "succeeded somehow in rising above the situation, above the sufferings of the moment" (p. 73). From this distance, he

[6] Viktor Frankl, *From Death-Camp to Existentialism* (Boston: Beacon Press, 1961).
[7] *Ibid.*, p. 49.

was able to "form a clear and precise picture of it," and to take stock of his situation from a wider point of view (p. 74). In this new, "noetic" perspective, as Frankl calls it, he was able to seek for a meaning in his threadbare and painful existence.

Commenting on this break with the senseless routine to which he was becoming chained, Frankl says: "Man is the only being which is able to transcend himself, to emerge above the level of his own psychic and physical conditions." This is the only way toward the giving and finding of meaning, and "again and again we have seen that an appeal to continue life, to survive the most unfavorable conditions, the most dire distress, can be made only when such survival appears to have a meaning" (pp. 102–03).

B. THE SEARCH FOR EXISTENTIAL MEANING

This search for meaning was of critical importance. Those who failed simply gave up. "Woe to him who saw no more sense in his life, no aim, no purpose, and therefore no point in carrying on. He was soon lost" (p. 76). The prisoners had to unlearn the traditional view that they were in a position to question the meaning of life as spectators, and that this meaning might be given to them with no effort on their part. No! We had "instead to think of ourselves as those who were being questioned by life—daily and hourly" (p. 77). If an answer was to be given, we (the prisoners) had to work it out for ourselves. And this answer required neither thought alone nor action alone, but thought and action together.

There were always ambiguities, challenges, and chances if they could be seen in the right light. As Frankl says: "Most men in a concentration camp believed that the real opportunities of life had passed. Yet, in reality, there was an opportunity and a challenge. One could make a victory of those experiences . . . or one could ignore the challenge and simply vegetate, as did a majority of the prisoners" (p. 72). One had "the chance of achieving something through his own suffering" and death (p. 67). Opportunities differed for different individuals. But they were there, and once perceived, a meaningful project could be formed. For one prisoner this was to return personally unscathed to a child in a distant country; for another it was to complete an unfinished book on science by jotting down notes on scraps of paper (p. 79). This project must be supported and surrounded by a world of meaning. But meaning is not enough. The world must be concentrated in daily tasks to be performed. And to embark on these tasks a decision must be made here and now.

C. THE GIVING OF MEANING

In the death camp, prisoners were afraid of making decisions. There was a strong feeling that fate was one's master. "At times," when responsibility was involved, "lightning decisions had to be made, decisions which spelled life or death" (p. 56). To carry out such a decision the prisoner "must accomplish concrete, personal tasks," and at the same time "he must realize that unique meaning which each of us has to fulfill" (p. 100). To do this, two things are required. First of all, the situation must be accepted just as it is, in all its stark misery. As Frankl puts it, "he [the prisoner] will have to accept his suffering" (p. 78). But this is not a passive response. It is the active acceptance of "his suffering as a task" (p. 78).

This means actively "taking the responsibility—to fulfill the tasks which life constantly sets for each individual" (p. 77). In becoming responsible for the situation, it is taken up into a new and wider horizon of meaning which makes sense to the active agent. We can "give meaning to our lives" not only "by creating and being, but also by suffering: by the way and manner in which we face our fate, in which we take our suffering upon ourselves" (p. 105). This "way and manner" is the wide horizon of our understanding, into which the narrow regions of our misery are taken up, and through which they can make sense for us. As Frankl says of his fellow prisoners who struggled with him for meaning: "for us, the meaning of life embraced the wider circles of life and death, of suffering and of dying" (p. 78). It is through the finding of such global meaning that we become responsible and free.

Is this phenomenon of responsibility, which we have now analyzed and described, the same as some special mode of causation? As we have already noted, this view is widely defended.

The Traditional Assumptions Are Not True

Let us now turn to the common assumptions which ordinarily underlie discussions of free will, as it is called, and determinism. In the light of our phenomenological examination of responsibility in previous sections, we are now in a position to see that they are false. Let us consider them briefly, one by one.

A. TO BE RESPONSIBLE FOR SOMETHING IS THE SAME AS TO BE ITS CAUSE

Unless our analysis of responsibility is basically false and Frankl's account of life in the camp is radically distorted, we can see that this traditional assumption, which goes back to Aristotle, is unjustified. Whether it is internal or external, a cause cannot gain any distance from itself. It can gain no freedom from what it is. It cannot negate itself. It is not able to cause in various ways, or not to cause at all. It simply operates. This operation is neither responsible nor irresponsible. It belongs to an entirely different genus which we may call pure action without a meaning (or lack of meaning) of its own.

A cause does not act *for* anything *to* anything. It simply acts. It does not carry a meaning, and is not answerable to itself or to anyone. Furthermore, it does not take anything over nor give meaning. It simply produces its effect. Aristotle made a basic mistake from which we are still suffering when he classified responsible, purposive action as a kind of internal cause (final cause). Such action is not purely internal or subjective, as we now say. It is spread out into a world that is radically different from the objective perspective in which causal uniformities appear. Thus in common usage we say: Arsenic was the cause of death, but X, the son in debt, was responsible. He murdered his father. To be answerable for an act I have performed in a world that makes sense to me, is not the same as to cause an effect. The two are worlds apart.

It may be supposed that, since causal efficacy can always be found in a responsible act if we look at it in a certain way, causation is a necessary condition for responsibility. But this again is a reductive mistake. When we shift our whole perspective in this way, we are not discovering a necessary condition of the original phenomenon in its own horizon. We are concerned with a different phenomenon in a different horizon, though the two may overlap in certain respects. Suppose, for example, that a first-degree murder has been committed by a revolver shot. I might then say that a perspective necessarily could have been found from which the murderous act might have been photographed whether by night or by day. This statement is certainly true. Such a perspective can always be found. But it does not reveal a necessary condition for the shooting, which may have taken place with no photograph. The perspective has been changed. The original act of murder and its horizon may overlap in certain aspects with the filming of the act from an external point of view. But the two are quite different, and the latter is in no sense a necessary condition for the former. As we may repeat again, they are worlds apart.

This strong statement may gain further force as we examine the other two common assumptions which have grown out of the first, and which have been presupposed by traditional formulations of the so-called problem of free will vs. determinism. The second runs as follows.

B. RESPONSIBILITY (UNDERSTOOD AS CAUSAL ACTION) IS CONCERNED PRIMARILY WITH ACTS AND NOT WITH MEANINGS

Our phenomenological examination of common, linguistic usage and the lived experience of responsibility very clearly indicates that this assumption is false. Responsibility is a union of act and meaning in an act that, as we say, carries the meaning, as the musical sounds bear the symphony, and we can no more separate the meaning from the acts that carry it than we can separate the symphony from its sounds. Just as the composer is responsible for the order of the music as well as the sounds, so are we responsible for the meaning of what we do as well as for the acts.

Underlying our freedom of action, there is a deeper freedom of world constitution beset by those tortuous ambiguities and difficulties with which philosophy has been concerned. Aristotle made another radical and far-ranging mistake when he held that at the most basic "theoretical" level, as he called it, global meanings are already fixed and finished so as to be assimilable by a passive and empty mind. The struggle for meanings that on the one hand will fit the facts, and on the other hand will make sense to us, is always arduous and fraught with risk. But it lies at the heart of what we mean by freedom and responsibility.

C. RESPONSIBLE THINKING AND ACTING HAVE NO MEANINGFUL WORLD OF THEIR OWN

Since the time of Aristotle, and especially since the coming of natural science in the seventeenth century, it has been easy for us to regard ourselves and all things from a perspective of detached observation. This perspective abstracts from the concrete life-world, the world of the street, as William James called it, in which we pursue our chosen projects, exist, and face death; and sees only its objective aspects. It is from this perspective that science is now able to reveal those objective, causal laws which enable us to make predictions as to what will happen under conditions we can control, and on which our mass existence now depends. Into this limited perspective, responsibility and freedom are strange and unwelcome intruders only grudgingly admitted, if at all, into the narrow domain of a private subjectivity having no real, objective status.

But this perspective abstracts and selects its objects from a broader and richer horizon of the life-world, in which we not only observe objects and calculate their probable consequences but also live and exist. This is the world of freedom and responsibility which was glimpsed by Kant, and which is now beginning to be explored by the methods of phenomenology. This world is constituted by facts and structures quite different from those of objective reason and science. It is filled with ambiguity and surrounded with mystery. Any understanding of it requires a global interpretation, far beyond the competence of any objective science, that cannot be undertaken without risk. Nevertheless man is responsible for the working out of such an interpretation, without which no human life can be humanly lived. And, in fact, no human tribe, people, or civilization, and no free individual person has ever been found without such a global understanding of himself and the world in which he exists.

Many of these interpretations fail to fit the facts, and others are senseless and meaningless to man. Some are less imperfect than others. But no one as yet has been formulated which is not subject to damaging criticism. It is the purpose of philosophy, insofar as it does not evade its essential function, to exercise such criticism, in order that this human task may be undertaken less inadequately through the generations. The responsible person, often semi-consciously and sometimes consciously, is constantly engaged in this search for meaning. As he works out his way of life from day to day and his way of understanding the world, he takes over the meaning-less facts and causal sequences in which he is involved precisely as they are. But at the same time he takes them up, both by his action and by his thought, into a world of global meaning in such a way as to give them sense.

In this manner, the responsible person does what no cause can do: he gains distance, or freedom, from the immediate objects to which his attention is glued, and becomes responsible for his acts and meanings. Freedom is a partial, negative aspect of responsibility which is richer and more complete in meaning. We may become free from the immediate and yet remain irresponsible. We cannot become responsible, however, without also becoming free.

We shall here conclude our consideration of human freedom. In Part I, we described the present situation of philosophy in the West, and the new existential approach, inaugurated by William James and other pioneers, which is an original expression of the living thought of our time. In Part II, we gave an account of that phenomenological exploration of the human life-world to which this new approach has given rise. In Part III, we examined the sense in which it is true to say that this life-world is the world of freedom, and then, in the light of this development, we attempted to shed some further light on what we call freedom and responsibility. In Part IV, we shall now approach some ancient questions in a new way suggested by the methods we have been using, and the conclusions at which we have arrived.

The first of these will concern the nature of what we refer to as value vs. disvalue, or the authentic vs. the unauthentic, as illustrated in the distinction between devotion and fanaticism.

A New Approach to Some Ancient Questions

Chapter 9

Authentic Existence
and Value

What we now generally refer to as "value" is the very heart and soul of meaning. When we cannot place a thing, when we fail to see what it can be for, we find it meaningless. When we are confronted with a proposition, or a proposal, that has no appeal for us, we say that it makes no sense. As we have seen, our versions of the life-world are ordered around some project directed toward an ultimate value and, in the last analysis, to grasp the meaning of an act or a thing is to place it in this world. It has long been recognized that science and objective reason in general are unable to help us in making basic judgments of this kind. It is often said that science is neutral to value; though, as we have suggested, what we have in mind is better expressed by saying that its perspectives are too narrow for any grasp of the overarching structures of the life-world.

As a result, the disciplined consideration of the so-called problem of value has been turned over to philosophy which, in recent years, has amounted to a polite way of neglecting it. In this chapter, we shall have to be brief, and shall divide our discussion into three parts. First, we shall offer some criticisms of the traditional, objective approach to this problem. Second, we shall suggest the new approach, which phenomenology has made possible, by an examination of the terms *authentic* and *unauthentic* and their meanings. Finally, third, we shall try to clarify the meaning of this basic distinction by a phenomenological interpretation of what ordinary language calls devotion and fanaticism.

159

Abstract Theories of Value

Traditional theories of value have accepted the assumption that meaning can be broken down into fixed essences abstracted from existence. They have paid little serious attention to lived existence, and have regarded it as a successive realization of the forms, essences, and laws which reason apprehends rather than as a world with overarching structures of its own. In accordance with this assumption, values also have been understood as static properties, virtues, or natures which could be examined in themselves without any references to the world of existence from which they have been abstracted. The rationalist first hoped that he might arrive at a single system of value essences and moral principles, which would be timelessly valid for all mankind, and would ultimately explain the world. But this failed to do justice to the human capacity to create new meanings, and led to rigid forms of dogmatism that stifled human freedom. This faith in *objective values*, as they are called, is still alive, but it has been gravely weakened by criticism, and has given way to another form of value theory.

This type of theory tries to avoid dogmatism by doing justice to so-called "subjective" factors which are always at work in the setting up of values. In the formula of R. B. Perry, value is "any object of an interest." This, indeed, makes room for hundreds, for thousands, indeed an unlimited number of value entities which may be abstracted from human history, and then carefully analyzed and described. No one of these has any qualitative supremacy over any other. There is no aristocracy in the realm of values. Democracy here reigns supreme and poetry, as Bentham maintained, is intrinsically no better than pushpin. The end is conceived in quantitative terms, as the maximum realization of the greatest number of interests. And it must be granted that just social policy should, in fact, be guided by such utilitarian procedures of compromise. But grave questions can be raised, as we shall see in the next chapter, as to whether these social procedures can be applied, without serious reduction and distortion, to the freer and wider ranging reflection of the existing person. One reductive consequence of this type of value theory has already come clearly into the light.

If it is possible for us to be objective about our own subjectivity in this way, and to fit our free existence into such an observable frame, how is relativism to be avoided? We may say that "selfish" values, which interfere with others, should be eliminated on quantitative grounds. But any integral way of understanding the world, which is lived through with passion, would seem likely to interfere with the serious concerns of others. It would apparently be better for us to get rid of those impassioned commitments, which give direction and meaning to our lives, and to replace them by a large number of diluted interests which can be readily adjusted and compromised, because nobody cares much about them anyway. But who really wants such a life? The utilitarian solution to the problem of value by compromise would seem to be the cultivation of an objective indifference which leaves us with no real interests to compromise.

As a matter of fact, this general sense of indifference, or meaninglessness, is very widespread in our culture. Recent forms of subjectivist value theory have avoided the dogmatism of their objectivist ancestors only by nurturing a relativistic indifference to meaning which is not merely remote from life but actively hostile to it. They have reached their end in those endless academic discussions of meta-ethics which are now thinning into a "clarity" of pure emptiness.

We may summarize the situation of traditional value theory in the form of a dilemma. Either provincialism and dogmatism, or relativism and indifference. We may take our choice. It is now doubtful whether ethics as a separate, abstract discipline will survive. But the disciplined consideration of basic human issues is another matter. If this is to be revived, the dilemma of traditional moral theory must be avoided. And for this, a new approach is needed. Phenomenology offers us such a new approach, which we shall now consider.

An Existential Approach to "Values"

First of all, we must reject the traditional assumption that values are fixed essences which can be examined in themselves apart from the historic world in which we struggle to exist. All the values in heaven are no good to me, if I cannot exist in them. This existence is not a mere neutral staging of pre-existent values. It opens into a world-horizon which, though filled with ambiguity, has values and meanings of its own. There is no special region or realm of value.

The life-world, as we have seen, is never neutral. It is deeply pervaded from beginning to end, in all its realms and regions, with "value" and "disvalue." It is, in fact, the locus of real meaning and value. What is worthwhile for us is to be in the world. What is not worthwhile is not to make sense, or not to become what we really are. This issue—to be or not to be—is not restricted to any special region or phase of our existence. It affects every region and every phase. It is not the special object of a special kind of ethical, or moral, reflection. It belongs to that care for our being in the world which is involved in every object of every kind of thinking, whether it be moral, aesthetic, scientific, ontological, or religious.

This approach to what we now call "values" does not attempt to defend an abstract system of essences and principles as a moral guide for all mankind. It does not try to win victories over opponents by logical controversy and argument. It tries only to reveal and to clarify the "values" that are already implicit in our lived existence. One tiny grain of insight is worth a hundred syllogisms. As we have seen, truth cannot be revealed without partiality and error. But as long as the empirical spirit remains alive, it must be open to revision and correction. There is, of course, nothing more dogmatic than the claim of an individual to be nondogmatic, and I shall not make this claim. But if the spirit of radical inquiry can be justly charged with dogmatism, it is hard to see how the charge can retain any meaning, for nothing can then escape.

Nor can phenomenology be identified with any traditional form of relativism. It recognizes the unlimited variety of cultural patterns and individual interpretations which history has brought forth, and is, indeed, profoundly interested in exploring these different versions of the world as they are lived and expressed by the peoples and persons themselves. But this is only the beginning of a further inquiry which attempts to penetrate back of what is said and what is done, which is variable and temporary, to the conditions of this human freedom, such as oriented space, human time, historicity, feeling, anxiety, death, and conscience, which are stable and lasting. These conditions are not fixed properties of a human substance, that can be abstracted from existence. They are ways of existing, existentials, that cannot be understood apart from the historical being that they characterize.

Phenomenology is neither absolutistic nor relativistic in the accepted senses of these terms. It offers us a new approach which simply by-passes this, as well as other threadbare antinomies and dilemmas of traditional philosophy.

Properties, essences, and laws can always be abstracted, and analyzed in a timeless frame. They come and go. But the ways of existing that condition our finite being remain. As long as men exist, time and history will go on, and they will face death. In so far as we can snatch these flowing forms from the dimness of the "obvious" and bring them into the light of the truth, we can gain some hints from them as to the structure of the one world into which these different versions open, and the meaning of real existence in this world. If this were to happen, the so-called problem of value, which experts still hope to solve, would become the mystery of being in the world, which all men have to face and to answer, not only by thought and word, but by thought and word and deed.

But we will be asked: What has all this to do with how I should live?—and what I should do? What are these existential values, and how do we arrive at them? Let us now sketch out briefly a new way of answering this question.

First of all, we must face a difficulty that radically distinguishes the situation in which this question places us from any situation in science. As we have often noted, the objective thinker is able to observe his object from a detached point of view. From this external position, he tries to form propositions which agree with its properties and relations to other objects. He, too, of course, makes mistakes and falls into error. But once detected, falsity is quietly ushered off the scene and disregarded, except as an aid in the training of initiates. The skilled practitioner, however, does not have to bother with falsity. He can focus exclusively on what is already known, and on the further advancement of this knowledge. For him, the ancient saying of Protagoras holds good: the true alone is; the false is not.[1] Indeed, it is hard to see how he could function at all effectively, if he were forced to concern himself not only with the truth but with a Babel of conflicting falsities surrounding him on every side, and drowning out his words. But fortunately for him, he is saved from any need of dealing with existing subjective falsities, and is able to maintain a separation of the true from the false that is sharp and clear. The truth alone is; the false is not.

The philosopher and the humanist, on the other hand, are concerned with world truth. They do not enjoy this kind of peace. They cannot jump out of the world to observe it from a detached point of

---

[1] Cf. Plato, *Euthydemus* 286C, and *Theaetetus* 167A.

view. Any truth that they may achieve must be revealed directly out of lived existence as it goes on in them, and in the others with whom they can communicate. This truth does not come from a super-human reason in which they only participate. It comes from a purely human, finite reason that belongs to them. When they make a mistake, it affects their way of understanding the world and their way of existing. If they try to ignore it and forget it, they are forgetting themselves and disintegrating, for this past belongs to their being, the only being they have. They cannot simply toss it aside. They must rather accept it, give it some meaning, and take it over. Mistakes of this kind are known as guilt.

In this broader horizon of the life-world, error, deception, illusion, distortion, and reduction cannot simply be ushered off the stage and disregarded. They exist in ourselves, in our friends, in our enemies, and in the public life of all tribes and peoples. The objective thinker "solves" this problem of evil by simply eliminating it. If we were to follow his example in the life-world, we would have to destroy half the human race and then commit suicide. In this world, we cannot defend the clear-cut distinction between truth, as what is, and falsity, as what is not. Here the saying of Protagoras does not hold good, for here falsity *is*. It seems that it *is* even more, in terms of aggressiveness, clamor, and noise. But perhaps the real existence, where "value" really lies, cannot be judged adequately in terms either of seeming success, or of the mere presence of properties. It must be judged, rather, existentially in terms of those temporal ways of existing which condition our being in the world. Value lies not so much in what we do as in how we exist and maintain ourselves in time.

To express this new sense of existential value, a new terminology is required; though as we should expect, the basis for this is already latent in ordinary language where we find words, like *authentic, genuine, real*, and *really*, commonly used to convey a sense of basic, existential value. Thus we speak admiringly of works achieved at the greatest cost, with the full devotion of every human power to the highest degree of intensity, as *genuine* and *authentic*. Or we speak in the same way of a *real* artist and, at the climax of a masterful performance, we say that he is now *really* playing. Beginning with Kierkegaard, these usages have been taken up into the literature of existential thought. In a more quiet and less obtrusive way, they express those more basic "existential values," as we may call them, which underlie all the valuable things that we do or say. Since they characterize our ways of existing in the world, they are universal in scope, and apply to every phase and region of our care. There is nothing that we say, or think, or do that may not be done either authentically, with the full devotion of our powers up to the very last limit, or unauthentically in a noncommittal, half-hearted way. They are not "values" at all, in the traditional sense of this term, for they cannot be understood apart, in any special realm of their own. They are patterns of our lived existence in the world.

Every clarification of the limits and conditions of our finite existence sheds light on an existential value of this kind. To ignore, or to suppress any such limit, or condition, is always inhuman and unauthentic. Anxiety, guilt, death, and the gulf between my present self and the self that I could be, are necessary conditions of our existence. Hence any attempt to evade them, or to explain them away, divides us from what we really are and have to be. It disintegrates and dehumanizes us. Different ways of working out these evasions are peculiar to different cultures. But the conditions themselves, and even the general tendency to evade them, are found everywhere. Hence they provide us with an ontological basis for certain value judgments that hold universally. Self-evasion and disintegration are not good.

The light shed on these phenomena by recent ontological studies, like that of Heidegger in his important work *Sein und Zeit,* has, therefore, rendered a significant service to psychiatrists and therapists throughout the Western world, who are seeking a more stable foundation for their procedures than the variable customs and fashions of their particular cultural patterns. These judgments of suppression and evasion are largely negative in character. But it is possible to go further than this. As we have suggested, every clarification of a necessary ontological pattern is normative in character. This is true of the existential structures we have been considering in this work. Every one of them has normative implications which it may be worthwhile for us now briefly to indicate.

If the account of the human life-world we presented in Chapters 3–5 is on the whole sound, we may say that world comprehension and the attainment of existential truth are important for man everywhere. As we have indicated, the traditional terms, *reason* and *understanding,* are no longer adequate to express this "value," since they are concerned with more specialized functions. For example, feeling also is necessarily involved in what we are calling *comprehension*. We are desperately in need of new usages. But the phrases *existential awareness*, and *openness to the world* may perhaps convey what we have in mind.

In Chapters 6–8 we were concerned with patterns of freedom and responsibility, which can also be readily translated into normative terms, provided that we guard against the accepted meanings of traditional language. Thus we can say that the gaining of distance from himself and his version of the world is always important for man. But this distance must be understood in temporal rather than in spatial terms. We cannot gain this kind of transcendence by observing ourselves as objects from an external point of view. It is only by moving ahead of ourselves to our last possibilities, and back to the past, that we may grasp our lived existence in the world as a whole, from the inside. The term "self-transcendence" may perhaps convey this meaning.

We identified the second element in the pattern of responsibility as the search for meaning in the historical situation confronting us. This ability to find meaning is a constant need of man, whoever and wherever he may be. With the proper context in mind, we may perhaps express this as *global insight*, or creative originality in the finding of meaning, or making sense. The final stage of this existential pattern, which includes the others, is the active taking over of the situation intact, exactly as it stands, and the placing of it in a new field of meaning. The term *responsibility* may, perhaps, still be used to convey this existential value, though we must here be on guard against the usual, abstract connotation that suggests little more than the exercise of a blind causation.

We have also referred to the existential pattern of personal wholeness, or integrity, which is closely related to responsibility, but more inclusive and, therefore, distinguishable from it. This pattern has important normative implications, as analytic studies of many kinds of personal disintegration have made clear. These studies have discredited traditional theories of a personal essence, or substance, that automatically ensures self-identity and integrity. It is now evident that these "values" are not guaranteed to us in any such timeless way. They may be gained, or they may be lost in history. They are guided only by global understanding, constant effort, responsible choice, and repetition. They are lost by blindness to meaning, drifting, and self-abandonment to present distractions, which bring forth

privative or unauthentic modes of personal existence. These priva-
tions cannot be reduced to the mere absence of some property in a
thing that is present before the mind. They are absences in a
temporal history which calls for them, and in which they always
exist in a suppressed or distorted form. Every one of the values we
have considered can temporalize itself in an authentic or unauthentic mode of this kind.

It must not be thought that we have presented an exhaustive list
of existential values. This ontological approach has only recently
been inaugurated, and a dim, initial light has been shed on certain
basic patterns of personal existence. But further studies are required of the ontological foundations of other values in the fields of
both personal and social action. We are in desperate need of
further light.

In order to work out our meaning more clearly for the reader, we
shall conclude this chapter by a brief phenomenological study of an
important value whose real meaning is so deeply hidden beneath the
cloaks of the "obvious" that its authentic and unauthentic modes are
often confused. But so far as this vital distinction is still preserved,
we use the term *devotion* for its authentic, and the term *fanaticism*
for its unauthentic manifestations.

Devotion and Fanaticism

These ways of existing, fanaticism and devotion, have their an-
alogies in the realm of objective theory and opinion—dogmatism and
breadth of mind. But the former are neither opinions nor ways of
holding opinions. They are ways of thinking and existing in the
life-world. Is passionate care, or devotion, merely a polite way of
speaking of bigotry? Or is there a real distinction between the two?
Both R. Niebuhr and G. Marcel have dealt with this distinction in
recent works.[2] But their discussions rely, for the most part, on
psychological categories, and fail to do justice to the sense in which
two different ways of constituting the world are involved.

The most thorough treatment with which I am familiar is that of
W. Zuurdeeg.[3] In spite of his use of the psychological term *conviction,* he is aware of the depth of the issue involved, and realizes that

[2] R. Niebuhr, *The Self and the Dramas of History* (New York: Scribner's,
1955); G. Marcel, *Man Against Mass Society* (Chicago: Regnery, 1950).

[3] W. Zuurdeeg, *Analytical Philosophy of Religion* (New York: Abingdon Press,
1958).

it lies at a level more basic than what this term would ordinarily suggest. However, though he makes many pertinent remarks, to which we shall refer, his failure to distinguish between *the* world and *versions of* the world, leads him, in the end, to question the very distinction that his penetrating observations would seem to justify (pp. 83–84).

Let us now turn to these two ways of being in the world, the devoted and the fanatical—Kierkegaard and Hitler, for example. Can they both be subsumed under a single concept, like that of fanaticism? Or is this a confusion of types? Is there a real difference between the two?

One difference is suggested by a bare reference to these two names, though they must not be thought of as paradigm cases. Other equally pertinent examples can be found. The world of devotion is ordered toward a mystery absolutely transcending our finite powers of understanding and appropriation. In Kierkegaardian language, it is a world of *infinite passion*. It is important to note that he does not say a passion for the infinite, since the infinite is no object, which we can observe from the outside. It is a presence coming from beyond us, and yet working in us, so that this passion itself, when it is felt, belongs to the mystery. The world, whose presence is felt through such a passion, must transcend any human version of it, including that of the one who is feeling and thinking it. Hence it is characteristic of such thinking to recognize itself as only a version, but as a version open to the transcending world. There are also other versions. But there is no need of trying to absorb them in a great synthetic whole, for this one is capable of infinite deepening. This way is not the only way. But it is felt to be open and authentic.

The world of the fanaticized consciousness, as Marcel calls it, on the other hand, is not open in this way. Here the distinction between my version and the world of which it is a version is blurred, in a way that is not always revealed by any examination of the words and concepts used. The language may be filled with extreme and hyperbolic terms. The confusion lies rather in the direction and movement of the thinking itself, which seems to be enclosed within inflexible limits and to be elucidating what is already there, instead of breaking through boundaries and opening itself to what is beyond. This kind of world-version becomes rigid and fixed, and, finally, in place of any further exploration and creation, it gives itself over to aggression and defense against other views. Instead of an authentic way, it thinks of itself and its friends as the only way. Between the fanatical world and the world of impassioned devotion there is this basic difference. The one understands itself to be a version; the other to be the world itself. The one is open. The other is closed.

Both the fanatic and the man of devotion are engaged in tasks. But here we may see another difference closely connected with the one we have noted. Without betraying the ethos of his way, the zealot may give himself to a cause which might be fully realized and completed in human history. In fact, many examples of such fanaticism can be given. Hitler, for example, was fanatically concerned with the conquest of the world. This might have been actually achieved. What then? But the man of impassioned devotion, described by Kierkegaard, could not give himself to any such realizable goal without betraying the ethos of his devotion. This is because the infinite passion is concerned with and enveloped by a mystery which can be penetrated but never comprehended. Some advance, some satisfaction may be hoped for. But one cannot imagine the philosophic passion of Socrates ever being realized or satisfied in this life. It is an infinite passion which is capable of an endless deepening. But no matter how far it goes, it needs to be endlessly reinterpreted and re-enacted by each succeeding generation. This is what Socrates meant in his *Apology*, where he speaks of human knowledge as worthy of little or nothing (23A), and of the young men coming after him (39D). And as Kierkegaard remarked in his study of Socrates,[4] this infinite passion, called forth by mystery, though never fully expressible by concepts and theories, can nevertheless be expressed by irony. Here is another basic difference. The fanatic can attack his enemies by ridicule and satire. He is incapable of a self-reflecting irony.

From an objective and intellectualistic point of view, devotion and fanaticism are merged together under such general terms as emotional commitment, feeling, and especially passion, which has undergone an important change in meaning during our Western history. For the Greeks, this term *pathos*, Latin *passio* referred to the internal, subjective effect of some external agency. Such feelings, or passions, disturb the rule of reason, and must be suppressed or controlled so far as possible. Feelings are a kind of suffering in which

[4] S. Kierkegaard, *Der Begriff der Ironie* (München: Kaiser Verlag, 1929), pp. 225–226.

we lose our rational autonomy, and simply give in to random influences from the outside. The word still carries this ancient rationalist meaning, and we still speak of someone as being upset, or disturbed, by emotion. But we have now become aware of the cognitive value of feeling, and of certain things that we can come to know in no other way. The most exhaustive intellectual and physical analysis, for example, could never tell us the meaning of a friendly gesture. Hence we now speak of *feeling our way, feeling a person out,* and *having a feeling for art or music.* We are prepared to grant that feeling is even more closely connected with action than conceptual thought; and in our common speech, we often recognize that rational discourse, without feeling, is abstract and "cold." By personal "warmth," and "warmness of heart," we refer to attitudes which overcome this separation, and which involve a noteworthy interpenetration of thinking and feeling. Thus by "a warm-hearted person" we do not ordinarily refer to someone who is unstable, but rather to someone whose thinking and feeling work together in a harmonious way.

There are several ways in which this kind of integrity can be approximated. There are those who achieve an integrity of thought by wide-ranging systems of ideas. But they do not come very close, because their lives may remain distracted. Kierkegaard referred to them in his famous remark about the philosopher (Hegel) who built a spacious palace on a beautiful hill, but lived in a mud hut on the swamp beneath. On the other hand, there are those, with no overarching insights and little perspicacity, who try to achieve integrity by sheer intensity of feeling alone. Instead of dwelling with this feeling and thinking it through to the depths, they attach it to some purpose, or cause, that they find already under way in their environment. Instead of taking this over responsibly, and lifting it up into a new field of meaning of their own, they give themselves over to it with an intensity of blind feeling that may substitute for understanding.

Against such violence of feeling, the charges of irrationalism and irresponsibility are certainly justified. But this is a simulated passion, as we may call it, which is quite distinct from the infinite passion of devotion. It is outwardly directed toward something objective which abstracts from lived existence. This objective purpose, as we have seen, is one that may be achieved or realized by a quantitative proliferation in breadth rather than in depth. Finally, it is only a false imitation that is achieved, not genuine unity and integrity. Underneath this false façade there is a buzzing swarm of competing loyalties and unities that must be ignored or suppressed, and which bring forth a sense of insecurity in the agent. This is answered by a further outburst of passion for the one great cause, in a vicious circle which is characteristic of fanatical existence. From the outside, this vicious circle is evident, as Zuurdeeg remarks,[5] even though it may be, for the most part, concealed from the person himself. It is also attended by further manifestations which are not found in the world of devotion, to which we shall now turn.

One of these is the element of possessiveness. The fanatical consciousness is not wholly and integrally on the way which it has chosen. Many parts of it are uncommitted, or tending in other directions. But it wishes to be on the way, to be totally identified with it. Unable to attain this by giving itself to the way, it tries, by a reverse operation, to do something to the way, to bring it as close as possible, into a position where it can be governed and controlled. The closest relation I can have to an external thing with which I wish to become identified is that of possession or ownership. Such a thing I can make my own by owning it, and by using it for my purposes, if I know what they are. Instead of taking the way and becoming a Marxist, for example, and being it through and through, I hold it as a set of opinions which I have, and a set of regulations which I follow to the letter. I am more concerned with the curves and dips of the way which lie immediately before me, and over which I can exert some control, than with the ultimate end. This seems very distant and remote.

Nevertheless, having gained some external control over the instruments of the way, such as walking boots, binoculars, and a cane, it is easy for me objectively to identify the way with its ultimate end. After all, they are connected as objects, and part of it is already mine. So I soon hear myself thinking of my way, my devotion, my faith, and my God, as though the whole path, from beginning to end, were already in my possession; as one who is ambitious to play, and owning an instrument, but as yet knowing only a few scales and bars, may readily identify with exquisite finished productions, and may speak not only of his instrument, but also of his style, and his kind of music.

Zuurdeeg has noted this tendency of the religious fanatic to

[5] N. Zuurdeeg, *op. cit.*, pp. 80–81.

identify the ultimate end with the way thereto, so that he himself, and the group to which he belongs, are taken up into the divine, and with little effort on their part are also holy. He points out that the term *fanatic* is derived from *fanum*, meaning temple. For the bigoted believer, his group is a privileged and holy domain where he is relieved from all worries and insecurity.[6] He himself, his *fanum*, and his God all belong together in a special, sacred area, apart from the trials and problems of everyday life, and not subject to ordinary standards and criticisms. This type of fanatical devotion is not restricted to religious groups. It is found wherever groups are bound together by basic, global purposes which are not easily understood, and where intense feeling has replaced careful and disciplined thought, as in the existing nation-state, the superior white race, the Communist party, and the like.

In spite of the ubiquity of such devotion, there is another kind. Though easily confused with the unauthentic, when regarded externally from an objective point of view, it can be distinguished, in those rare cases where it actually occurs, by those who will take the trouble to use their imaginations in following this type of existence as it is lived from the inside. Such authentic devotion, as we may call it, differs from the fanatical type in all the respects we have just mentioned. In the first place, intense feeling is not only directed to a global view of life, but this view is carefully thought through, as in the case of Kierkegaard, and related to concrete daily tasks. Through this union of thought and feeling in a grand and overarching passion, the whole of life may be taken over in full responsibility, and lifted up into a coherent world which makes sense to the living person. He is then in a position to choose a way of existing that is supported by this world, and through this choice to achieve a genuine integrity, following his way with the whole of himself, all that he is and has been, up to the end, death.

Nothing will have to be ignored or suppressed. He will not need to hold himself back and gaze on the way with a longing detachment. He will be on the way. He will not try to have and to hold it as a possession which he can identify with himself. He will try rather to identify himself with this way and to *be* it. He will no longer speak of my devotion, but of my devotion *to* _____. He will think of the way as a whole, and especially of its final destination and source, rather than of the immediate twists and turnings. With respect to

[6] N. Zuurdeeg, *op. cit.*, p. 81.

these, he will remain flexible, and will be indifferent to specific regulations, and to the use of this instrument or that. He will rather constantly aim to be on the way. And while he is moving toward it, both with his thoughts and his limbs, he will never be able to confuse himself and his mobile position with that of his destination. This will be especially true if he is climbing upward, and if his goal has any transcendence in it. He will be quite clear that this goal is not, and never will be, in his possession, even if he reaches the mountain top. It is not a thing or a place to be possessed. It is rather a mystery that may be compared to a sunset, or a sweeping view from the heights, that is not obtained but suddenly given and granted.

By devoting his every effort to climbing higher and thus transcending himself, he becomes aware of heights to which he can never climb, and of that which completely transcends himself and all that he ever can be. No one actually devoted to a project of this kind will ever confuse himself and his group and his instruments with the goal that is luring him on. It is by his own blood and sweat that he knows the difference. These are human, all too human. He has no access to any special area separated from the trials of everyday life. This is only a false escape. These trials and problems must be taken over and given meaning. It is precisely in and through them that he must find his way. Once we get a sense of such devotion as it is actually lived, we see that it is sharply distinct from the fanatical type. But there are other differences which are even more clear.

The unconditionally committed person is supposed to be subjectively certain of his own beliefs, unable to bear the thought of being disappointed, unwilling to stand serious questioning, and hostile toward other groups and persons following different ways. These criticisms certainly apply to fanatical modes of existence. Insofar as I fall into one of these modes—and there are very few of us who do not—it is not only myself but my relevant doctrines and feelings that become identified with the divine end, and come to share in its infallibility. One can say that this is especially true of the doctrines, since I myself am never fully and integrally committed. But the doctrines I possess concerning the holy are identified with the holy. Hence they are absolutely certain. They cannot lead me astray. The very thought of missing the promises they contain is unthinkable and unbearable. Since the fanatical mind, like any other, can and does think such a thought, it is goaded to more and more frantic actions and protestations of faith.

This attitude is sharply contrasted with that of the centurion in the New Testament who said: *I believe, O Lord; help thou mine unbelief* (Mark 9:24), and with that of a "believer," like Kierkegaard, who recognized that there could be no objective or divine certainty in matters of faith. There is a risk involved, as in the accepting or nonaccepting of any global interpretation of the world. Kierkegaard goes even further than this in his discussion of infinite resignation,[7] where he says that the believer must be resigned to ultimate disappointment, and the frustration of all his hopes. This kind of devotion is not to be confused with the objective proofs and certainties of fanatical belief. It is true that the fanatic mind resists questioning, and is unable to question itself. But if we are right in thinking of Socrates as an example of impassioned concern for an unfinishable project, it is hard to believe that every commitment belongs to this type. It is hard to deny that he questioned himself. And Kierkegaard is another example.

The fanaticized consciousness is aggressive and hostile to other ways than its own. They offer threats to its sense of security. Hence it is interested in universal agreement concerning matters of life-interpretation, and in the quantitative proliferation of its point of view by numbers of adherents. But there is a devotion which, though it recognizes a real risk, is sure enough of itself to be on the way. And once on his way, the devoted person is free from such threats. He knows himself to be taking one way, and that there are others also open to the truth. He has enough questions and difficulties of his own to face. So he has no time for hostility and aggrandizement against others. He defends himself against them only insofar as he must defend himself against himself. He does not feel strengthened by crowds on his side. He is able to stand alone.

I think we have now shown that there is a contrast between two types of devotion, one that is authentic and open, and another which is fanatical and closed. The authentic type is guided by an overarching union of thought and feeling we now call passion, and understands itself to be a version. The other is guided by uncriticized feeling, and thinks of itself as the only way. Fanatical consciousness thinks of its way as an object, which it possesses from beginning to

---

[7] *Abschliessende unwissenschaftliche Nachschrift*, Zweiter Teil (Jena: Diederichs, 1925), IV.

end. Authentic devotion, on the other hand, is on its way to something transcendent. With respect to rules and regulations, the one is flexible, the other literal and strict. The one thinks of its faith as a special region apart from the problems and questions of profane existence, while the other works out its way in and through the trials and difficulties of daily life. Fanatical commitment finds itself to be certain of its beliefs, is unwilling to face serious questioning, and is aggressive toward other ways. Authentic devotion, on the other hand, is aware of the risks of its global project, self-conscious, self-critical, and unaggressive. This is the nature of the contrast we have suggested.

But before closing, we must underline a warning first cogently presented by Zuurdeeg.[8]

We have referred to ideal cases in our attempt to bring out a distinction that is only implicit and latent in everyday life. From an objective point of view that simply observes behavior and language, the two types are indiscernible. The same observable acts may be performed; the same words and expressions may be used. To grasp the distinction clearly, it is necessary to follow the lived experience imaginatively from the inside, and to grasp its meaning for the agent. But even here, though the boundary is clear, it is readily crossed from the one to the other. Each type in our lived existence is usually mixed with the other, and is hardly ever pure. Authentic devotion, in particular, is constantly threatened by the danger of fanaticism. Nothing, in fact, is more fanatical than the claim to be the nonfanatic view. Authentic devotion in its purer forms, as we have suggested, is very rare and difficult to maintain. It is, nevertheless, a distinct, existential mode to which every person has access, and which can be achieved in varying degrees. Fanaticism, on the other hand, is something far more familiar. It is proper for us all to realize that if we have not already fallen into it, we are very near the edge.

But now we shall conclude and raise a further question. The distinction between fanaticism and devotion, which we have attempted to clarify, is found in ordinary language. It seems to be commonly recognized, and neither arbitrary nor artificial. Why then, we must ask, is there the widespread tendency, at least in certain contexts, to slur over it and to confuse the two? We have already suggested an answer to this question by distinguishing between two perspectives,

[8] N. Zuurdeeg, *op. cit.*, pp. 83–84.

that of objective reason and science, and the horizon of the *Lebenswelt*, as we have called it, in which we exist both as individuals and as members of active groups. In the former, we observe and theorize about objects from a detached point of view. This is the perspective of science, in which we try to abstract from bias and other "subjective" factors, in order to get an impartial and objective view. But this attitude extends far beyond the limits of science in the strict sense. In much of our ordinary conversation, we assume this attitude of objective impartiality, trying to take account of all the observable facts, and to synthesize them into a sweeping view. From the time of the Greeks until recently, our Western philosophy has been dominated by this kind of objectivism. From this standpoint, it is better to suspend judgment than to run the risk of error by jumping to hasty conclusions. Authentic thinking of this kind demands suppression of personal feeling and bias, detachment, and a tentative withholding of judgment.

What we have called *devotion*, however, involves a violation of all these standards. It is dominated by personal feeling and passion, is completely committed, and is, finally, based on a global decision which goes beyond the available evidence. So it is not surprising that, from this point of view, what we have called *devotion* is identified with fanaticism as a kind of dogmatism which is a constant threat to objective clarity and breadth of mind. This confusion arises from an exclusive concern with what we have called "the objective universe" (Chapter 5), and a neglect of the life-world.

But this is the world in which we have to exist. And here, as James pointed out, we are confronted with forced options. We cannot wait indefinitely for further evidence to come in. We have to live in one way rather than in another. Hence we have to make global decisions of the most far-reaching kind on insufficient evidence. Furthermore, the scientific evidence never would be adequate, even if it all came in, for it abstracts from "subjective" factors which have to be taken account of in life, and the life-world also involves obscurities and mysteries which will never be exhausted by any mode of approach. Hence it is also not surprising that, in this horizon, the distinction between devotion and fanaticism, with which we have been concerned, makes sense, and that it is found in ordinary speech, the language of the *Lebenswelt*.

As human beings, we participate in two noetic enterprises. One is that of objective reason and science, which are concerned with all objects that can be observed from a detached point of view. This calls for suppression of bias, and for other specific intellectual virtues. Authentic thought here is impartial, tentative, and wide in scope. Unauthentic thinking is dogmatic; that is, partial, biased, and narrow. The other is an attempt to understand our own existence in the life-world. It is concerned not only with objects, but with our own subjective attitudes and meanings as we live them. We cannot detach ourselves from this world to gaze at it from the outside. We have to understand it, if at all, from the inside by a thinking that attends our action, and reveals it as it goes along. We must here be guided not only by conceptual insight but by feeling as well. This calls for global understanding and integrity, for passion and depth; in short, for the authentic devotion we have described. Its proper vice and corruption is fanaticism.

We have now criticized traditional, objective theories of value; have explained a new existential way of investigating value by a consideration of authentic and unauthentic existence; and have, finally, illustrated this distinction by a description of two ways of existing in the world, devotion and fanaticism. Our aim in Chapters 8 and 9 has been to show how phenomenology now offers us new approaches to basic human questions. The next question that we shall consider in the following chapter is: What is the relation of the free, individual person to society?

Chapter 10

The Individual
and the Group

In the early editions of Thomas Hobbes' *Leviathan*,[1] there was a prefatory picture which summarized the gist of this most lucid and influential book. We see the social *Leviathan* as a great giant in human form, with a confident expression on its face, and with symbols of authority in its hands. Millions of tiny homunculi have been captured and are now contained within its gigantic frame. Those who still retain any individual identity have a bearing of resignation, indicating that nothing can be done. The rest have already been absorbed into the tissue of the giant. They are bone of his bone, and flesh of his flesh. They are now nothing but the obedient organs of the omnicompetent state.

This gives us a vivid image of the conflict between the individual and society, which has constantly marked our Western history from its origins in ancient Greece and Palestine, and which is now sensed by many of our contemporaries who feel lost and deformed in performing their routine functions in a vast, social body over which they have lost control, and whose meaning, if any, they no longer understand. This conflict is now tearing apart what we have been calling *the* human life-world, and we need to examine it with some care to see if we still have any right to refer to it in the singular.

In Hobbes' picture, we see the English philosopher's one-sided,

[1] Cf. *Leviathan or the Matter, Forme, and Power of a Commonwealth Ecclesiasticall and Civill*, by Thomas Hobbes of Malmesbury: London, printed for Andrew Crooke at the Green Dragon in St. Pauls Churchyard (1651).

178

totalitarian solution of the issue, to which he was forced, as he thought, by cold logic, the only alternative to an individualistic chaos where life is "nasty, brutish, and short." In the light of the common assumptions accepted by both sides in traditional discussions of this issue, there is no doubt that he made a very strong, perhaps the strongest, case. But the *Leviathan* picture also provides us with a suggestive point of departure for a consideration of these common assumptions which it clearly suggests. If we can get hold of them, and then subject them to a careful criticism, we may be able to clarify the new approach to social questions that is now emerging from the existential thinking of our time.

Traditional Assumptions Concerning the Individual and Society

Let us now consider four basic presuppositions of social philosophy in the West which are indicated by the Hobbesian picture. In the first place, both the individual and the group are taken to be things, or substances, enclosed within themselves, rather than stretched out into world horizons. This ontological atomism, as we may call it, goes back to Aristotle's doctrine of substance. It dominated medieval anthropology, and through Descartes' definition of man as a thinking thing, played a dominant role in modern philosophy. It is, indeed, still very much alive at the present time. By nature, the human individual is enclosed within himself. His relations to other things and persons are later developments which do not affect his original, substantial nature. Similarly, it is not necessary to think of society in terms of the public world in which it exists. It is conceived rather as a gigantic, physical thing, including many individual bodies and forces, or as a great spiritual thing, absorbing men's minds within itself. This atomism has been accepted by all parties in the major debates of social philosophy in the West.

In the second place, it is assumed that the individual and the social giant exist in the same way, simply as objects before the mind, and that the only difference between them is a quantitative one of size. The group is much larger than the individual. We shall call this the assumption of an objectivist ontology, which is clearly suggested by Hobbes' picture, and which was shared by many of the most influential social philosophers in our history. Thus Plato, in his *Republic*, says that the state is the individual writ large, implying, of course, that the individual is simply the state writ small. For Aristotle, ethics, dealing with norms for individual action, is a branch of politics, dealing with norms for more inclusive, social action. Hence the latter takes precedence over the former. The same is true of Aquinas, and also of Hegel, who taught the supremacy of objective spirit (*objectiver Geist*) over that of the individual subject (*subjectiver Geist*). To look at someone existing, of course, is not the same as the existing of this someone, as felt and understood from the inside. But Hobbes makes little effort in his picture, or in his theory, to penetrate into the lived existence of the objects with which he is concerned. The picture and the thinking are spatial and static. It is like a snapshot taken at a moment. How do these beings temporalize themselves? How do they realize their lived existence? Do they exist in the same way? These questions are never raised.

In the third place, we must take note of two further, allied assumptions that have been widely held, but which emerge with peculiar clarity in the thought of Hobbes. The first is the idea that the human individual, imagined as an isolated substance, is ontologically prior, and perhaps even temporally prior, to the society which is later, and in any case derived. According to Hobbes, in the original, anarchic state of nature, each individual substance pursues exclusively his own desires, and wars to the death with the others, until a protective community is established. According to this interpretation, there is no reason, and, indeed, no real possibility of escaping from the *Leviathan*, once it has been established. It is here that supreme power and authority always must remain. There is no real way of controlling the monster. The only escape is into the jaws of death.

This leads to a fourth and final assumption concerning "values." As we noted in the last chapter, the "values" we take seriously are concerned with our way of existing in the world. Hence if the individual person and the group exist in the same way, and if, once established, the more lasting, inclusive, and powerful existence of the group takes precedence over the weaker and less inclusive existence of the individual, it will follow that the social values of survival and realization will take precedence over other values and ways of life which may have an appeal to the free, individual person. As a matter of fact, this subordination of personal ethics to the public ethics of self-realization is clearly marked in our Western history. Such an ethics has been applied, both to the state and to the individual with only minor variations, ever since classical hedonism and the eudaemonism of Plato, Aristotle, and the Stoics. The basic aim of man is to realize the interests he already has, with power. This basic pattern is found not only in the modern idealistic ethics of self-realization, but in the various ancient and modern forms of utilitarianism. It has been certainly the dominant type of secular, moral theory in the West, and in the Middle Ages it was taken over by scholastic philosophy as the only rational and objective way of interpreting Christian ethics. The end of man is to attain the maximum realization of the desires we have, and the only way of doing this effectively is by giving absolute sovereignty and obedience to the state.

These four assumptions have been taken over by the major schools of social philosophy in the West. In the previous chapters, we have brought forth evidence in the light of which these assumptions can be questioned. Let us now try to interpret this evidence in a critical manner that may suggest the new phenomenological approach to social questions which is developing in our time.

The Public World and the World of Freedom

Man is never isolated from the things around him. Even less is he isolated from the other human beings with whom he exists in the world. Our original awareness dwells in our action. Hence in responding to the gestures of those attending it, the child must be aware of the two together in a diffused, dual consciousness, like that of the tennis player who must feel the response of his opponent in preparing for his own. In his penetrating studies of children's play, George H. Mead has shown how the child understands his own role in a game only by learning to play the roles of the others.[2] In baseball, the catcher has no meaning apart from the pitcher and the man at bat. If his consciousness were locked up within a subjective container, he could never play the game. The child feels himself as a member of the family, the boy as a member of the team.

Mead also shows how the child, as he grows up, eventually learns to take the position of the generalized other who embodies the norms of his society, and before whom he prepares and plays his various roles.[3] Even his silent thoughts and images are submitted to this con-

2 *Mind, Self, and Society,* pp. 150–152.
3 *Op. cit.,* pp. 154 ff.

stant onlooker who watches and judges them, and it is to him that the child becomes responsible for everything that he does. When he is first asked to say who he is, to give his own name, and to express himself, he will run to his mother and bow his head. Though he feels that this is expected of him, he has no self of his own. His awareness is not yet self-centered but still diffused in the family group. Not being now what they know him to be, he is stricken with shame before them. When he takes over his life and becomes responsible to himself, this self-division takes on another form. He is now ashamed that the others have taken him over, and that he is not on his own. But while he is still struggling to become responsible, and even when he has achieved it to some degree, this being-before-others remains as a dimension of his existence from which he can never escape.

His feelings and acts are not merely intentional, as Husserl and the earlier phenomenologists supposed. The self is not only intending its objects by actively thinking them, desiring them, fearing, and hoping for them. It is also harassed, oppressed, ignored, praised, and admired by the others. I am not merely ashamed of a base act, and proud of a fine one. I am ashamed of this and proud of that *before the others*. This double intentionality, as it has been called,[4] has been neglected by past phenomenologists, which has led them into a self-centered and solipsistic point of view. It has given their thinking an antisocial tone that has often been noted.[5]

The child is never cut off as an isolated substance from the other members of the primary group, especially the family, into which he has been born. He exists with them, and faces the world with them through a consciousness that inhabits their shared endeavors. It is out of this diffused awareness that his own self-consciousness arises. He says *I* only over against the *you*, and becomes himself only in the small primary group, as over against the others who nourish him, help him, and love him. It is out of this shared world, with its common projects and objects, that the individual person and his personal world emerge. This world involves meanings that only he can understand, and acts that he alone can perform.

It is also out of this shared existence that the public world of a tribe, or people, emerges. Thus, at the present time, I exist not only

[4] Cf. Anders, *Die Antiquiertheit des Menschen* (München: C. H. Beck, 1956), pp. 65 ff.

[5] As by E. A. Tiryakian in his recent book *Sociologism and Existentialism* (Englewood Cliffs, N.J.: Prentice-Hall, 1962).

in the public world of the West but in a special version of it which is governed by my own global interpretations. These two versions of the world, the public and the personal, are later developments from a shared existence that lacks this tension between the public and the personal which are very different. It is to the main features which sharply distinguish them that we shall now turn.

The public world is a vast, human contrivance, depending on complex systems of action and mass communication. It is not a thing, nor any collection of things. It is rather a way of looking at things, a horizon in which any thing or person may be placed. It is the shared world of a people or a nation. For many of us living today, it is the only world which is consciously understood—the real world in which we exist. As anthropologists and sociologists are beginning to recognize, this world is quite different from what we have called "the universe of science," though it is similar in many respects, and can be readily, though mistakenly, identified with it. The public world is also quite distinct from the world of the responsible person.

This public world is organized around common concerns already established in the past, and observable in objective works and institutions. The personal world, on the other hand, is organized around personal projects worked out in lived existence, and expressed through existential communication. The common concerns of a modern large-scale group, like the nation, do not originally belong to this group, for, ontologically speaking, there is originally no such entity having subjective existence of its own. For example, I can never find the United States and identify it with any existing subjectivity that I can interrogate, and ask what it is doing. At best I can find only one of the officers, or committees, who represent it and speak in its behalf. It would be false to infer from this strange fact that the nation has no public interests, no public policy directing them, no public opinion, no feeling, and no national existence. It possesses all of these, but they are not originally its own. The common concerns are first portrayed, or formulated, in objective terms which can then be understood and accepted by the common consent of primary groups and individuals who exist in and for themselves, and loan their actual concern, understanding, feeling, and subjectivity to the nation. After being first loaned to the group, they must then be taken over from succeeding generations by a constant pressure of force, propaganda, and coaxing, as long as the state endures.

This is the real meaning of the giant's greed in the Hobbesian picture. He lives only on the feelings and powers of smaller groups and individuals, whom he must ceaselessly devour and digest to stay alive. This greedy ingestion is usually taken to be a sign of strength, but it is also a sign of weakness. The giant is only a vast contrivance with no subjective consciousness of its own. It exists only in and for its members, as an object of their consciousness. Of course, these primary groups and individuals need the giant and his strength. They may let themselves be devoured and absorbed into their own gigantic artifact, as in the picture. But this does not need to happen.

By the responsible use of insight and feeling, and with the help of their more courageous fellows, they may open up the monster and bring him under control. This is the real meaning of what we call democracy and the free world. From the public standpoint of the other world, this looks like anarchy and private selfishness, which it very often is. This other world is devoted to science, technology, efficiency, order, power, and self-realization to the highest degree. The predominant trend of social philosophy in the West, from Plato and Aristotle through Aquinas and Hobbes to Hegel and Marx lies in this direction. The larger, public world of society, with its common values, takes precedence over the private, "subjective" perspective of the individual.

This public world is spatially centered in a large capital city, or temple, that is readily observed by all. The personal world is centered in the lived body of a fragile and fleeting individual person, though this does not mean that its horizon is narrower in range. The circumference of a circle has nothing to do with the size of its center. The perspective of public opinion is determined by the common values and meanings to which the group is committed. This perspective, if left to itself, abstracts from everything that is distinctive of personal existence, to focus on the common tasks and concerns of the group. What is friendly to them is true and good. What is alien to them is false and bad. If these common meanings have emerged from the special history of the group, without sustained criticism, they become rigid and closed in a narrow fanaticism, which is unable to communicate with other versions of the world.

The world of the responsible person, on the other hand, having emerged from a transcendence of such limits, and having glimpsed other alternatives, can become open. It is from this wider and more flexible horizon that basic social criticism takes its origin. As William James pointed out in his suggestive essay, "Great Men and Their Environment," the responsible individual is the spearhead of social change. Such a perspective is not limited to objective, mythical interpretations of human history. Though no society has yet succeeded in doing so, the responsible person can exist without myth. He does not have to restrict himself to the observed similarities in human behavior, to common feelings and common concerns. While taking account of these, on the basis of his firsthand experience of self-transcendence, he can also penetrate into the dynamic, lived existence of other persons, both in his own and in different cultures.

Unlike public opinion, which takes its global meanings for granted, he will be concerned with the clarification of his basic presuppositions and, therefore, will be involved in philosophy, though he may never read about it in books. He will be constantly dissatisfied with the fixed forms of the living language he has inherited from the past, and will struggle to develop it in the expression of new meanings which are relevant to his own existence and the situation of his time. He will recognize the need for the transmission of factual information, but since this can now be done just as well by machines, he will be more interested in language as a way of expressing his own feelings and meanings in a living dialogue with others who live responsibly in different world versions of their own. Through such dialogue, he may come to recognize ever more clearly that his own global understanding and that of others are only versions opening into *the* one world which, while it must include them, nevertheless transcends them.

Man is neither an objective thing nor a set of things, as the tradition has widely assumed. He is always a way of existing in a world horizon. Hence, in comparing the individual and the group, we are confronting two worlds that are basically distinct. The public world is organized around common interests that can be understood objectively. We are deeply in need of further light on its structure. But we have seen that it has no subjectivity of its own, and that it lives on ideas and feelings borrowed from others. It is centered in a common object, like a capital city or temple, and, without constant criticism, is apt to become fanatical and closed. The world of the free person, on the other hand, is ordered around a global project that originally involves subjective as well as objective factors. Once he comes into being, the responsible person exists in and for himself, with his own feelings and meanings. His world is centered in his lived body, and is open to transcendence. In humanistic disciplines, like history, literature, music, and the other arts, we are concerned with these worlds of existing persons, their distinctive pattern, their radiating power, and the sufferings that brought them into being.

We have just contrasted the world of the person with the public world of a large-scale group. But wherever we find different worlds we find different ways of existing. Let us now, therefore, try to focus these two ways of thinking and existing: that of the individual, on the one hand, as responsible; and on the other, as self-abandoned and taken over by the group.

Public Life and Personal Existence

If men are to work together voluntarily, a clearly defined objective must be brought before their minds, which is readily understood and appealing. In primitive communities, where the whole of life is shared, these ends are expressed in the form of myths; in more "advanced" cultures, in the form of written or unwritten constitutions, though always with some mythological background. These constitutions determine the basic order of the common life. In addition to the common end, they prescribe the necessary laws, or rules, that must be obeyed, and the necessary functions, or means, that must be performed to realize the end. When new situations confront the community and decisions on public policy must be made, the end is usually taken for granted, for to change the common end means revolution and a disturbing upheaval of social life. Hence, until the eighteenth century, political deliberation has followed the Aristotelian dictum that man, in general, deliberates about the means only, and never about the end.

It is fair to say that the objective, political life of a community, as our Western tradition has maintained, is a process of realization which is dominated by the past. The needs of man are supposed to be firmly ingrained in our human nature. They have been already recognized and accepted. At any given time, they exist in a potential state. They can be realized if the proper means are carried out. Once achieved, the community can rest in this stable and orderly state. Public opinion, or what we often call *common sense*, proceeds in this framework of self-realization; and within certain limits, it is unavoidable in the consideration of public action, which is openly taken for the sake of something else—namely, the free existence of individual persons.

But when this mode of common-sense thinking is applied to them, as has happened throughout the whole course of our Western history, serious questions arise, as we have suggested. The individual is then regarded as though he were a little state—the state writ small, as Plato said. He is supposed to be provided at birth with a constitution inscribed in his nature, and the whole aim of his existence is simply to realize himself to the highest degree, and then to rest in this realization. In order to do this, he must follow exclusively the same legal code that governs the life of his community, and must perform the necessary works for which his nature has fitted him. Then he can rest in them. In his practical life, it is wrong for him to think philosophically and to raise basic questions about the end of his existence, for this end has been fixed by nature. He should deliberate about means only, as Aristotle said.[6]

This view is a justification of the Hobbesian picture. The individual has no world of his own. He exists in the same objective manner as the state. He is what he is seen to be by the others, and his acts are the works that he can perform for them. He is, in fact, only a part of the society. He is responsible to it, and, through it, ultimately to nature. With no world and no existence of his own, he is no longer responsible.

This is a reductive analysis which fails to do justice to the distinctive features of personal existence. This existence is a total becoming with an autonomy and an integrity of its own, which are ignored and lost insofar as it is analyzed into successive steps in a process of realization. Its authenticity and unauthenticity cannot be analyzed into fixed states, or qualities, that terminate intervals of change. They are concerned with existential modes of becoming, how it is held together, or allowed to disintegrate into a piecemeal succession. My lived existence cannot be neatly separated into instrumental intervals having no value (means), and periods of static enjoyment (ends). Either the whole becoming is authentic or it is not. This becoming is neither a means, for it may have value, nor an end, since it is ever unfinished and on the way.

What is to be enacted is not some stable goal in the future. It is rather a responsible way of existing which, if it is to be achieved

[6] *Nicomachean Ethics*, III, iii, 16.

at all, is to be achieved here and now. In any case, this "end" is not fixed in advance, like a state constitution. Owing to revolutionary changes in the eighteenth and nineteenth centuries, even our state constitutions are subject to amendment and revision, so that, in spite of Aristotle, political deliberation is now actually concerned with ends as well as means. This is even more true of the human person who, insofar as he is free and responsible, reflects philosophically about the whole of his existence in the world, and thus, unlike a society, can live in a perpetual state of revolution. In any case, his "ends" are open to choice.

The state of the society and the human condition into which he has been thrown, however, are not open to choice in this way. The basic needs of himself and the others, with whom he lives in the world, must be met. To help meet them, he must play certain roles, and perform certain works, as directed by his society and its meanings. In doing these works, he must see himself as others see him, and meet their judgments of praise and blame. But he need not accept them and their meanings as they stand. He produces his works, and is responsible for them to social authorities. But something else is left over—he himself, who is doing these things as a center of meaning.

Who is he?

Perhaps only a Hobbesian man, who has let himself be taken over by the *Leviathan* he is serving, and who is nothing but his works. Many of us are like this most of the time. But by pressing the question, I may gain a distance from my works, and myself as I am seen by others. Then, by working out a pattern of meaning that I understand, I may come to myself and take over the whole field of my objective, social being by lifting it up into a new world. I may then do the same things as before. No difference may at first be visible to an external observer. But I am doing them in a different way, in a different field of meaning. I am no longer just the self whom I and the others see and regulate. It is I myself who am acting. And the things that I do are no longer mere works which I have caused, and for which I am responsible to an external authority. They are my acts which belong to me. I live in them, and am them. This is not the way of Hobbesian man. It is the way of freedom and responsibility, toward mastering the *Leviathan,* and toward regaining that dynamic unity of the life-world which he and his brother robots have lost.

Escaping from the Leviathan

No escape is even suggested in Hobbes' picture. The tiny individuals are too weak, and, on the whole, this is the traditional view. They must simply resign themselves to being absorbed in the all-encompassing order of the state. In Chapter 8, however, we have seen how certain prisoners in the death camp, while living under the harshest and most barbaric oppression, were able to make an escape. This is essentially that gaining of responsibility which we described and analyzed with some care. We shall now briefly summarize the necessary steps in this process, in a way that may bring out its general, social significance.

In moments of silent concentration, alone by themselves, certain prisoners were able to set themselves at a distance from their immediate situation. They did this not so much by simply gazing at what was going on around them as by running ahead of this situation into the future. From this vantage point, they were able to get a sense of its whole temporal style and its future possibilities for them. Without a sense of possibility derived from a grasp of the ever ambiguous future, the prisoners were left to die without life-giving hope. But in the light of this temporal self-transcendence, some of them were able to work out a world of meaning to support concrete projects, making sense to them. It is in the very same way, usually under less harsh conditions, that the human person, feeling trapped in the social world that seeks to take him over, gains a distance from this world, so that he may become free from it, and responsible.

Humanistic disciplines, and especially philosophy, may give him a sense of the radically different alternatives that are open to him, and may stimulate him to work out global meanings of his own. They will never fall into a coherent pattern, however, until they are organized around a project of his own that calls for daily tasks to be performed. In this world, ideas carry no real meaning, unless they are lived out day by day and year by year. The philosopher whose ideas are not reflected in his life is merely playing games.

The last step in becoming responsible is the decision which cuts one off from the public world and its duties, and yet, at the same time, takes it over just as it is. It is important to emphasize once again that this public world must be taken over intact, precisely as it stands. From the point of view of a social observer, no difference may at first be seen. The responsible person may go on playing his roles and performing his functions just as before. But if we are willing and able to communicate with the person himself, we will find that the observable acts are being performed in a different way, with a different sense. He is no longer producing these works for the sake of social rewards of money or prestige. He now acts them out with the whole of himself as part of the total life that he is living. He is no longer finally responsible to a public authority for what he does. He is now responsible for the works, the rewards and punishments which go with them, and for the authority judging them, if he accepts it, to himself. In this way, the whole public world, which has taken him over, is now taken over by him and placed in a wider world of meaning.

This is enough to show the one-sidedness of the Hobbesian picture, and the inaccuracy of the traditional view that society is always bigger than the individual, and includes him, as a whole includes its part. The discovery that the person and the group cannot be separated from their respective worlds places the whole situation in a different light. The picture portrays one possibility that has perhaps dominated our past history, though certainly not without important exceptions at its turning points. The individual is weaker. He can easily allow himself to be taken over, as in Hobbes' picture. But this is not inevitable. He can now become responsible and, in his own peculiar way, take over the meanings of society. When this happens, his world is "bigger" than the other, though the categories of whole and part are unable to convey the sense of this basic tension in our human existence. The two worlds are not merely different in quantitative size. They are basically and qualitatively different.

If this is true, we can no longer accept the traditional perspective on the social meaning of our Western history. The individual is in no sense prior to the group. Both ontologically and historically, the group is prior to the individual. Primitive societies have now been found, and carefully studied, where personal self-consciousness does not yet exist in its own right. The individual lives no life of his own. He is not a person, but rather, as we may say, a personage, whose existence is exhausted in playing the role to which he is assigned in the all-encompassing, communal myth.[7] The great *Leviathan* is not something radically new in our Western history, as Hobbes and

---

[7] Maurice Leenhardt has given us a penetrating description of this completely shared existence in his *Do Kamo* (Paris: Gallimard, 1947).

others have supposed. He is merely an altered manifestation of the primordial, socialized condition of man, now opposing itself to the responsible person and the historical dynamism that has come with him. It is the free individual, not the giant, who is new. The meaning of this history is not the gradual socialization of an untamed individual, but rather the gradual personalizing of an untamed society.

Our history began with the emergence of weak and fragile individuals who began thinking for themselves in the Greece and Palestine of the seventh and sixth centuries B.C., and it is only through the sacrificial devotion of their successors that it has been kept alive and moving. At the present time, with the coming of mass technology and the triumphs of objective reflection, this history may be nearing its end. On the one hand, there is the great *Leviathan*, stronger than ever before; on the other hand, millions of individuals partly prepared for freedom, but wondering whether it is really worth the cost. Will they resolve to take over the giant, or will the giant simply continue to take them over?

We are confronted here with a basic opposition that is found in all the nations of the free world at the present time. What we have been calling *the life-world*, in our preceding chapters, is really split in two: on the one side, order, loyalty to state authority, respect for its dignity, obedience to its commands, and vigorous realization of its common interests, with power. But in our time, the other is even more poignantly expressed: freedom, the dignity of the individual and his decisions, rebellion against the objective standards of public authority, and the integrity of the person without power, come what may. The life-world has been divided into a public world, and myriad personal worlds; though this is not exact, for there are also many giants. We are all now acutely aware of the existence of other societies radically different from our own.

So we are left, on the one hand, with a plurality of great societies, each with vast powers, objective orders, and universal standards valid for all mankind; and on the other hand, vast numbers of free individuals, thumbing their noses at these great power complexes still supported by majorities, and running off to live freely on their own. Many say that this is the meaning of democracy, a center of power stable enough to support individual anarchy. It would even seem that this interpretation is supported by our preceding argument, for have we not seen that the public world is quite different from the world of the individual, and that the two exist in quite different ways? Why then is this not the proper climax for a history that has slowly prepared the way for the most radical and far-reaching freedom, that of the individual person?

In terms of the Hobbesian image, we might picture the present situation in the following way.

At first, the armor of the giants held firm. They were able to move around effectively, to catch plenty of little homunculi, to devour them, and to hold them inside. This is the stage portrayed by Hobbes. The tiny men may as well allow themselves to be digested by the monster into whose hands they have been thrown. For if they run free, they are weak and helpless. They will only interfere with each other, be stepped on, or finally digested by some other brute. So they may as well be resigned and stay where they are.

But now, in our time, history has moved, and the sun shines on a different scene. The great dumb monsters have collided with one another, and this has aroused their rage. These collisions have opened gaping wounds in their armor through which millions of tiny men are escaping, climbing down the great brute limbs and running off on their own in the wilderness. For the monsters are now in trouble. This the present picture would have to show. Of course, millions of tiny men stay inside, since they remember the words of wise old Hobbes who told them about the dangers faced by little men, running around by themselves in the wilderness.

So some of the craftier little men inside have taught their monsters to make vast weapons, fit for a giant, of monstrous destructive power. Now the brutes stand scowling at each other with these weapons in their hands. And it is clear that when they start throwing them around, there will be no more monsters, and no more little men. This is what the picture would now have to show. Also that there are two clubs of monsters now threatening each other. On the one side are those less badly wounded. They are more or less whole and intact and retain their pristine vigor. A few little men escape through the holes, but the vast majority are still resigned, sleepy, and content to remain inside. From the outside, they look much stronger and more intact, since they are close to the original human state portrayed by Hobbes. Under them, in the picture, the caption *communism* would appear.

The monsters on the other side are seemingly in a more desperate state. They have been badly damaged in the past, and the great wounds in their armor are deeper and more gaping. Through these wounds, many millions of little men are pouring out to climb down to the ground and run away on their own. And from the inside comes a confused murmur of dissension, for even those who remain are now awake, and often disagree as to what their monster should do. So he often makes false starts, and his behavior is on the whole less predictable, which is a headache for the other side, as they make their aggressive and defensive maneuvers. Under this side in the picture, the caption *democracy* would appear.

The Democratic Way

But is this caption true? However we might draw our pictures, many of us would think of democracy in this way. But would we be right? Is this what the term really means? Let us pretend that we do not have to think and do what our monster tells us. Let us suppose that at last our feet are on the ground, that we can look around for ourselves. What will we say to this question? I do not think that we can say "yes." This may be the beginning. But it is not the real meaning of what we call *democracy*. The history may soon end. But it is not over yet. And we cannot grasp a historical meaning without projecting ourselves into the future to which it points.

How is the split between the world of the group and the world of the free individual to be healed? How is the life-world to become one? I believe that our descriptions of freedom and responsibility (Chapters 7 and 8), and of fanaticism and devotion (Chapter 9) indicate a sound way of answering these questions, which we shall now summarize.

The gaining of distance from the situation in which we exist is only the first step in what we have called *responsible existence*. Freedom is only the beginning, not the end. This negative movement may take us momentarily away from a rigid and closed fanaticism. But by itself, it will never lead us toward a free and open devotion. Instead of this, it will either destroy itself, together with its enemy; or, if it continues to live over against its enemy, this will be only by developing a new fanaticism of its own. Provincial versions need to be opened into *the* world by the development of self-consciousness and breadth of view. But this will never be achieved by negation alone. The distance we need for understanding will not be gained by running away. It will be by running away, and then stopping and turning around. The narrow group version must be dealt with on its own ground. It is only here that it can be opened up.

The primordial group needs to become a community of free men, and, for this, rebellion is indeed required. But rebellion by itself is not enough. Unless the group itself is transformed and taken over into a wider field of meaning, the result will be only the forming of new groups and new versions in addition to the old which remains as it was, with its fanaticism intensified. This may be a necessary step on the way. But I cannot believe that it is the final meaning of democracy—an endless breaking down of tyranny, now facing either total destruction or new tyrannies about to form. What then is its meaning?

The answer, I think, is suggested in the notion of responsibility. As we have seen, this is more than just negative freedom, though it contains freedom within it. After the responsible person has gained distance, he must work out a world of meaning that makes sense of the real situation. He may, of course, fall into another closed fanaticism of his own. But two factors may enable him to avoid this trap into which our group life is so apt to fall. In the first place, he has moved beyond the tight structures of the public world into which he was born, and, once started, this motion will tend to proceed. If it does, it will make him more self-conscious, and more likely to discern the limits of his own conclusions. This critical factor will be strengthened by existential communication with others like himself to whom he should now be open.

The shock of meeting another whose world of meaning is quite different from my own is a severe but salutary shock. If, after really listening, I emerge with a sense that each of us has seen what the other does not clearly see, this can give me a keener sense of the limits of any human perspective, including my own, and of mystery lying beyond, which I now know that I do not know. From the conflict of fanatical public worlds comes only destruction and nothingness. From the conflict of more open, personal worlds comes a feeling for transcendence. I then see that my world is not *the* world, but only a version. This widened horizon is no longer centered in the capital city of a human group, nor in the lived body of an individual. It is centered in transcendence.

This is a critical discovery which, when it is really made, can heal the many divisions of which we have been speaking, between objective perspectives and public and personal worlds of meaning. All of these are radically diverse, and relative to different interests and points of view. No one of these can succeed in absorbing the rest without radical distortion and reduction. And yet deep in his heart every man knows that the world in which he and the others exist is one. This thought, if he presses it hard, will lead him to the notion of a single transcendent source, toward which the world is centered. Only in this world (if it is a world) can we find a place for all that is seen in finite perspectives, for the perspectives themselves, and for those many things beyond (if they are things) which we know that we do not know.

This opening into *the* world leads us to seek for further light beyond all the answers we are given from different points of view. Each of these, no doubt, reveals something concerning that of which we must take account. But they do not tell us its real place in the world. Hence concerning any scientific fact, we may always ask, What is it really?—of any human meaning, What does it really mean?—and of any existence, Is it authentic? These questions involve mystery which cannot be comprehended. Nevertheless it can be penetrated to various degrees. There is evidence, especially that of our lived existence, which is relevant to our answers. But these answers cannot be objectively calculated and deduced. They must be understood from the inside; and finally they must be lived.

This sense of transcendence not only enables us to recognize the life-world as one. It also gives us a different feeling for the others existing with us in the world. They are no longer comrades who follow the same leaders and the same cause. We simply agree with them and ignore them. In either case, the matter is readily disposed of at a single glance. But to other free men, existing in the world with us, a different attitude is required. A single look is insufficient. They are free men, thinking and acting on their own, like us. No matter how strange and alien they may seem to be, what they say has arisen from the depths of struggle and suffering. What they say must be heard. Their version may be authentic. So we must *look again*, rethink for ourselves what they are saying, and respect them. Discussion in depth is required.

In a group of this kind, where such discussion takes place face to face, in public forums, even in mass media of communication, a new sort of thinking together takes place, which is neither agreement, nor disagreement, nor a mere combination of the two. It is rather a balanced decision which takes account of all sides, even of those who totally disagree, for the possibility of further evidence not yet known is always admitted. What emerges is neither a charismatic command which we simply accept, nor an arbitrary preference we simply ignore. It is rather a *consensus* which calls for our respect, whether we agree or disagree.

Out of such a consensus there may emerge projects for social action which, though they do not represent the interests of any special groups, nevertheless do justice to what has been said on every side, to the weight of the past, and to grounded hopes for the future. The social action which emerges will not be merely the realization of present interests, nor the kind of personal wholeness, or integrity, that can be maintained in personal existence. It is rather the kind of social realization, with integrity, that we call *justice.* The individuals who participate even negatively in just action are no longer merely free. They have worked out a field of meaning together which makes sense out of the situation, and in the light of which they may take it over. They are no longer loaning their minds, their feelings, and their bodies to be taken over by that great artifact, the state, which they have constructed. They have taken it over. They are not only free; they are also responsible.

The society that performs such action is no longer enclosed within a world of its own contriving. It is an open *community* in which free men can participate. The world of such a community is, in one sense, larger than that of one of its free members. This is because it includes many more individual versions without being able to integrate them, except by the precarious process of consensus. But it can include them only by listening to them, respecting them, and remaining open to them; and this will depend on a living sense of transcendence. But the responsible person also possesses this sense, which opens him to the world. Hence in this respect, the two worlds are equally inclusive.

We have now tried to show that there is a democratic way which is neither tyranny, nor anarchy, nor a mere combination of the two. It requires a way of thinking and acting on the part of its individual members, which is neither the passive acceptance of the social order as it stands, nor the negative rejection of it; but rather the responsible taking over of this order, and the placing of it in a broader field of meaning, achieved by a consensus. This, of course, is only a version of the world which will need to be transcended. But insofar as this is self-consciously recognized, the version will be open to *the* world, and may, therefore, move forward. A group that can move in this way is rightly called an open society. That which makes it *open* is a sense of some source of unity and meaning beyond. Without this, it must sink into either tyranny, or anarchy, or some futile and immobile combination of the two. The world, in which things, persons, and societies really exist, is centered neither in the human group nor in the human individual. It is centered in transcendence.

We have no time here to work out the image of this democratic process and its values. We shall throw out a few hints, and leave the rest to the reader.

The tiny men who escape from the bowels of their protecting monster find themselves, as Hobbes predicted, in a difficult and threatening situation. Accustomed to the dim light of the interior, the sunlight hurts their eyes and, as in Plato's story of the Cave, they move at first only at night in the light of the moon, and sleep by day. But the monsters have absent-mindedly taken them into a harsh and mountainous region where food is hard to obtain. Many die of starvation. Others, unable to see well in the shadows of the night, stumble into wild animals who tear them to pieces, or fall over cliffs. Finally some of them, growing lonely and anxious about their destiny in the vast expanses of the world around them, which they had never before really seen, gather together to consider their situation, which they had never before really done. Many say they have had enough of freedom, and decide to return. But the monsters have grown weak and sluggish, and those inside, unwilling to share the diminishing nutriment, will not let them in. The few remaining gateways are crowded by despairing ones coming out, and many are crushed by the threshing of the giant limbs.

Then a few daring ones, having accustomed themselves to the light of day, climb a rugged mountain, from whose summit they see a fair and fertile land far away, in the light of the sun that they cannot see. They come back with a plan to get control over some of the monsters at least, by means of certain hidden devices inside, long forgotten by the little men but still remembered by a few. Then, using the giants' superior strength for refuge, food getting, and locomotion, they may reach the better land. Many lose their lives in the struggle that ensues. But at last, with the aid of certain friends inside, the devices in their giant robot are discovered, and they subdue him to their wishes. With his strength, they get control over other monsters, and start on their way, boring holes in the faces of their carriers so that some of them can see. Further prospects open up as they advance. But more distant horizons keep beckoning them toward something they only partially see, which lies beyond. They are no longer at the mercy of their own gigantic contrivances. They have taken them over and on their way.

The image of the *Leviathan* that appears in Hobbes' book clearly has little to do with democracy. But, like all that is human, it belongs to a history, and the first image that we suggested is a later stage. The image just presented, however, is still later, and it gives us a less dim picture of the democratic ideal. Following Plato, we have made the key to this image, the sun, or in conceptual language, the notion of transcendence which brings forth freedom. What is the meaning of transcendence for the existential thinking of our time? And what is the evidence for it? It is to these questions that we shall turn in the following chapter.

Chapter 11

An Existential Argument
for Transcendence

The terms *existentialism* and *existential* suggest to us postwar neurosis, irrationalism, and a morbid preoccupation with such gruesome themes as anxiety, death, and the absurdity of life. While this impression may be justified by a brief acquaintance with some of those sensational versions which attend any revolutionary movement of thought, it will be corrected by a deeper study of the responsible literature in this field. This literature, as we have tried to show, is far from being an explosion of irrational thought. It is rather an expression of the first persistent and disciplined attempt in our Western history to explore the dim and hazy regions of the human life-world. If by *rational* we mean scientific in the Anglo-Saxon sense, this long neglected investigation, which started in the twentieth century, is, indeed, irrational, for the world of our lived existence includes "subjective" factors which are closed to the objective methods of science. But if we mean the attempt to reveal the world as it really is, then this investigation is thoroughly and unqualifiedly rational.

The title of this chapter suggests a vital union between disciplined philosophy and religious faith, which brings forth criticism from both sides. Thus on the religious side, Protestant theologians have been eager to reject any intrusion of secular criticism and secular philosophy into the purity of the faith. And on the other side, positivistic and old-style, analytic philosophers are equally anxious to reject any vital concern with religion as a corruption of their

199

discipline by extra-rational bias. One of my colleagues in the East has recently argued that it is all right, in a free university, for scholars to talk objectively and scientifically *about* religion from a detached point of view, but not as though they themselves could be actually religious. Giving this thesis a somewhat wider extension, it would seem to reduce to this: it is all right in a free university for scholars to talk objectively and scientifically about life and its problems from a detached point of view, but not as though they themselves could be actually alive.

Religion belongs to the human life-world, and will only be misunderstood and reduced if it is squeezed into an objective perspective. The present chasm between lived religion and philosophy, I believe, has an unfortunate effect on both, artificially insulating religion from an understanding criticism, which might check its tendency to become incoherent, fanatical, and closed, and at the same time artificially insulating philosophy from vital contact with lived existence, which might check its tendency to become an academic playing of linguistic games.

Existential phenomenology is an attempt to bridge this chasm, which has increasingly yawned between scientific reflection, in the narrow sense of this term, and life as it is lived in the concrete. In the field of religion, it has already produced many new ideas concerning the meaning of religion, and careful descriptive studies, like that of the great Dutch phenomenologist Van der Leeuw,[1] which have given us a new understanding of religion as it is lived, and have opened up many new vistas for exploration. I wish now to direct our attention primarily to this chasm, and to a possible way of bridging it which I shall suggest. This will take the form of an existential approach to transcendence, a type of "argument" which, I believe, may bring religion into a new and more vital relation with philosophy.

Existential Philosophy and Religion

We have seen that existential phenomenology has emerged from a union of two independent streams of thought. The first, existential philosophy, is grounded on Kierkegaard's profound criticism of

---

[1] *Phänomenologie der Religion* (Tübingen: J. C. B. Mohr, 1956), translated into English under the title *Religion in Essence and Manifestation* (London: Allen & Unwin, 1933, now out of print).

Hegelian idealism, the reigning system of his time, and in those penetrating studies of personal existence in which he suggested most of the essential themes of contemporary, existential thought. The second, phenomenology, grew out of the critique of British empiricism inaugurated by Brentano and Husserl at the end of the last century. This has developed into a new approach to the human life-world (*Lebenswelt*), called *radical empiricism* by William James, and a new intentional, or relational way of understanding consciousness. It is often forgotten that all of these thinkers were concerned with religion, and more especially that, after many oscillations and experiments, the theistic concept of God became decisively important for Husserl at the end of his life. Thus in an unpublished manuscript of 1934[2] he says: "an autonomous philosophy . . . comes necessarily to a teleology and to a philosophical theology as a non-confessional approach to God." This was, no doubt, an important factor in his rejection of any metaphysical relativism.

The divine transcendence stands above our separate versions of the world, and leads us to recognize them, as we certainly do, as versions of the single world which excludes none of them, but transcends them all. However, since Husserl clearly rejects any abstract, causal argument which, for him, would not apply to the *Lebenswelt*,[3] and since he is speaking of "a non-confessional approach to God," his grounds for holding such a doctrine are unclear. This is also true of the living existential thinkers who recognize the phenomenon of transcendence.

Marcel is a Catholic Christian who is certainly committed to some form of theism. But since he also rejects all traditional rational arguments, his belief would seem to rest on personal faith or fidelity alone. In his later writing, Heidegger is clearly opposing subjectivism and relativism on the ground of his philosophy of being, which has been referred to as a *Seinsmystik*.[4] But since his thought on this

---

[2] E. Husserl, *Vorgegebene Welt, Historizitat, Trieb, Instinkt,* MS. 1934 Sign. E III 10, p. 18, quoted by S. Strasser, *Das Gottesproblem in der Spätphilosophie Edmund Husserls, Philosophisches Jahrbuch* 67, p. 142.

[3] Husserl, *Ideen zu einer reinen Phänomenologie und Phänomenologischen Philosophie* (Halle: Niemeyer, 1928), I, p. 111; James, *Varieties of Religious Experience, passim.*

[4] This mysticism of being might have been avoided if Heidegger had clarified the relation between being (*Sein*) and world (*Welt*) as he uses these words. In terms of the actual evidence he offers, the two seem equivalent. But then, in spite of this evidence, he slips into a strange transcendentalism which places being (*Sein*) beyond the world. This is open to serious question, for it is difficult

subject is still obscure and in transition, and since he has made it plain that *Sein* is finite and definitely not to be identified with God, it is not yet clear that he has offered coherent and communicable evidence for any genuine transcendence. Similar criticism can be made of other existential philosophers, like Jaspers, for whom transcendence is a category of central importance. But the evidence they offer is so ambiguous, and the conclusion so indeterminate, as to carry little weight in counterbalancing the subjectivism which otherwise pervades their thought.

Hence it is not surprising that many phenomenologically oriented thinkers in Europe have followed Sartre in openly embracing some form of relativism, which leaves us, on the one hand, with the partial, objective perspectives of science which are true but lacking in global meaning; and on the other hand, with a Babel of conflicting, subjective worlds which are global enough but not even possibly true. Such relativism justifies the judgment that life is absurd, and reinforces that widespread sense of meaninglessness which is so characteristic of our time. This relativistic point of view is not only defended by philosophers. It has also been taken up by theologians who feel that it indicates a bankruptcy of reason which will lead men to special revelations.

In my opinion, this position is neither philosophically nor theologically sound. It is philosophically inadequate, because it fails to account for the fact that almost all men, as they live and struggle in the *Lebenswelt*, recognize that this world transcends their different versions, and that it is one. It is theologically inadequate, because it tries to make us believe that the transcendent source of unity and freedom has left no signs of its presence to which all men have access, and has completely shut itself off from the millions and billions of men who are untouched by any special revelation.

I am ready to grant, with the present-day phenomenologists, that the traditional, causal categories are applicable, if at all, to the objective universe of science, and that the traditional arguments for a First Cause are incompatible with the facts we have learned about this universe through science. But does this then mean that an existential argument is impossible? Is there no way by which we

---

to conceive of anything that is as beyond the world. When we seek the real meaning of an entity, *what it really is,* we are seeking its place *in* the world, not beyond. For a fuller statement of this criticism, cf. my review of the recent English translation of *Sein und Zeit, Review of Metaphysics,* December 1962.

can briefly and coherently suggest the evidence that has actually led living men of all known times and cultures toward transcendence, without becoming trapped in a closed system?

I cannot believe that this is so.

Such an argument has, in fact, often been hinted and implicitly suggested, as by Kierkegaard and others in modern times. But so far as I know, it has never been formulated explicitly and clearly in an existential context. I believe that such an argument offers us an alternative that is beyond traditional dogmatism, as well as the relativism of such a thinker as Sartre. But what kind of "argument" is this?

What is an Existential *Argument?*

If we are to avoid the dogmatism of classical, natural theology, we must look for a demonstration that is existential rather than syllogistic, that grows out of life as it is lived rather than out of objective concepts and arguments. But as soon as we have stated this prescription, we are confronted with another serious objection. How is life, as we live it, to constitute a rational argument? How is any demonstration in terms of abstract concepts and deductions to apply to life? Even if we were to discover another rational "proof," it would lead us only to the Deity of the philosophers, to use Pascal's famous words, rather than to the living God of Abraham, Isaac, and Jacob. By our use of the phrase *existential argument,* are we not mixing together two incompatible regions and perspectives? Are we not faced with a downright contradiction between our existence, which is subjectively oriented, actively engaged, and ever-moving, and our rational thought, which is objectively oriented, disinterested, and fixed in timeless essences? Before we proceed, we must pause to consider this objection, which springs not only from thinkers like Pascal and Kierkegaard, but from the living thought of our own time as well.

We shall grant, first of all, that we are not here using the term *argument* in the traditional logical sense of either induction or deduction. We shall not be subsuming separate instances under a law, or abstract concept. Neither shall we be deducing a conclusion, that God exists, from two or more premises. We shall be formulating an argument of another kind, concerning the meaning of certain facts of our lived existence. First, I shall call the reader's attention to certain facts of this kind with which almost all men are familiar in higher or lower degrees of clarity. Then I shall describe these existential facts as accurately as I can. This will be the first step of the argument. Finally, by reflecting on these lived facts, I shall try to clarify them, and to show that they point to what we have in mind. This reflective clarification of the only meaning that fits the facts, or gives them sense, will be the second stage of our argument.

Before proceeding, it may be well to point out again that the word *argument* is still commonly used in this sense. Thus we have already noted[5] how we speak of an attorney for the defense in a criminal case as *arguing* that all the relevant facts can be fitted into his theory, or of a physician as *arguing* with his colleagues that his diagnosis is the real meaning that fits the facts of the case. It is in this sense that we are speaking of an existential argument here. But even though we may be willing to grant that the term *argument* may be applied to cases of this kind, we may agree with Pascal that religion must be lived through and experienced in the first person to be understood, and that any attempt to reason about it from a disinterested, rationalistic point of view must end in reduction and distortion.

We shall, of course, grant that there is a kind of abstract rationalizing that is really out of touch with the facts, and that even tries to replace them. This must end in irrelevance and reduction, like the diagnosis of an untrained medical student, or the case of an inexperienced prosecutor who is out of touch with the facts of life. No doubt a vital experience of religion is even more important. Pascal had good reason for contrasting the God of the Bible with the God of the Cartesian philosophers of his time, and no doubt, if he had lived later, with the conceptual absolutes of other modern thinkers. But this kind of abstract reflection is not reflection at its best. It is not the only kind. Not all doctors are untrained; not all lawyers are naïve. Nor do we believe, in spite of the depressing evidence that can be gathered from the history of philosophy, that all philosophy of religion, especially if it is phenomenologically oriented, need be objectively rationalistic and reductive in the traditional manner.

Let me try to defend this attitude by recalling the distinction we have previously made between *primary thinking* and *secondary reflection*.[6] We must remember here that our lived existence is far

5 Chapter 4, p. 71.
6 Chapter 4, pp. 62–63.

from being blind and thoughtless. There is a primary mode of awareness that attends our actions in the very act, and which works out, sometimes half-consciously or subconsciously, our patterns of life and thought. In different degrees, it is proceeding within us all through the day as we eat, walk, perform our duties, and make our minor decisions, and even through the night. This spontaneous thinking comes out of the depths of our being. It is original, creative, and global in scope, but it is apt to be confused, incoherent, closed, tribal, and fanatical. The great religious answers to the questions of life have grown out of this mode of thought, which lives and works near the heart of our lived existence.

Over against this, there is a secondary mode of thinking with which all men living in what we now call advanced civilizations are familiar. This is the self-conscious reflection on our existence-in-the-world which comes only in calm moments, and which attempts to be disinterested and critical. It can be elicited by genuine, existential communication with others whose styles of life may differ radically from our own, and who put our views and attitudes to the sternest possible test. Such encounters often lead us to serious self-examination, with a view toward further clarification and correction of our ways of life and thought. So important has this exercise of disciplined self-criticism been judged to be by the opinion of mankind, that a place for it has been reserved in the colleges and universities of advanced cultures, including our own, under the name of *philosophy*. When thus institutionalized and endowed with a privileged leisure, there is always a danger that philosophy will lose touch with existence as it is lived in the concrete, and will embark on grandiose, systematic projects for the total explanation and rational assimilation of life, or even for its replacement by an all-inclusive system. Many philosophers, in thinking about religion from their sheltered, academic havens, have far exceeded their critical competence, and have tried to develop, under the disguise of philosophy, new gods and religions of their own. Against this more or less common academic practice, the protest of Pascal is justified.

After the failure of such grandiose enterprises in the past, academic philosophers have often yielded to the opposite temptation of simply sneering at the simplicity of the average man, of breaking off all relations with concrete existence, and then devoting themselves exclusively to the playing of artificial, intellectual games of their own. As we all know, this has happened in our own tradition in the recent past. The coming of phenomenology, however, gives me hope that this epoch of academic chess may be passing, and that philosophy may be returning to the exercise of its more humble, and more essential, critical function. In the field of religion, this means that the philosopher will no longer attempt to devise religions of his own. He will rather attempt, first of all, to understand religion as it is spontaneously lived and practiced by existing men (phenomenology), and then to reflect critically on these phenomena in the attempt to achieve further clarity.

The following argument will proceed in this manner. It will start with certain lived experiences, or world facts, as we have called them,[7] with which we are all familiar. It will then attempt to clarify the meaning of these facts. This is what is meant by an existential argument.

The Argument

The world fact from which we start is the restlessness of our existence-in-the-world, which drives us beyond any fixed form or pattern, and works in us as a first, creative ferment in our human history. In the well-known words of Augustine:[8] *Inquietum est cor nostrum donec requiescat in te.* As Kierkegaard put it: *in the beginning was boredom.* There is a strange anxiety in man which prevents him from feeling at home in any fixed pattern of life or framework of ideas, no matter how comprehensive or coherent it may be. Our human existence is marked by an openness to what is other that constantly goads it beyond itself, and that justifies the now familiar judgment that man is never what he is, but always beyond himself and his constructions. This being-open-to-otherness first stretches man into a spatio-temporal world-field where he encounters things and persons radically different from himself, and enables him to love them and hate them in different ways, depending on his needs and the accidents of his history. Then it leads him to remove himself from these immediate attachments and to question their meaning. Why is it only this way and not otherwise? What is the sense of these facts?

These questions underlie that quest for meaning which works at the center of our human history. They lead man to work out answers

[7] Pp. 51–52 and 66–68.
[8] *Confessions* I, 1.

which gather the disparate facts together, and give them a global unity in the light of which his existence gains some sense. But no sooner is such a system formulated than it is subjected to further questions. The meaning turns out to be confused and ambiguous. The facts are only partially explained. Why should it be only this way and not otherwise? The system is incoherent and disunified. It rests on arbitrary choice, and, if allowed to persist, will obstruct our freedom of thought and imprison us in untruth. But freedom, by itself, leaves us with a disordered array of meaningless facts, and the freer we are, the deeper becomes our thirst for the unity of meaning. So other interpretations are constructed, only to be revealed, once more, as incoherent and partial. Human history is a story of this kind—the rise and fall of systems of meaning which become incorporated into social institutions.

At the beginning, when these institutions are bright with the fire of a new creative unity, they bring men together in the cooperative fulfillment of a single purpose. But then individual critics and rebels appear. Instead of being freely elicited, social unity has to be enforced by power, or the threat of power, and the structure becomes rigid and dead, until its stiffened remains are swept away and it is replaced by another pattern, calling forth the fierce devotion of a new, creative unity. It is not to be denied that certain things have been learned from this history of creative disillusionment. It has been discovered that forms of undiluted tyranny and those of anarchic freedom are unworkable. Only those patterns which combine a maximum of freedom together with a maximum of order seem to be authentically human. But these words express an ideal that can be only remotely approximated, and no institutional order that has ever been, *or ever will be* actually established, seems likely to escape from the force of creative criticism.

In those cultures where there is some respect for individual freedom, and where personal existence has been possible, a similar history has been recorded. The freedom of the individual person is more radical than that of the group. Hence in the records of personal life-worlds, which constitute such an important part of our Western literature and history, there is a more searching and destructive criticism, as well as a wider variety of styles of life. But here again we find the same dialectic of freedom and order. Pure freedom, after negating every fixed pattern, becomes uncreative, and wastes itself away. Unity, on the other hand, as soon as it is established and freed from tension, becomes rigid and dies. Freedom needs order, and unity needs freedom, but in the imperfect modes which we can achieve, neither can bear the other. And yet as long as we remain human, we are lured toward a perfect order and a perfect freedom which would somehow coincide.

In what we call the history of Western philosophy, this dialectic is given a clear expression. Unlike the history of science, as we have seen in Chapter 7, this is primarily a history of individuals, which cannot be separated from individual names. Here we find not merely theories, but different worlds of meaning in which great world explorers of the West have been able to think and sometimes to exist. And not only in the systems themselves but in the history as a whole, there is the same restless tension between unity and freedom. Meaning itself is a search for unity which first gathers up the disparate facts into a single type or structure, and then points beyond to further meanings. Hence it is not surprising that we find great deterministic systems, like those of Aristotle, Spinoza, and Hegel, where the freedom of personal existence is taken up into a great structure of unified meanings, and reduced to patterns of action dictated by the absolute, or *in accordance with reason,* as the classical tradition has maintained.

Such systems have the grandeur of an overarching unity-in-many. But they take the life out of freedom, and reduce it to the acceptance of a single and arbitrarily chosen pattern of life, as against which there are certainly viable alternatives. They become associated with hardened patterns of social and individual life. As Kierkegaard showed in his criticism of Hegel, they are artificial constructions which lack the flavor and contingency of life as it is lived in the concrete. Over against these systems, there are other worlds of meaning, like the existential philosophies of our time, which subordinate unity to freedom, and which end in a subjectivism or relativism of some kind.

What then, let us now ask, is the ultimate sense of the restlessness of which we have been speaking? It is moving away from passive receptivity toward active radiation, from sluggish repetition toward creative originality, from fixed determinateness toward perfect indeterminacy; or now, integrating these motions into the single direction under which they fall, from a servile dependence toward a self-determining freedom. At the same time, it is moving from a senseless multiplicity toward an ultimate unity that gives meaning. Or in broader terms, if we think of that being-open-to-otherness which lies at the heart of this dialectic, we may say that it leads toward what is wholly other—radically transcendent. Or finally, in terms of the concept of the finite, which gathers the starting points together, it is moving from the passive, uncreative, determinate, and multiple toward an infinite which is active, creative, indeterminate, and purely one.

This dialectic, of course, takes many diverse forms in different cultures, and shows even more diversity in the experience of different individuals. It may be lived through by the uneducated and illiterate, in passing from an ego-centered to a nonself-centered style of life; by students of history and literature, in passing from a narrow, utilitarian point of view to that of a great poet, or literary artist, which is far richer, more unified, and filled with meaning; by students of philosophy, in passing from a more limited horizon, like that of objective science, to another wider horizon, like that of the life-world; by ordinary men, in passing through what we call a religious conversion; and in countless other ways. What is essential is that an actual passage be made, and existentially experienced, from one more limited perspective to another that is wider and more unified.

This is an existential argument from motions rather than from notions. One must live through this passage to really understand the *argument,* which simply brings out the sense and clarifies the original, lived experience, not merely of the individual himself, though this is essential, but that of other individuals and other cultures as well. There are, in fact, very few persons who have not experienced passages of this sort, though the meaning of these liberating conversions may be almost wholly closed to them. The argument lies simply in a reflective mode of thought which brings out the latent meaning. The conclusion of the argument is this: the free action which lies at the heart of cultural, and even more of individual history, points to a transcendent unity, which is the ultimate, creative source of meaning and being, and of the unity of the world.

An Answer to Objections

But before we proceed to further clarify this meaning, we must meet a basic objection. This dialectic appears as a human phenomenon, in the passage of our human history, where, as we know, many spurious ideals and delusions have arisen. To interpret it, therefore, as indicating the existence of a real, transcendent being is merely to express a special bias. Is it not more realistic and more true to the facts to interpret this as a purely human phenomenon, generated by human forces alone? In the last analysis, this transcendent being is a construction of man himself, perhaps necessary for his comfort, or perhaps for his betterment, but nevertheless a human ideal, or delusion, depending on one's point of view. Instead of man being made in the image of God, as the tradition has it, it is God who, as Feuerbach suggested, is made in the image of man. Religion is man's attempt to idealize himself. Theology is anthropology.

We can break this objection down into two distinct questions. First, why is it not to be understood as a motion produced by human energies alone? Second, why is the idea calling it forth anything more than a human construction, answering some human need?

In considering the first question, we must remember that the motion, of which we have been speaking, takes us beyond any human, social order, beyond any individual pattern of life, beyond any intelligible system of meaning. As we may know from our own lived experience and from the lessons of history, none of these can withstand free criticism; none of these can leave us fully satisfied. This restlessness takes us beyond any human achievement, or sense of self-satisfaction, spoiling our human joys, disillusioning us with our human victories, leading us constantly toward something we ought to be which is always beyond what we are. There is, of course, a sense in which this motion is essentially human, for it lies at the heart of our human history, and constitutes its ultimate meaning. But in recognizing this, through our participation, no matter how slight, in the dynamic life of the human spirit, we are forced to expand our conception of the human. We are, in fact, recognizing, no matter how dimly, that in addition to all the finite dispositions and determinations which belong to man by nature, he is also touched by an indetermination that cannot be held within any determinate limits. Is it reasonable to believe that, all by himself, man can lift himself above his own shadow, that finite forces can take him beyond the finite?

As to the second question concerning *the idea* inspiring such a dialectic, if this word can be used, we must note that it lies beyond the intelligible formulation of any human purpose, whether it be social or individual. Such purposes have given unity and integrity to many human lives. But the unity they give is always partial and imperfect, not unity as such, but only a one-in-many. Hence none of them can be identified with *the* end of man. The attempt to defend such a conclusion always turns out to be dogmatic and closed, and is finally abolished by free criticism. The idea which elicits this freedom is beyond any intelligible system of meanings. Any such system, or level of meaning, is again imperfect, for it is only a one-in-many, and points beyond to something that is purely and strictly one. Hence every such final system of ideas, or absolute, is open to criticism as a relative human construction; and in the history of philosophy, we find them destroyed soon after they are formulated, and passing away one by one, though the search for unity, that elicits this freedom, constantly leads to renewed reformulations, none of which can ever meet the test.

To argue that the idea calling forth this freedom is a human construction, faces many difficulties, for it is this idea, whatever it is, which places man in question; all that he has been, all that he is, and all that he hopes to be. It is only through this idea, and its shattering of our projects, that we come to recognize our weakness and our finitude. Before it, man is nothing. To conclude that this idea, if it is an idea, is a human construction, a final achievement of man which witnesses to his power and glory, would seem to be a flagrant denial of the sense of the situation, a stubborn running against the facts. This idea works immanently within our existence, and within our human history. But the idea that inspires this dialectic can be accurately described only as an intention of transcendence, a pure unity, transcending all that we understand and are.

But now we must face a further question. What *is* this transcendence to which we have referred, with some doubt, as an "idea"? What kind of idea is this which transcends; that is, lies beyond everything that we can do or understand? If it is transcendent, then it must be indefinable and uncharacterizable in any way. If ineffable, how can it be given any meaning, or called by any name? What then are we speaking of? How is it more than a breath of air, a meaningless sound, a word?

We answer this by saying that we grasp something of its meaning by what it does in us, or what it leads us to do; and again not just by gazing at this in others, but, first of all, by living this through in ourselves, these passages from one style of life to another, from one whole horizon to another that is more filled with meaning. Such passages, which usually require long periods of preparation, are the turning points of our existence; they are the heart of our human history. As we have noted, these changes arise from the exercise of a radical unity we never find, but nevertheless approximate in varying degrees. Unless we achieve some unity, we cannot act at all, and our action becomes freer only on the basis of a purer and more inclusive unity. This correlation between freedom and unity can be observed at every level of our action and thought. Thus a society broken by factional conflict cannot act; a disintegrated individual with no singleness of purpose can do nothing; and one whose world is pulverized into a chaos of meaningless facts and disordered ideas can neither think nor act.

In speaking of the dialectic of freedom and order that runs through the whole of our Western history, we have noted how the imperfect forms of inflexible order that we achieve have been broken down by freedom, and how freedom, torn loose from order, is dissipated and wastes away (Chapter 10). We have also noted how the greatest, creative works of the human spirit have been achieved only through the total integration of all the personal powers of feeling, thinking, and striving in the impassioned pursuit of a single purpose (Chapter 9). Does this not give us a meaningful hint concerning the first source of this self-transcendence? Does it not point to a principle where perfect unity and perfect freedom coincide in one?

Here we must, of course, grant that freedom and unity are only imperfect, human categories, bound up with systems of meaning that are finite and relative to man. We know what freedom is only by living through the passage from one perspective to another. But this freedom is always partly determined by the given facts of the situation, restricted to the mere alteration of something already there, and reciprocal in its action—involving the agent himself in some change. Such freedom is never fully creative. But in its varying degrees, it points toward an unrestricted freedom that is purely indeterminate and purely active in the creation of something other, without being altered in itself. We realize only partial unities, a one-in-many, a plurality that is held together by force, by form, or by purpose, that is never strictly one. But in and through our passage from a less integrated level to one that is more unified, we may grasp the sense of that pure unity toward which we are moving.

These approximate freedoms and unities are quite distinct and even opposed to one another. As we have noted, the human order we establish crushes freedom, and the exercise of our human freedom destroys order. But as we live through this dialectic, and pass from one less radical horizon of freedom to another, we may gain a sense of that single, creative source which is luring us on, and in which unity and creative indeterminacy are one. We do not hold this, or possess it, in any concept or idea. We tend to it by an intention that moves us toward it. In itself, it can be defined only negatively as that which is wholly non-multiple and indivisible, strictly and simply one, that creative source of being and meaning that lies beyond all that is, and beyond us and our versions of the world.

The Argument in Relation to Traditional "Demonstrations"

This argument is quite distinct from traditional, causal arguments for the existence of God, for the following reasons. In the first place, it does not proceed from the abstract point of view of detached observation, but from the concrete horizon of the life-world. It belongs not to the objective universe of reason and science, but rather to the order of life and existence. Hence the mystery toward which this "argument" points is not to be identified with a thing, or object, of any kind. This mystery transcends objects as well as subjects and, indeed, the whole world of human meaning.

Hence, in the second place, it cannot be assimilated into any order of finite categories, or relations, as the first being among other finite beings, or the first cause in a series of finite causes. Any such assimilation must lead to a dilution of pure transcendence. If this creative source is to be called a "cause," this must be only on the condition that it "causes" no attribute or structure that is like itself, but only what is radically different. Order is finite and created. The transcendent is beyond all order and intelligibility. What it conveys to us is neither order nor meaning, but rather the creative energy of freedom that moves through them toward transcendent unity.

Finally, in the third place, we may say that traditional absolutes and ideas of the divinity are too often open to the charge of answering some final, explanatory need in a human system. That which explains must be, in some sense, continuous with what it explains. It is a human construction which may be meaningful and useful for certain purposes. But the transcendent cannot be a construction of this kind. If this were the only alternative, we should have to define the theist as one who does not know that he is the author of his own ideas. The transcendent is not a cause which gives certain properties of itself to its effect. It may lead us to glimpse the possibility of meaning in our existence. In this way, it may help us to understand; but it explains *nothing*.

The argument we have suggested is closer to the ontological argument than any other traditional formulation, because of the dialectical movement in Anselm's "proof"—which leads us to pass from the concept of what is lesser to a greater and a greater . . . than which nothing greater can be conceived. It is through this motion of the mind that the presence of transcendence itself, not merely one idea among others, is revealed. Certain later versions of the argument also preserve this original claim to the divine presence. Thus Gilson notes concerning St. Bonaventura's version of the ontological argument, that there is no passage from the mental idea of God to the divine existence, since for him, the "idea," to which the dialectic moves us, is itself a manifestation of the divine presence.[9]

This version is close to the argument we have suggested, which may be regarded as an attempt to translate it into existential terms. But the logical language, in which the argument was originally formulated, opened it to later interpretations, like that of Descartes, where the *concept* of perfection plays a crucial role, and where the passage from this concept to real existence can always be questioned. We must emphasize that in our argument there is no such passage from the idea of transcendence to its being. What is really transcendent is beyond being. The passage is rather from its hidden presence, as subconsciously lived, to its existence as freely and openly recognized. This presence cannot be enclosed within the range of any objective concept. It can only be intended, to use a phenomenological term, by an intention of our whole moving, living existence.

An argument of this sort offers us a way through the relativism of our time, toward a nonsubjective, existential philosophy. The relativist fails to recognize the sense of mystery. For him, the comparative study of cultures results in a set of separate patterns, each fixed and frozen within itself, and that of the history of philosophy in a succession of separate, incommunicable systems, each closed within

---

[9] *La Philosophie de St. Bonaventura,* 2nd ed. (Paris: Vrin, 1943), p. 110.

itself. It would be futile to deny that many such frozen patterns of individual and social existence are to be found. The effects of dogmatism and fanaticism are never far from us. The subjectivist sees only these.

But there is something else that he misses, something else that is found rather in the free existence of individual persons than in the more sluggish life of institutions and groups. This is the restless urge toward self-transcendence, which is, perhaps, the image of the divine in man. Thus if we look hard enough, we can find a sense of mystery and transcendence in every known world culture. It is this sense of mystery which leads each of them to distinguish between its version of the world and *the one* world transcending all versions.

The history of philosophy cannot be reduced to a bare succession of closed systems. Even those which at first seem most self-sufficient and complete are open to further development. Thus Platonism is transformed into Neo-Platonism, Thomism into Neo-Thomism, and Hegelianism into Neo-Hegelianism. Philosophers of opposed schools do communicate. If we penetrate back of these fixed results to the underlying spirit of this history, we find a creative urge toward unity and freedom, which points beyond any system of human meaning, any human order of any kind. Those of us who participate in this life of the human spirit (and are there any of us who do not to some degree?), if we reflect upon this experience and seriously reach for its meaning, may come to recognize it as the working of transcendence in human history, apart from any mystic union, or special revelation. This is our argument.

Without such an argument, phenomenology and existentialism must end in some form of subjectivism, or relativism, and a non-relativist existential philosophy will be impossible. We cannot escape from the final conclusion that life is absurd. With it, or with some argument of this kind, we may pass through subjectivism and humanism without denying those human factors which, as we now know, pervade every aspect of our human existence in the world. We may be led to conclude that, while our existence cannot be explained by any system of human categories or meanings, neither can it be finally judged as absurd. For it is only to a confirmed, dogmatic rationalist that transcendent mystery is the same as the absurd. Furthermore, we shall be able to understand why, for all men, in spite of the world differences of which they are aware, *the* world is one.

Part V

A New Foundation for the
Humanistic Disciplines

Chapter 12

Philosophy and the Humanities:
A Concluding Note

In the preceding pages, we have attempted to give the reader a firsthand account of the worldwide movement of thought that has been given such different names as *existential philosophy* and *phenomenology* in Western Europe, and *radical empiricism* in our own country. We began by comparing it with other contemporary trends of thought, and by placing it in the context of our present situation in history. After this, we turned to the central project of this philosophy, the exploration of the human life-world, which we do not merely observe from a detached point of view but in which we actually exist, think, pursue our chosen projects, and face death. We tried to clarify this notion of the life-world, or *Lebenswelt*, and to show the reader how any disciplined exploration of it must concern itself with a different kind of fact, a different mode of understanding, and a different type of truth.

We then turned to the radical kind of freedom which belongs to this world, and which involves not only our human action but our human thinking as well. We presented evidence to show that this freedom is an aspect of a wider and richer phenomenon, generally known as responsibility. Finally, we offered to the reader some further examples of the phenomenological method in actual practice, showing him how it could clarify the phenomena of fanaticism and devotion, the relations of the individual to the group, and the experience of transcendence.

We shall now attempt to gather together what we have said,

and to give the reader a general sense of the meaning of this movement by making a few concluding comments, first, on the present situation of philosophy and the humanistic disciplines, and then on the new prospect it offers to them in our time.

The Present Situation of the Humanistic Disciplines

Since Plato's time, as we have noted, the primordial world of immediate experience, as it came to be called, has been constantly discounted and discredited as unstable, distorted, and subjective. In modern times, it has been claimed that it offers us no objective, verifiable facts, or meaningful structures, no intersubjectively testable mode of understanding, and no stable truth. Reason alone gives us access to such objective truth. Of course, the generations of men came and went. Individual persons continued to exist in their strange, irrational life-worlds where they struggled for their separate dreams, suffered from conflict and misery, and finally died. But as time went on, it was increasingly held that these different world views, which separated culture from culture, and man from man, were really included within the brains, or mind-containers, of the people holding them. This idea of private experiences being contained within an isolated subject turned out to be a convincing way of discrediting the world of our lived existence. As a total world horizon, which it is, it stood as a formidable obstacle to objective explanation and research. But if this world could be reduced to private experiences in the mind, it seemed less independent, and less formidable. Hence such steps were taken, even before the time of Descartes, and reason was left free to investigate the uncontaminated objects of the real, external world.

But the path of objective reason has proved to be difficult and filled with obstacles. Reason, when freed from subjective mythology and left to itself, should have produced a single, systematic account of the external world as it really is, which could then be gradually refined and perfected by the labors of great minds. And for many centuries, philosophers and schoolmen were guided by an image of this kind. But instead of a single system, the history of philosophy in the West alone soon produced a vast plethora of conflicting systems; and occasional rebels, like Berkeley, were heard to proclaim that everything we can directly know is subjective and contained within the mind of someone, or of God. It was hard to control these sudden explosions of a hidden and neglected subjectivity, and convincing answers are still hard to find.

But on the whole, where reason and logic failed, silence and indifference succeeded. This process was furthered by the continuous budding off of respectable scientific branches from the philosophic mother stem. These scientific shoots abandoned the grandiose claims of their maternal source. Each of them took over a limited province for disciplined investigation adapted to the nature of its special objects. But the basic, objective perspective established by the Greeks is still the same. What is real is an object out there before the mind and the senses. All genuine facts are of this objective kind. Understanding is to be achieved only through the checking of different hypotheses by a detached observation, which avoids subjective interest and bias. In this way propositions can be formulated which agree with the independent facts, and laws may be discovered through which the events of nature may be predicted and controlled.

When regarded from this point of view, the human individual becomes a complex object, swarming with his fellows on the surface of a small planet in one corner of a minor galaxy. He moves in a physical space of some non-Euclidean type, and in a clock time which is conceived as a succession of nows, every one exactly the same as any other except for its relative position in the sequence. The only real phase of time is the present now. The past was once a real now, but at present it is a no-longer-now that is dead and gone. The future, when it becomes actual, will be a real now. But at this moment it is a not-yet-now, a mere unreal projection. The past in itself, as it really was, was made up of the objects that could have been then observed by a detached, unbiased observer equipped with the proper instruments. We have access to this past in itself, and to certain aspects of what will happen in the future by our knowledge of the laws of nature. This enables us to pass from some present fact to a past or future event with which it is connected by some law. In this way, we may discover what really happened in the past, and may predict the future.

It is this conception which has led some historians to believe, especially in the last century, that they could gain a position outside of history from which they could penetrate through all subjective biases so as to observe, in the famous words of Ranke, "how things actually happened." It is this point of view which has led American psychologists to think of memory almost exclusively in terms of that ability to recapture some factual detail, like a name or a date, which is of immediate service to action, and to ignore that capacity to re-live a whole world of the past, which the French now call *affective* or *concrete memory,* as a mere subjective construction. It encour-aged psychiatrists to disregard the world of the disturbed person, to treat his disease as wholly internal and mental, and to proceed ob-jectively to induce responses which would more effectively adapt him to the same objective world which all of us actually inhabit.

From this point of view, everything in the world is actually deter-minate and clear. Obscurity and ambiguity are dismissed as *sub-jective* failures of knowledge, with no objective status. Living men have questioned the implications of this objective perspective for human freedom and responsibility. But in the age-long debates which this controversy has called forth, we have noted how the determinists have always had the better of the argument, and in-deed this was inevitable. For when the question is raised in an ob-jective frame where everything else is determinate, and where the basic concern is for mastery and control, freedom is an unwelcome and homeless intruder, an uncaused cause, an indeterminate deter-mination. So in the end, freedom has had to be either denied, or at least restricted to a single, human faculty as what we now call *freedom of the will,* that feeble compromise which still manages to maintain an insecure status in our common speech.

I need not speak here of the remarkable successes of this method and its underlying perspective in its modern, scientific and techno-logical developments. I need only point to the evident fact that it has now revolutionized the whole way of life of those who have taken advantage of it, and has even altered our landscape and geography. Were it not for these achievements in the conquest over nature, we should not be here. For our very lives depend on them. We humanists must certainly grant that this objective perspective on things, as we may call it, has a penetrating, revealing power. In-deed, there is no entity, including man himself, on which it cannot shed a certain light. At the present time, it would be simply absurd to deny this. But these successes have also strengthened the orig-inal, Greek claim that this perspective provides us with the only pathway to the only kind of truth. This claim is still widely influ-ential, but, as we have tried to show, open to serious question. Let us glance for a moment at certain consequences of this prevailing attitude for the humanistic disciplines, and for our human existence in the world.

Starting with the ancient discipline of philosophy, this was first conceived as a guide for living men to find their way through the world. But now, from an objectivist point of view, its functions seem to have been removed. Having given birth to the different, objective sciences, there is nothing left for it to do, except language and logic, and eventually these two will become sciences. Philosophy has no facts, no stable structures to uncover. All genuine facts are scientific facts. There is no super-science of the world to be achieved by a priori methods, and by unchecked intuition. This is a mythical dream. The world as it really is, together with its laws and structures, will be revealed, if at all, by the objective methods of science. There is no other mode of verifiable understanding, no other mode of truth than agreement with the objective facts. Deprived of any world of their own, philosophy, art, literature, and religion have had to be interpreted subjectively, and even admired as edifying expressions of human emotion and faith, but as lacking any real revealing power. They may have been needed in prescientific ages, but now their usefulness has passed. Thus the French philosopher Renan says in 1883:[1] "The time will come when the arts will be a thing of the past . . . a creation of nonreflective ages which one will admire, while at the same time recognizing that nothing can be done with them now."

Even the humanist, who would strongly reject such a positivistic judgment, feels the absence of any common frame of reference which might provide a stable basis for communication between the different humane disciplines. The scientists have such a common frame of reference. They can communicate and cooperate, so that real advances can be made. But in the humanities, each worker lives in a world of his own, and seems to communicate only by accident. In this realm, if it can be referred to in the singular, one can appeal to no higher standard than an individual judgment that is unconfirmed. A sense of chaotic isolation and relativism fills the air. The humanities are still respected because of the past. But at the present time, they seem to be on the defensive, and have little to say for the future.

[1] *Dialogues Philosophiques* (end of second dialogue on *Probabilities*) in *Oeuvres complètes de Ernest Renan* (Paris: Calmann-Lévy, 1947–49), Tome I, p. 600.

224

This disintegration and weakening of the humanities has served to strengthen the social and technological forces which are everywhere tending to objectify and standardize the forms of personal expression. More and more we think of ourselves in terms of the functions we perform. This woman is a housewife or a nurse. He is a doctor or an engineer. From time to time we are checked over and overhauled. We are good for so many more years. Then we must be shelved, and replaced by another. Guiding public opinion into concerted policies by the use of mass media, the welfare state calculates and organizes for the satisfaction of every objective need. It is futile and mistaken to attack this mass organization. Our very existence depends upon it. Nevertheless we must note the widespread mental *malaise* and disillusionment that have attended the growth of this intricate web of institutional structures. Caught like a fly in one such web, the individual, after a wearing struggle, escapes from it only to fall into another. Everything has been taken care of, everything seems to have its place, except himself and the strange, irrational world in which he exists.

On the one hand, there are vast ranges of scientific fact. These are certainly true; who can doubt them?—but humanly meaningless for him. On the other hand, there is a welter of global meanings, values, and faiths, all relative, all in conflict, and therefore not objectively true. The naïve questions of the individual are unanswered, and the meaning of the whole is lost. This threat of the meaninglessness of existence calls forth a feeling of anxiety which is manifested in many ways, one being the prevalence of mental illness, and the unprecedented elaboration of techniques for psychotherapy. In literature and the arts, we find a spirit of discontent and rebellion against traditional pictures of cosmic order and beauty, as well as the poignant expression of a sense of emptiness in the constructions of technology, and the objective universe of science. At the same time, we often find a troubled groping for some new world where the individual person, unhampered by traditional codes, may find himself in those inconspicuous corners of life which are now dismissed by objective reason as fleeting, subjective, and paltry.

A New Prospect for Philosophy and the Humanistic Disciplines

The contemporary development of a radical empiricism, which we have been studying, is, I believe, the beginning of a new strengthening and revitalizing of the humanistic disciplines. I know no better way to remind ourselves of the general sense of this world-wide movement toward concrete, existential thinking than to quote once again from William James. At the end of his lectures on *The Varieties of Religious Experience,* he says: "I *can* of course put my-self into the sectarian scientist's attitude, and imagine vividly that the world of sensations and of scientific laws and objects may be *all.* But whenever I do this, I hear that inward monitor of which W. K. Clifford once wrote, whispering the word *Bosh!* Humbug is humbug even though it bear the scientific name, and the total expression of human experience, as I view it . . . invincibly urges me beyond the narrow 'scientific' bounds. Assuredly the real world is of a dif-ferent temperament—more intricately built than . . . science al-lows."[2]

The life-world, and the ordinary language through which it is lived and expressed, include not only objective factors but subjective factors as well. This horizon is richer and more inclusive. The facts which the historian studies include not only objective, measurable factors but human meanings and interpretations as well, which belong to these world facts. From a logical, or positivistic point of view, such world facts seem to be confused and "sloppy." In con-trast, the abstract facts of science are simple and clean. Neverthe-less, historical facts, like your reading of this book in your room at such and such a time, are given to us with the same constraining evi-dence. It is as absurd to doubt the one as to doubt the other. Nor, in spite of the positivistic judgment, are they a mere chaos of confusion. As James says, they are more intricately put together, and fall into different patterns of their own.

The global meanings we require for the interpretation of this life-world are not principles of reason in the traditional sense. Sci-ence may ignore them. And yet they carry a philosophic sense which is required for our concrete existence in the world. No human cul-ture, no matter how primitive or how advanced it may be, has been found which lacks such a global interpretation of the meaning of its life—nor any free individual in a society which respects personal freedom. This life-world has a different temperament, a different feeling tone. If it is to be understood, it must be understood in a different way, which, as James saw, is open to a different kind of

[2] James, *Varieties of Religious Experience* (New York: Modern Library, 1955), p. 509.

truth. The disciplined exploration of this *Lebenswelt*, which James called *the world of the street*, is possible. In fact, it has begun, and is now proceeding as a cooperative task which not only philosophy but other human disciplines, such as anthropology, sociology, and especially psychiatry, are already contributing. This is, in fact, the world of man.

It is no longer necessary for the humanistic disciplines to depreciate their own activities as being concerned with disordered, "subjective" phenomena which will eventually be taken over by some objective science. It is now fair to say that this need never happen again. These phenomena may be discounted and disregarded, as they have been throughout long ages of the past. But they are facts, *world-facts*, with distinctive meanings and structures of their own. The humanistic disciplines now have a world of their own which is closed to the special approaches of the objective sciences, but which is open to other responsible and confirmable methods of investigation, now widely known as *phenomenological*, though little depends on the name.

In our examination of human freedom, we have noted that it is not an objective fact of science. It does not belong in this kind of frame. We have also referred to the philosopher Kant, who saw clearly that freedom belongs in another horizon, another world of its own. Perceiving that this world was closed to the objective categories of traditional reason and science, he concluded that this world was noumenal or unknowable, though he managed somehow to say quite a few significant things about it, especially in his *Critique of Practical Reason*. It has now become clear that this is the human *Lebenswelt* of which we have been speaking, and that far from being noumenal, it is, and can be, understood by disciplined methods of humanistic study. Hence a new future now confronts these disciplines.

Science, as we use this term, is concerned with objective facts which do not interpret themselves. The humanistic disciplines, on the other hand, are concerned with human existence in the world, which is always self-interpreting. Freedom is not restricted to a single choosing faculty concerned exclusively with practical action. It is concerned primarily with meaning and the interpretation of the world. It ends only with the responsible taking over of the total situation, precisely as it is, into a world project which can make sense out of it. This freedom of world-constitution, as we may call it, pervades the whole life of man, his thinking as well as his will. If one doubts it, let him think for a moment of the freedom of groups to reinterpret their history, and the freedom of repentance where the individual person reinterprets his whole world and style of life, past, present, and future. Let him also think of the radically diverse versions of the world that are found in different tribes and cultures, and even in the life and thought of free persons in a culture that we call the same.

This world is closed to the perspectives of science. For example, it requires global interpretations from which the sciences abstract. It has meanings, structures, and logics of its own that require different approaches in the humanistic disciplines, which are concerned with this life-world in its various major forms and manifestations. With a firm foundation in a world of their own, we may hope that these disciplines may soon be able to communicate, and to cooperate more effectively, and in unprecedented ways with one another. By revealing existence as it is lived from the inside, in its authentic possibilities, they may be able to elicit and to nourish freedom in novel and unfamiliar ways, which will, in turn, stimulate them. If this should happen, the humanistic disciplines may now be entering into a future to which their past, important as it is, has been but a faint, preliminary prelude.

As for the ancient discipline of philosophy which, from an objective, scientific point of view, seems to have budded off so many factual sciences that little seems to be left except secondary studies of logic and language—we can now interpret this history in a different way. The present situation is certainly to be welcomed by anyone seriously concerned with the future of this discipline. It is to be regretted only by those who think of it as a great, objective super-science concerned with objective facts. But there is no super-science of this kind, as is now clear, not only from the history of philosophy in the West, but from what we know of the history of philosophy of other cultures. This history can now be read in a different way. It has not taken the form of an objective science concerned with objective facts, which it gradually learns to predict and increasingly master throughout the generations. This kind of task is much better performed by the different sciences. And if this is the only kind of knowledge, philosophy must be abandoned. Some of our contemporaries are predicting that it soon will be abandoned.

But philosophy is not an objective science concerned with scientific facts and scientific methods. It is an altogether different kind of discipline, concerned with a different world, and a different mode of understanding. In its history, as we have noted, we certainly do not see a continuous progress in the mastery of a definite region of nature, nor in the mastery of nature as a whole. We never should have expected to find this. We find rather a radical discontinuity in the working out, by individual minds, of different versions of the world in which they were able to think, and *sometimes* to exist. I do not need to engage in this style of thought in order to gain any control over a limited region of nature. I need it to understand myself and the life-world, and to exist as a free man in history. Any help I can get, through communicating with other free minds, will be a different kind of help, which must be given, if it is given at all, in a different kind of way. The difficulties involved in eliciting and strengthening such communication in depth between free men are very great indeed. The struggle to overcome these difficulties must be renewed in each generation, if freedom is to endure.

To bring this struggle into the light, to understand the conditions under which it takes place, to give it guidance and support, a discipline is needed. At the present time in our situation in history, I believe that of all the different, academic disciplines, philosophy is the least unfitted to perform this task. It is not concerned with scientific facts of nature but, like history, literature, and the fine arts, with world-facts of the *Lebenswelt*. Unlike these disciplines, however, it is not so much concerned with individual acts of freedom, and particular versions of the world, as with those general limiting conditions under which freedom is always exercised, and the structure of the world itself, such as world-space, world-time, historicity, choice, and death.

By continuing to shed some light on these common structures of the life-world, it may act as a binding link between the different, humanistic disciplines, enabling them to communicate more effectively, and to cooperate in exercising that therapy for sanity of thought and life which can strengthen and maintain responsible freedom in a free community. As we consider our past history, we can see that philosophy has often, almost inadvertently, performed this therapeutic function, and has actually elicited and supported freedom of mind in the human community. But the misconception of philosophy as a rational science has hitherto interfered with the exercise of this critical function. With the removal of this misconception which is now under way, we may look forward to a revival and renewal of philosophy as a basic discipline of freedom.

With the coming of a clearer understanding of man and the life-world which is his dwelling place, it will be harder to regard him as a mere complex object, and to misplace him in an alien, deterministic frame. This should help us in working out an answer to the vital question, on which our very survival now depends, of discovering the proper place of science and technology in an authentic culture, and of finding viable ways of subordinating and using these essential tools for authentic existence, without being engulfed and dominated by them. Their objective perspectives will be valued and respected. But ultimate meaning will not be sought in them. It is rather the wider horizon of the life-world and its mysteries which call for radical speculation and ultimate faith. Here, no doubt, original speculation and the widest diversity of conviction will be encouraged; though, at the same time, willful eccentricity will be subjected to careful and searching criticism. By such criticism men will be reminded that freedom is not the same as license, and that it is the dogmatism of the closed mind which brings forth relativism and the sense of meaninglessness.

Versions of the world will be sharply distinguished from the one world, and constantly opened to the mysteries which lie beyond. Responsible freedom is not the destroyer of meaning, but its human ground and source; and in the last analysis, every institution should be judged by the degree to which it nurtures and supports this personal freedom. By avoiding regimentation and by thus encouraging the individual, so far as this is possible, to think for himself and to work out his own style of life, we may hope that a free world community may eventually be established.

Bibliography

I. Important works in phenomenology and existential philosophy. These texts in English will be of interest to those wishing to gain an orientation in the field.

Aiken, H., and W. Barrett, *Philosophy in the Twentieth Century*, Vol. III. New York: Random House, 1962. A well chosen anthology of phenomenology and existential philosophy.

Barrett, W., *Irrational Man*. New York: Doubleday & Company, Inc., 1958. An illuminating study of living existential philosophy and its artistic and literary background.

Berdyaev, N., *Slavery and Freedom*. New York: Charles Scribner's Sons, 1944.

Blackham, H. G., *Six Existentialist Thinkers*. New York: Harper & Row, Publishers, 1952.

Buber, M., *Eclipse of God*. London: Victor Gollancz, Ltd., 1953.

————, *I and Thou*. Edinburgh: T. and T. Clark, 1955.

Bultmann, R., *Theology of the New Testament*. London: Student Christian Movement Press, 1952. Shows the relevance of existential concepts to the interpretation of the *New Testament*.

Clive, G., *The Romantic Enlightenment*. New York: Meridian, 1960. Especially Chap. III on existential themes in William James.

Fallico, Arturo B., *Art and Existentialism*. Englewood Cliffs, N.J.: Prentice-Hall, Inc., 1962.

Heidegger, M., *Introduction to Metaphysics*, trans. Manheim. New Haven: Yale University Press, 1959.

————, *Being and Time*, trans. Robinson and Macquarrie. New York: Harper and Row, Publishers, 1962. In the original German, this is the most basic and most disciplined study of the life-world and its existential structures that has as yet been written. Parts of this translation are usable. Cf. my review in *Review of Metaphysics* (Dec. 1962).

Husserl, E., *Cartesian Meditations,* ed. D. Cairns. The Hague: Nijhoff, 1960.

James, W., *Principles of Psychology.* New York: Holt, Rinehart & Winston, Inc., 1893.

——, *Essays in Radical Empiricism.* New York: Longmans, Green & Co., Inc., 1958.

——, *The Will to Believe and Other Essays.* New York: Longmans, Green & Co., Inc., 1897. When read with some understanding of present phenomenology, these essays can show the careful reader that existential philosophy is firmly grounded in our native, American tradition.

Jaspers, K., *Man in the Modern Age.* London: Routledge & Kegan Paul, 1951. A widely read analysis of present-day Western culture by a well-known German existential philosopher.

——, *Perennial Scope of Philosophy.* New York: Philosophy Library, 1949.

——, *The Way to Wisdom.* New Haven: Yale University Press, 1951.

Kierkegaard, S., *Concluding Unscientific Postscript,* trans. Swenson. Princeton: Princeton University Press, 1941. The most important philosophical work of the first modern existential thinker.

——, *Either/or; A Fragment of Life,* trans. Swenson. Princeton: Princeton University Press, 1944.

Macmurray, J., *Persons in Relation.* New York: Harper & Row, Publishers, 1961. A lucid expression of radical empiricism, worked out independently by a British philosopher, which has much in common with continental phenomenology.

——, *The Self as Agent.* London: Faber & Faber, Ltd., 1954.

Macquarrie, J., *An Existentialist Theology.* London: Student Christian Movement Press, 1955.

Marcel, G., *Man Against Mass Society.* Chicago: Henry Regnery Co., 1952. A penetrating study of our present cultural condition.

——, *The Mystery of Being.* Chicago: Henry Regnery Co., 1950.

May, R., ed., *Existence.* New York: Basic Books, Inc., 1958. A number of cases analyzed by well-known psychiatrists from an existential point of view.

Merleau-Ponty, *Phenomenology of Perception.* New York: Humanities Press, 1962. A careful and detailed study of the world of our preconceptual experience.

——, *In Praise of Philosophy,* trans. Wild and Edie. Evanston: Northwestern University Press, 1963. In this short address, a great French phenomenologist gives a lucid sketch of his whole philosophical position.

Ortego y Gasset, *Man and People.* New York: W. W. Norton & Company, Inc., 1957. A penetrating study of social life by a Spanish thinker deeply influenced by phenomenology.

Reinhardt, K. F., *The Existentialist Revolt*. Milwaukee: Bruce Publishing Co., 1952.

Sartre, J.-P. *Being and Nothingness*. New York: Philosophy Library, 1956.
————, *The Transcendence of the Ego*. New York: The Noonday Press, 1957.

Scheler, M., *The Nature of Sympathy*. New Haven: Yale University Press, 1954.

Schrag, C., *Existence and Freedom*. Evanston: Northwestern University Press, 1961. An interesting comparison of the thought of Kierkegaard with that of Heidegger.

Spiegelberg, H., *The Phenomenological Movement*. The Hague: Nijhoff, 1960. An accurate account of the world-wide movement toward a genuine, empirical philosophy from Brentano and Husserl to the present.

Thévenaz, P., *What is Phenomenology?* ed. J. M. Edie. Chicago: Quadrangle Press, 1962. An excellent introduction to French phenomenology as it is now being practiced in our time.

Van den Berg, G. H., *The Phenomenological Approach to Psychiatry*. Springfield: Charles C. Thomas, Publisher, 1955.

Wild, J., *Challenge of Existentialism*. Bloomington: Indiana University Press, 1955.

II. Works referred to in this volume.

Anders, G., *Die Antiquiertheit des Menschen*. München: C. H. Beck, 1956.

Aristotle, *Nicomachean Ethics*, The Works of Aristotle, Vol. IX. Oxford: Clarendon Press, 1925.

Augustine, *Confessions*, trans. Pilkington. New York: Liveright Publishing Corp., 1927.

Barnes, W. H. F., "On Seeing and Hearing," in *Contemporary British Philosophy*. New York: The Macmillan Co., 1956.

Campbell, C. A., *On Selfhood and Godhood*. New York: The Macmillan Co., 1957.

Clive, G., *The Romantic Enlightenment*. New York: Meridian Books, Inc., 1960.

de Saussure, F., (*Cours de linguistique générale*) *Course in General Linguistics*, trans. Baskin. New York: Philosophical Library, 1959.

Frankl, Viktor, *From Death-Camp to Existentialism*. Boston: Beacon Press, 1961.

Gilson, E., *La Philosophie de St. Bonaventura*. Paris: Vrin, 1943.

Gurwitsch, Aron, *Théorie du champ de la conscience*. Paris: Desclée de Brouwer, 1957.

Hume, David, *A Treatise of Human Nature*, ed. Selby-Bigge. Oxford: Clarendon Press, 1958.

Husserl, Edmund, *Krisis der Europäischen Wissenschaften und die Trans-zendentale Phänomenologie.* Haag: Nijhoff, 1954.

——, *Ideen zu einer reinen Phänomenologie und Phänomenologischen Philosophie.* Halle: Niemeyer, 1928

——, *Vorgegebene Welt, Historizitat, Trieb, Instinkt,* MS, 1934, Sign, E. III 10 p. 18.

James, William, *Pragmatism.* New York: Meridian Books, 1959.

——, *The Principles of Psychology.* New York: Holt, Rinehart & Winston, Inc., 1893.

——, *Varieties of Religious Experience.* New York: Modern Library, 1943.

——, *The Will to Believe and Other Essays.* New York: Longmans, Green & Co., Inc., 1897.

Kierkegaard, S., *Der Begriff der Ironie.* München: Kaiser Verlag, 1929.

Leenhardt, Maurice, *Do Kamo.* Paris: Gallimard, 1947.

Marcel, G., *Man Against Mass Society.* Chicago: Regnery, 1950.

Mead, George H., *Mind, Self and Society.* Chicago: University of Chicago Press, 1934.

Merleau-Ponty, M., *Phénoménologie de la perception.* Paris: Gallimard, 1945.

Nagel, Ernest, "Determinism in History," *Philosophy and Phenomenological Research,* XX (1960), 305.

Niebuhr, R., *The Self and the Dramas of History.* New York: Charles Scribner's Sons, 1955.

Plato, *Euthydemus,* trans. Lamb. Cambridge, Mass.: Harvard University Press, 1937.

——, *Theaetetus,* trans. Fowler. New York: G. P. Putnam's Sons, 1928.

Renan, E., *Oeuvres Complètes de Ernest Renan.* Paris: Camann-Levy, 1947.

Rickman, "Philosophical Anthropology and the Problem of Meaning," *Philosophical Quarterly,* X (1960).

Thévenaz, P., *What Is Phenomenology?* ed. J. M. Edie. Chicago: Quadrangle Press, 1962.

Tiryakian, *Sociologism and Existentialism.* Englewood Cliffs, N.J.: Prentice-Hall, Inc., 1962.

University of California Associates, "Freedom of the Will," in *Readings in Philosophical Analysis,* eds. Feigl and Sellars. New York: Appleton-Century-Crofts, Inc., 1949.

Van der Leeuw, G., *Phänomenologie der Religion.* Tübingen: J. C. B. Mohr, 1956.

Von Uexküll, J. G. *(Theoretische Biologie) Theoretical Biology,* trans. Mackinnon. New York: Harcourt, Brace & World, Inc., 1926.

234

Warnock, G. J., "Analysis and Imagination," in *Revolution in Philosophy*. New York: The Macmillan Co., 1957.

Wild, John, "Contemporary Phenomenology and the Problem of Existence," *Philosophy and Phenomenological Research*, XX, 2. Buffalo: University of Buffalo, 1959.

Wittgenstein, L., *Philosophical Investigations*. Oxford: B. H. Blackwell, Ltd., 1953.

Biographical Index

Subject Index

238